The One That Got Away

Helen Greenfield

HEAR PUBLISHING
hearpublishing.com
2017

Hear Publishing, LLC

Copyright © 2017 by Helen Greenfield

All rights reserved. Except for brief quotes used in reviews, no part of this book may be reproduced in any form or means without the prior written consent of Hear Publishing.

Published in Johns Island, South Carolina, by Hear Publishing.

Hear Publishing titles are available at special quantity discounts for bulk purchases for sales promotion, premiums, fund-raising, educational, or institutional use.

This novel is a work of fiction. Names, characters, organizations, places, and events that are portrayed are either products of the author's imagination or used fictitiously.

HearPublishing.com 843.889.8260 Johns Island, SC 29455

Library of Congress Control Number: 2017914541

Names: Greenfield, Helen, 1959, author

Title: One that Got Away / Helen Greenfield

Description: First edition I Johns Island, SC, 2017

978-0-9992460-0-9 First Hear Publishing Electronic Edition: September 2017

978-0-9992460-1-6 First Hear Publishing Trade Paperback Printing: September 2017

Subjects: Law of Attraction, Shift to love-based, Unity Consciousness, Imagination, Mother Earth Preservation, Peace, Wisdom, Meditation, Yoga, Veganism, Fairies, Mermaids.

Printed in Charleston, South Carolina, United States of America

Gratitude
Steve, Sharon,
and the Goddess Isis

"Every living being is an engine geared to the wheelwork of the universe. Though seemingly affected only by its immediate surrounding, the sphere of external influence extends to infinite distance."

FUTURIST NIKOLA TESLA

ONE

The sound of salt water against the floating dock brings me out of my morning Spiritfly-meditation. I give gratitude to my guides before adjusting my eyes from dark hues to dawn colors.

"Whewsuu, Whewsuu," I whistle. Ouida flaps her expansive wings and swoops down for me to pet her luxurious feathers.

"Yes ma'am, you are a gorgeous pelican."

I get a hit.

Guide says, "Change is a-coming."

I tilt my left ear up to get a better signal.

"Soul desire will shift humanity to love-based."

Guide's voice fades. I see a red flag and then a mailbox. My heart races. Something is going down.

I change-up my morning swim routine, whistle for Ouida, and head out to check the mail.

In the Deep South, my half-mile driveway is called an avenue of oaks. I slow down my pace under the shade of a living canopy of grand oaks, planted by my ancestors and Indigenous Guides.

Yippee. A letter from Grandmama Sharon. What's this? Savannah School Board said the final vote was next month. And why would Dr. Cross and Mr. Nicopane write separately? Odd. I walk back to the house holding the letters to my heart.

"I am planting seeds for the next seven generations. I am moving in accordance with my inner knowledge. I am a Shaman Warrior.

"Great Spirit, Mother Earth, Isis, Sophia, Osiris, Horace, Shiva, Shakti, Krishna, Kali, Buddha, Jesus, Ra, Etherals, Aspirants, Masters, and Enlightened Avatars, please, let me be the light that shifts humanity to love-based."

Mr. Nicopane and Dr. Cross have zero power over me.

Guide says, "Green calms."

I squeeze tubes of cerulean blue, light ochre, raw umber, and titanium white on my palette. I dab my brush and grab the rough tooth of the canvas surface.

I 'imagination-paint' the tiny yellow-brown leaves on azalea bushes, tree-sized camellias packed with tight lime buds and glossy blue-green leaves, and a magnolia tree that is dripping with emerald green and crimson umber leaves.

I imagination-paint the resurrection fern on the sunny side of a grand oak tree when two teenagers reaching around the tree, arms barely shy of touching, pop into my head. Skin tones, features, lines, shapes, and curves swirl in my imagination.

A unique chirp in the island bird symphony catches my ear. I find dozens of painted buntings roosting in the dogwood trees. I study their indigo heads, violet head feathers, blue-green shoulders, red-orange bellies, and yellow tail feathers. A toddler, intrigued by the rainbow-colored birds, pops in my mind. Thank you, muses.

Ouida swoops down, tucks in her wings, catches a low wind, soars down the avenue at a fast clip, flies a hundred feet straight up, and heads back to the river.

The river calls me, but I go to the office.

Mr. Nicopane's letter reeks of ill omen. My ego wants to rip it open, but my soul takes me to the art room.

I grab charcoal and a sketch pad and study the fluttering wings of the painted buntings. Why would the school board respond early? Was anyone even listening to me? I study the lover's urge to touch and the spirit of the toddler.

Warriors have no regrets. Warriors don't ask how.

After I sand and prime three new canvases, I take a break.

I put on Jacqueline du Pré playing Elgar. Riveting. When the CD ends, it's green smoothie time.

I blend a banana, blueberries, dried Turkish figs, and kale leaves, all organic, into pure energy. Oh jah.

I take ten minutes to stretch out my back before I head back to the art room.

I slip on my smock, prepare my color palette, and start the process. By late afternoon, quantum things move to Newtonian reality, proving they coexist.

Guide says, "Polarity. Two worlds."

When I have to stop for the paint to dry, I hear my father's high, tenor voice, from the other side, say "worst first."

I head to the office.

Lizard brain spits, "Six months of flying experts from San Francisco, LA, NYC, and Seattle to speak at Savannah School District Board Meetings, and nobody ever said thank you."

I sit at my desk and conjure ancestral power from the three generations of my Father's fathers who built and lived in this house.

Why have the Howards all died so young?

Monkey brain chatters, "And Mr. Nicopane acted holier-than-thou the whole time. Has he ever stopped prophesizing, hating, and discriminating for a minute?"

I wonder about the bad karma I've built with Mr. Nicopane.

Why is he my next-door-neighbor? Why was he my third-grade teacher, and why wouldn't they let me out of his eleventh grade English Lit class? Why?

Will Mr. Nicopane and his small band of Primitive Calvinist devotees always haunt me? Will I ever get the 'God Hates Unbaptized Sinners' sermon, which he preaches over a bullhorn every Sunday, out of my head?

In my head, I see Mr. Nicopane's yellow-grey eyes, bushy eyebrows, and vulture-shaped nose, smirking at me when my expulsion from May Howard School was final.

How did Mr. Nicopane get away with preaching the Old Testament in public school English Lit class? And who in their right mind promoted him to Curriculum Director? Yuck.

Lizard brain spits on Mr. Nicopane.

"Easy fella," I say.

After six months, the school board knows in their hearts that banning factory farmed meat, eggs, and dairy from school lunch programs drastically improves the health of our children, community, and the planet. And, even if they didn't get the interconnectedness of factory farm suffering, they had to get that FDA-USDA-approved chemical additives in commodity food is carcinogenic.

Twelve public school superintendents shared their organic plant-based lunch programs with us. Each claimed that switching to clean food made kids happier, more engaged, and want to stop bullying. And they all had a school lunch budget reduction that averaged around five percent.

They said 'for profit,' Mr. Nicopane and Dr. Cross. Isn't that your antiquated greedy sellout dream this incarnation?

Guide says, "Unity."

When I pick up Mr. Nicopane's letter, I drown in disgust. Unreal.

I think patience before Guide gets a chance to correct me.

Wouldn't the school board at least vote to ban red and blue dyes, aspartame, fluoride, BPAs, GMOs, pesticides, high fructose corn syrup, Kellogg's, General Mills, Nestle, and Coca-Cola?

Come on, Savannah School Board, organic edible education is the best investment we can make for our kids. Clean food is a no-brainer, an evolutionary win/win.

I spin around in the swivel chair. My work is fruitful. I am worthy of the fruits of my labor. Love, love, love. As above, so below, and so it is done. I am so ready for love-based.

We gave the school board a plethora of plant-based meal plans that are popular with both students and lunchroom ladies alike.

I watch Ouida perched on her floating dock piling.

Daydreaming, I get a hit. The good-old-boys are still too dense. Ground zero. Heartbreak.

I stop little 'e' ego. I'm here to quash false belief systems with the truth. I am planting seeds. I will stop greed from killing Mother Earth.

I decide to open Grandmama Sharon's letter first.

Dingle in Kerry County, Ireland   7/7/09
Dear Mary,

I hope you are well. I am happy to hear you are working to make school lunches healthier. Remember to stay upbeat: your goal is not to change the crystallized minds of antiquated administrators' huge egos, but to splatter New Age ideas like seeds in the wind.

Speaking of seeds, your kitchen garden inspired us to plant out a four-by-four square in the adjacent vacant lot. My how the kids from the orphanage love to tend the newly sprouted seedlings!

Last night was orientation. The Diseart faculty sends their love! We have twelve Fairy Magic freshmen this year and my what a joy they are!

How is your painting coming along? Have you been in contact with Patrick since you've been home?

Mary, last night at 11:11 P.M., the ominous hour of the twin flame connection, I awoke to the soft voice of Isis, asking me to read for you.

Groggy, I'd been in a deep sleep, I fumbled around to light the kerosene lantern and gather the Runestones.

The moment I tossed the stones, it was exactly as if you were sitting next to me at my kitchen table.

Mary, exciting news from the other side. You have been invited to receive your third ring of power.

Love, it is your choice to accept or decline. Time is an illusion. But if you should accept, your will-to-do-good will be amplified beyond imagination.

Your guides have invited you to Daufuskie Island, September twenty-third when a severe tropical storm aligns with the full harvest moon.

The other side ensured me of your safety and urged you not to listen to trickster establishment media spouting off fear-based speculations written by Madison Avenue advertisers.

Mary, love, the real danger lies next door. As you become a bright lamp of humanity, Mr. Nicopane will become more immersed in hatred and revenge.

Polarity is our cross to bear in the physical.

When I turned over the last stone, Isis said that the size of Mr. Nicopane's stomach would determine when you should act as a Change-Agent. And then poof, she was gone. Odd, I've never heard of such a thing before.

I threw the stones a second time, hoping for clarity, but instead got some fairly juicy relationship updates.

Alright, dear, time will tell, but the stones say that you will be married two times; the first marriage will perfect your dharma and the second marriage will be your happy ever after. That's all I got, love.

Mary, everything is now and potential. Be in the moment and dive deeper into your imagination. Continue to invite true strength and divine wisdom to be with you. Practice rituals for psychic protection, go to Daufuskie with sacred intent, open your senses, work with animal spirits, and learn from different teachers. Pray and perform actions with respect and gratitude.

You will be tested again and again, but remember, love, every crisis is an invitation to perfect your soul. Keep faith in your power and know our spirit energy is united, even across the Atlantic Ocean.

Love, Love, Love,
Grandmamma Sharon

More tests? Really? Recurring lucid nightmares of Daddy's bloody death on my twelfth birthday haunt me. I had to endure the May Howard School expulsion humility test when I was seventeen. And Mama's green Jaguar wrapped around the Grand Oak at the entrance of the Oglethorpe Inn haunts me like it happened yesterday.

I'm twenty-four. Enough tests already. Please, just let me be of service to humanity already. I grab my straw hat and head outside.

The humble garden fairies greet me. I curtsey to my elemental companions who guide me to the garden shed.

I load the wheelbarrow with a stirrup hoe and a digging shovel and tackle the aggressive quack grass invading the perimeter of the veggie plot.

After an hour, I'm drenched. I send love to worldwide farmers working for slave wages in toxic fields. Crumble Grocery Manufacturers Association. Crumble FDA. Crumble USDA. Crumble antiquated greed.

When I'm finished working my way around the plot, I get on my hands and knees and pull dollar weeds from around the tomatoes.

What in the world? Ewe, stinkbugs. I manage to catch one before it flies away. I squish its armored body. Gag.

I am an organic gardener. I squish stinkbugs. Word.

Alright, the heirloom Speckled Butterpea lima beans have sprouted. My spirit soars seeing new life emerge. I succession plant a second row of beans in hopes of a continuous fall harvest.

I feel Mr. Nicopane watching me from the face of his house. How do I stop the good-ole-boy system from blacklisting free spirits?

I stop myself. Shaman Warriors don't ask how.

I squeeze soil in my hand and open my receptivity to solutions coming to me via my intuition.

I have unbending intent to quash greedy establishment politicians, puritans, media, textbook lies, ROTC, PISA, DARE, and corrupt legal systems.

The Universe is abundant. We will build a love-based society that distributes clean food, water, shelter, and peace to our people.

I sow buckwheat seeds where I pulled up turf welcoming the bees, beneficiary insects, and butterflies.

I walk to the dock. The tide is coming in. I imagination-paint a river spirit with flaxen curls falling to her bare bottom. She seduces me, and I dive into her rich estuary.

Ouida squawks her strange tune and joins me. Sunlight filters through fast-moving clouds, casting sparkles on the rippling water.

TWO

When the tide is dead high, husband number one pops into my head. He has a square jaw, dark wavy hair, muscular shoulders, dark olive skin tones, and the Hollywood-dimples that have always been my fantasy. He'll be fun to sketch tonight.

Then Mama pops into my head. She's focused on her upcoming show at Hauser and Wirth Gallery, New York. Was she ever not under the wire?

A long ash floats down from the cigarette hanging from her painted red lips as she labors with her tiny signature brushes. I plead with her soul to talk to me. Has she noticed I'm developing breasts? Is it time to wear a bra? I wait, but she never looks away from her crystal ball. And Marshall's mom ended up taking me bra shopping. Yuck.

The tide turns and the wind shifts. I turn back and swim hard. Right when I'm getting out of the river, Mr. Nicopane, Flambé, and Juicy are walking out on their dock. Could Doberman Pinchers be anymore ferocious?

Ouida flies off towards Wassaw Sound. I hide behind the floating dock and wait for Mr. Nicopane to empty his crab traps. Flambé and Juicy go berserk when they detect my presence.

Unity consciousness with Mr. Nicopane is the unknown. I wait for Mr. Nicopane to get back to his house before I crawl out of the river.

I get a hit in my solar plexus. I need to ask the Universe for a bigger team. I go back to the house, grab a pencil and pad, and start scribing.

Fill the house with free spirits, nondevotees, six-sensors, healers, intellects, and positive thinkers. Develop the ultimate help-and-be-helped scheme. Use the Law of Attraction to bridge those who are conscious of the evolutionary plight of humanity, the planet earth, and the cosmos. Co-create a love-based New Age reality.

That's all I get.

I take a shower, condition my unruly red hair and Spirit-fly-meditate. Please let humanity have equal access to clean water and food.

I visualize small bands of self-empowered, free spirits destroying sell-out establishment politicians and journalists with nothing but the truth.

Will New Age Curriculum mushroom out of what already exists or does a total do-over make more sense?

I get nothing from my guides.

I open my eyes, stretch out my back, and slip on the same Levi cutoffs and tee-shirt I've worn since middle school.

I put on the Elgar Cello Concerto, again. I'm addicted. When the last note fades, I go to the office.

Standing in front of my desk, I pick up Mr. Nicopane's letter. Is it possible that Mr. Nicopane's stationery cost more than a school lunch?

Helen Greenfield

> *To: Miss Mary Howard*
> *From: Mr. Nicopane, Savannah School District Curriculum Director*
> *Date: 7/14/09*
> *Re: Steering Committee Response*
>
> *The Savannah School Board has voted unanimously to deny your proposal. It is not in our mission paradigm to make changes to the School Lunch Program. This denial is final.*

Lizard brain puffs up. A memo? Really? I collapse in the office chair. They *weren't* listening. Yuck.

I plop my head down on the desk and shut my eyes. No way. I won't allow them to kill my spirit. I am loved. I wrap up disgust, frustration, and disappointment into one negative mass and cast it into the ocean. I am a warrior. I have no regrets. Step aside, Mr. Nicopane.

I take a deep breath, visualize a positive response, and open Superintendent Cross' letter. The silky gold and red embossed letterhead is a proclamation to the pecking order.

> *Savannah School District Superintendent, Dr. Cross*
> *666 Bull Street*
> *Savannah, Georgia 31912*
> *7/13/09*
>
> *To: Miss Mary Howard,*
> *The Savannah School District Lunch Program complies with the Center for Disease Control and Prevention (CDC) and the National School Lunch Program (NSLP).*

We do not aim to dazzle with trendy things as much as fill the hungry bellies of our at-risk students while providing popular choices that won't end up in the garbage can.

As times change, so has our school lunch program. We now offer low-fat milk alongside the chocolate milk and whole wheat buns, even though the students and faculty prefer good old white bread. What has not changed, is the one dollar, per student, per meal, ingredient budget.

The 2008 Federal Meal Plan Standard calls for two ounces of protein at the centerpiece of each school lunch. After thirty cents for two ounces of chicken nuggets, forty cents for milk, ten cents for a wheat roll, and twenty cents for dessert, we haven't any wiggle room to shift to the elite menu you recommend.

FYI, I sent the transcript of your claims saying the National School Lunch Program is unhealthy to attorneys representing USDA, FDA, EPA, Monsanto, Dow, DHEC, SYSCO, and USKidpsychmeds™.

Meanwhile, as of 7/13/09, any itty-bitty-teeny-weenie slander against Savannah School District will merit you an Oprah-Winfrey/Beef-Industry-style lawsuit.

Regards,
Superintendent Dr. Cross

Superintendent Dr. Cross you have an itty-bitty-teeny-weenie. So, blacklisting is the same old, same old. They still deny bullying exists. I pace. Blasphemy. Dr. Cross and Mr. Nicopane must be in bed together.

I'm fuming. This stinks of dirty backroom corrupt subsidiary kickbacks. And what kind of false belief system are we creating by telling kids it's smart to eat mutilated chickens, growth hormones, GMOs, soy, chemical cocktails, Trans fat, and high sodium?

I reread Superintendent Cross' letter.

As if kids are any better off consuming ultra-pasteurized white milk and non-organic wheat rolls. Please. And not one word about banning Leukemia-causing hot dogs or French fries that compost slower than a leather boot. Could they be any more insensitive to the childhood obesity epidemic? Ignorant bubbas.

I'm burning up.

I head to the art room. How did Mr. Nicopane get away with calling me "scrawny behind" in front of my peers?

I question my status as a change-agent.

Guide says, "Change channels."

Lizard brain screams, "Fight back!"

My soul aches.

I work until dark, pour myself a Dogfish Double IPA, and dig in the fridge.

When Mr. Nicopane pops in my head, I cast him out to sea, say "love, love, love," and visualize free spirits healing Mother Earth for the next seven generations.

I stir-fry kale and Vidalia onions, steam zucchini and crookneck squash, and food process a thick sauce made with jalapenos, garlic, purple onion, dill, lemon, nama shoyu, cayenne, balsamic vinegar, Roy Day raw goat cheese, honey, and evo.

I fix a plate and sit down.

Universe, please allow this generation to distribute clean food and water to all of humanity. As above, so below, and so it is done.

Outrageously fresh. A masterpiece. The kale energizes my seven chakras. Chlorophyll surges lifeforce energy through my body.

After supper, with Grandmama Sharon's prediction looming, I slip on my smock, squeeze tubes of oil on my palette and start the process.

I set up the structure and define the plane.

I hold Husband Number One steady in my imagination as if he is sitting for me. Love, love, love, Law of Attraction.

Before long, the voices of all my art teachers, since I was three, creep into my psyche to encourage me to search for my unique path.

Polarity. Mystery. Romance. Peace.

By two in the morning, I have to break for the paint to dry.

On the third night, I finish blocking in the shades and shadow areas. Wow, Husband Number One is too good to be true, but, hey, the Universe is abundant, right?

Monkey brain rehashes denial letters, puritanical belief systems, cognitive dissonance, and government institutions that shun free spirits from creating World Peace.

I am so over blissful ignorance.

I take off my smock, clean my brushes, and surf the net.

Come on, Internet, navigate me to southeastern schools teaching Fairy Magic, Psychic Intelligence, and Meditation. Zero matches. I'm distracted by pop-up ads that feature girls with perky tits, bright teeth, and shiny hair selling corporate colonization.

Lost in the rabbit hole, I hear my Fairy Magic Professor warning us against online glamor gurus, positive ions, and electromagnetic radiation.

"Bank in the bank," he said.

I get a hit and write a blog post.

Helen Greenfield

7/21/09

Hello Free Spirits,

    My name is Mary Howard. I am an oil-on-canvas artist and a recent graduate of Diseart Institute, Dingle, Ireland, where I earned my MA in Fairy Magic.
    Are you a six-sensor, spiritualist, or self-healer of mind, spirit, and body? Do you have a passion for balancing nature for the next seven generations?
    If so, the Wilmington Island School might be right for you. At Wilmington Island School we will develop a New Age Curriculum focused on organic edible education, meditation, exploration, and intuition.
    Join Wilmington Island School and help shift humanity to our Love-Based potential by 2020!

Wilmington Island School Application, click here.
Questions and Comments, click here.

I press send. Please let me be of service to free spirits. I fall asleep as soon as my head hits the pillow. A few hours later, monkey brain wakes me with nonstop chatter.

"Don't call it a 'school.' School says rules, tests, and standardization. I rack my brain. Institute, retreat, what?

I walk to the verandah and crawl into my Yucatan hammock. Unaffiliated pops into my head. Unaffiliated, what? Degree-free what?

I watch the half-moon's reflection rippling across the river while the sound of the tide swilling in the marsh grass lulls me into my second sleep.

I wake up at dawn, say "love, love, love," and head to the dock. When Ouida sees me, she starts preening.

"Whewsuu, Whewsuu. Yes, ma'am, you are a beautiful pelican."

I get comfortable, close my eyes, and Spiritfly-meditate until my mind is a still river. I invite my soul to rest on my heart. I radiate love to my southern, eastern, northern, and western brothers and sisters. I transcend time and space and then return. I give gratitude to my guides and float my eyes open.

Ouida flies down a few feet from the floating dock and nabs a school of croaker. The tide is still racing out so I head back to the house.

I flip on the computer and check out the WIS post. Zero hits. I edit the post.

"Wilmington Island School is unaffiliated and degree-free."

That should keep the crowds down until I perfect patience.

I head to the art room. I slip on my smock and squeeze oil paint on my palette. Husband Number One is manifesting into a Technicolor splendor.

Monkey brain chatters, "WIS has zero tolerance for processed food, junk food, factory farms, GMOs, FDA approved chemicals, Big Pharma, or conglomerate agribusinesses."

Guide says, "Unity."

I start dry brushing in shadow lines.

Lizard brain spits on PISA standardized tests that completely ignore social, health, environmental, and happiness indicators. How is it that the Labor Market's desire to increase the Gross National Product would have the last say in what kids should know? As if life is a straightforward multiple choice test.

I finish the final shadow lines.

Guide says, "Teach your highest truth, reach out, tell the truth into ears who will hear you, and dismiss the naysayer with love."

I go outside and get on my hands and knees to validate my feelings. I ask for Mother Earth to ground me with her loving dirt, and I blanket Mother Earth with the nurturing energy she seeks and so rightly deserves.

When I head back to the art room, *Young Lovers*, *Child's Wonder*, and *Movie Star Man* pop into my head. I curtsey to my muses in gratitude for inspiration and ideas.

I finish priming and sanding three more canvases before I break. I head to the kitchen and make a coconut butter, cinnamon, maple syrup, pecan, coconut flakes, and raisin wrap. Scrumptious.

I check the WIS post before bed. Zero hits. Refresh. Zero hits. I stop myself from doubting Wilmington Island School will materialize. I'm learning to trust my intuition. The Law of Attraction will work. Everything will happen in Divine time.

I check Underground Weather. All is calm in the tropics.

I shut down the computer, turn on Koyaanisqatsi, and pick up *Quantum Mechanics of Many-Body Systems.*

How many times have I started this book? Why is dream-state so easy to paint and such an unsolvable puzzle to express with words?

I make it through the introduction and fall asleep. The next day, I wake up before dawn and walk out to the dock.

Ouida is off fishing.

I am calm in body, spirit, and mind during my morning Spiritfly-meditation. I align myself with the light and cozy up to the greater good. When I float my eyes open, I slip off my clothes and dive into the river. It's high tide and the water is as smooth as glass.

This is my idea of heaven on earth.

I get back to the house around noon and make the final touches on *Movie Star Man.*

Oh jah. I do. Kiss, kiss.

After lunch, I ask the feather-light River Goddess, lodged in my imagination, to come forward and model for me. I sketch her hands, fingers, and toes before taking a break.

It's late by the time I start supper. I put sprouted brown rice and garbanzo beans on to cook while I chop beet greens, onion, celery, garlic, wild ginger, and basil. Five minutes before the rice and beans are ready, I throw in the veggies. I season the pot with nama shoyu, lemon juice, and evo, and fix a plate.

When I sit down at the kitchen table, it dawns on me that this is my six-month pescatarian anniversary. Thank you, Animal Activists for live-streaming Youtube videos from inside Smithfield and Tyson factory farms.

Chlorophyll surges lifeforce energy deep down in my pelvic region. Wow. Five stars.

After dinner, I prepare my palette and start the process. By four A.M., *River Goddess* springs to life. I clean my brushes, take off my smock, and crawl in my hammock.

Midmorning I catch the high tide and swim half way across the river and back. By the time I get back to the house, it's late afternoon. After I sundry, I head back to the art room.

Movie Star Man is real, and we will hook up.

While I wait for *River Goddess* to dry I sand and prime canvases. When I'm finishing the second coat of primer, I get a hit to let Marshall know about Wilmington Island School.

I take a quick shower, slip on a clean pair of cut-offs and a white tee-shirt, and lock up the house.

Yuck, Mr. Nicopane is spraying harsh chemicals on his GE roses. When Flambé and Juicy see me, they go crazy. Please don't let those two dogs jump over that seven-foot wrought iron gate.

I slip into the garage. What am I going to do with Daddy's sculpting tools, his unfinished sculptures, and thousand-pound blocks of Carrera Italian marble?

When Mr. Nicopane goes inside, I jog down the avenue of oaks and hang a left on Wilmington River Road.

Across the street, middle-aged men traipse across the Oglethorpe Golf Course, oblivious to the lethal chemicals EPA approves for recreational green spaces. Really, EPA? Are you completely unaware of the bad karma you will incur by killing Mother Earth and Humanity?

I stop myself from feeding Establishment negativity, disgust, hate, or self-pity. I am learning patience. When I learn patience, I will teach others patience.

I walk up to Marshall's front door. No answer. I walk around to the kitchen. He doesn't answer but the door is unlocked, so I go inside. Very neat. Things must be going well with Rosemarie.

I stop in the living room to take in Mama's sixteen by twenty portrait of Benjamin One's father performing a Shaman healing ceremony with drums and rattles. Mama's invisible brush strokes illuminate the spirit world.

There's a father and son who have vitality and fire. I fantasize that Benjamin One is energizing my Ka body. Holy yes, please.

Gone, gone, gone. Our parents passed to the other side and left three twenty-four-year-olds in charge of shifting the planet to loved-based. Exit plans, yeah, yeah, yeah.

I walk out to the dock.

THREE

I find Marshall asleep in his Yucatan hammock. I nudge him, and he wakes up after a random snort.

"Hey, there," I say.

"Mary, hello, great to see you," Marshall says.

I lean into his 6'2" frame for a hug.

"Good book?" I ask.

"Yes, I started reading it yesterday afternoon and haven't stopped learning about the horrors of banana plantations ever since," Marshall says.

"*Green Prison?*" I ask.

"Corporate greed has created horrendous suffering and exploitation on banana plantations," Marshall says.

"Banana farmers are treated badly?" I ask.

"Dole and Chiquita profit off of slave labor," Marshall says. "And they have been genetically modifying bananas since the 1950s."

"I can handle more," I say.

Marshall twists one up and alters his psychoactivity.

"Scientists have engineered the Cavendish banana to have

a long shelf life, zip-off peel, uniform shape, and seeds the size of dots."

"I never thought about banana seeds."

"Neither did scientists when they decided to eliminate seeds and rely on cuttings. Not smart. Tropical Race Four blight is wiping out banana plantations across Southeast Asia and Australia and threatening bananas worldwide. Now scientists can't stop the blight's destruction. Why? They eliminated the seed. I started an online pledge to boycott Cavendish bananas."

"Did you get any response?"

"Overwhelming. Within twelve hours, I had hundreds of comments saying I was nuts. The masses aren't willing to boycott bananas for a single morning."

"Carmen Miranda's "Banana Song" worked."

"Only two people shared the Youtube video I posted that exposed banana farmers being drenched with toxic chemicals that have been banned in the EU and the US for decades."

"Shameful, I had no idea."

"Banana farmers make slave wages, work eighty-hour weeks, and have no access to running water or bathrooms. To make things worse, Cavendish bananas are so hybridized that humans can't absorb their nutrients."

"What a waste. What about fair trade and organic?"

"As of today, I am boycotting Dole and Chiquita," Marshall says.

"I am in solidarity, brother. Good riddance 5,000-mile carbon footprint. Now to get my head around green smoothies without bananas," I frown.

"Corporations brainwash us to believe we need cheap food even if it means polluting nature, depleting natural resources, and exploiting workers."

"Am I hearing the subject of your next book?" I ask.

"Perhaps. Since handing out leaflets, Cesar Chavez-style would get me banned from island grocery stores just like you."

"So true," I say.

Marshall goes over to the dock fridge and pops open two Dogfish Double IPAs. Heaven.

"How's lil' sistah?"

I wait for Marshall to read Dr. Cross' and Mr. Nicopane's letters. He shakes his head "no." I roll my eyes.

"Mary, I'm sorry."

It hits me how deep sad runs.

"They made their decision before this study even started," I say. "All of the guests administrators testified that changing to organic fruit, veggies, beans, grains, nuts, and seeds stopped bullying and kid-psych drug prescriptions, and organic plant-based lunches ended up being cheaper. Cheaper!"

Ouida flies over and nudges me. We have to laugh.

"The good ole boy system," Marshall says.

"Will I always be blacklisted?" Tears unhinge.

"Mr. Nicopane is a cruel irritant who teaches us the last lesson for our soul's perfection: patience," Marshall says.

"How do I achieve Unity Consciousness when Mr. Nicopane continuously kills my spirit?"

"Mr. Nicopane is the crisis that forces evolution. The question is 'what now?'"

I stand up.

"Okay, drum roll, please... Marshall, I've decided to take a leap of faith and totally throw myself into the Law of Attraction. I've sent a new thought pattern to the Universe."

"What's this brewing in your imagination, Mary?"

"I've invited free spirits to join our esoteric study group. I want to be of service to like-minded people who are open to the fundamentals of reincarnation and evolution. I'm using the Law of Attraction to make our love-based takeover plan more successful," I say.

Marshall holds his hit, communes with Great Spirit, and exhales.

"I figured out how to make an online blog post and sent Wilmington Island School out to the Universe," I say.

"Has anybody taken you up?"

"No. But we *are* talking one percent of the one percent if that," I say.

"Where will this school exist?" Marshall asks.

"In my ancestral home. I have seven empty bedrooms."

"Are schools legal in residential areas?" He grabs the hemostatic clamps.

"Marshall, the time is now to create a parallel reality free of rules, deadlines, requirements, and judgment," I say. "They can shove memorizing viewpoints of greedy kings and selfish queens who fought bloody for-profit wars in faraway places long, long ago."

"So you decided to ask for forgiveness rather than permission?" Marshall laughs.

"I always do," I say. "Imagine free spirits focusing on quality, joy, happiness, peace, understanding, justice, kindness, giving, selflessness, courage, faith, and trust."

"Salute, to the Wilmington Island School. Knowledge for the pursuit of good, truth, and beauty to experience the ideal realm," he says.

We clink beer bottles.

"Hey, what happened yesterday?" I ask.

"Rosemarie met me at the Isle of Hope Marina. After spending an incredible day on the river, we decided to tell Professor Lowe that we were in love."

Color me impressed. I curtsy to him in gratitude.

"Rosemarie is the fifth generation of Lowe's. Their mansion spans four lots of riverfront property."

"Who knew?"

"We found Professor Lowe in the library puffing on his Sherlock-Holmes-type pipe. He was perched on a white leather swivel chair behind an oversized mahogany desk. Noxious tobacco fumes filled the room.

"He interrogates me about my parents and the authenticity of their posthumous publications."

"Insensitive on steroids."

"He pushed for details until I shouted out that they were blown to smithereens in Citaltépetl when the Orizaba Volcano erupted."

"What a creep."

"Then he called me the laughing stock of academia and a philosophical hoax for uneducated hippies."

"Please, you were coined the overnight philosophical sensation by *Rolling Stone.* You've made the *New York Times* best-seller list two times. What more could Professor Lowe possibly need to know about your accomplishments?"

"All that matters to Professor Lowe is my Athens, Georgia, arrest six years ago," Marshall says.

"Who is against peaceful college protesters fighting to stop Big Pharma from illegally buying cannabis seed rights?"

"He's a Libertarian. He thinks the men in blue have the right to make hippies conform with tear gas, Taser guns, and billy clubs."

"Does he support the militarization of police and the privatized prison 'ninety-eight percent occupancy quota?'"

"He took the side of the CO who waited two weeks to issue our release papers. He thinks nonviolent offenders, the mentally ill, and hardened criminals should all rot together."

"People who think it is okay to lock their fellow brothers and sisters in a cube, strip them of free will, addict them to pharmaceutical grade opiates, and force them to survive on boiled eggs and spam are the ones I'd like to see in privatized prisons."

I get us another beer.

"What did Rosemarie say?"

"She called him a neoconservative, defense hawk, religious right, psychic vampire who sucks vitality and happiness from the human race."

"She's assertive."

"She is one to speak her mind," Marshall says.

"A lesson she had to learn the hard way," I say.

"You're not kidding. When she told him she loved me, he grabbed a Civil War-style shotgun and charged at me like a pit bull."

"Get out."

"He's a tall man with short legs," Marshall says.

"What?"

"He chased me halfway back to Isle of Hope Marina. When I motored past on *Driftwood*, Rosemarie was on her dock flagging me over. When I slowed down to pick her up, a bullet whizzed by my head."

"You're lucky to be alive."

"It was surreal. So now we practice patience and visualize Professor Lowe being receptive to Universal Love," Marshall says.

"Love and peace, Professor Lowe," I say. "Hey, did Crew start the Krispy Kreme and Coca-Cola ban yesterday?"

"Yeah, he stopped by for a beer last night. Day one was hard-hitting. Those boys were weaned on lard, cornmeal, and Dixie sugar. Changing Thunderbolt Valley Police Department will be like winning the Olympic gold."

"TVPD Change Olympics," I laugh.

"Crew has plotted criminal reform for as long as I can remember."

"He has lofty goals in the name of justice," I say. "Hey, I'm going fishing before sunset, so I better take off."

Marshall swings out of the hammock, and we walk back to the house. Ouida flaps her wings and flies upriver.

"Thanks for coming over," he says. "And congrats on Wilmington Island School."

"Now and potential brother-man," I say.

We hug goodbye. Reckless drivers on Wilmington River Road speed past in luxury sedans, racing to new gated communities that didn't exist seven years ago.

I get home, head to the office, turn on the computer, and Google bananas. After confirming what Marshall said about worldwide banana blights, I find a list of multinational companies like Coca-Cola, Exon Mobile, Dole, Chiquita, and Del Monte who routinely pay leftist guerrillas to assassinate Trade Unionists and Land Reform Activists. I read testimonies from terrorized peasant farmers, labor leaders, and union organizers who say off-the-bus abductions and forced-entry murders are routine.

I stop halfway through an article about global land grabs and fall asleep in my Yucatan hammock.

I am on the river by five in the morning. Ouida nestles beside me, and we motor to Wassaw Sound.

The river is as smooth as glass and winds are calm from the north. Before daybreak, I turn off the engine and Spiritfly-meditate. Please, if it is in accordance with the Universe, we will have more caring people than greedy people by the year 2020. Love-based seems light-years away after realizing how many third-world banana plantation farmers have died in the name of seeds the size of dots inside a zip-off peel.

At daybreak, I come out of meditation and adjust my eyes to the rich golden hues.

I motor to the mouth of Halfmoon River, nose up to the marsh, cast the net, and pull up a few pogies and a half dozen shrimp. Plenty of live bait for today.

About a mile down the Halfmoon River, Ouida flies off the bow and nabs a school of spot tails. I throw anchor and decorate my hook with a jumbo shrimp.

I cast my line and soon get a nibble. I keep the tip low and wait. Yes, a bite. I jerk the rod back. Gotcha. Nice size. After a twenty-minute fight, I start slowly reeling him to the surface: a doormat flounder.

Alright, fella. I scoop him into the net, hold him tight, and remove the barbless hook. When I'm throwing him in the cooler, the flounder wills me to look at him. I look into his black eyes and see the inside of a slaughterhouse.

I stop myself from sending mixed signals to the Universe. Gratitude Great Spirit. Thank you for my gift of divination.

I bait my hook and cast. Soon I get another bite. We dance. A whopper flounder surfaces. What a magnificent beast. I'm in my element. Ouida watches from the bow, immobilized by her catch.

I remove the barbless hook and look into the flounder's eye. 'I feel pain,' the fish screams. Goose pimples run up my arms and down my spine. I thank Great Spirit for providing and pull the anchor.

I drift over to the marsh grass and scoop up pieces of broken Styrofoam coolers. What kind of corrupt EPA goons would approve carcinogenic, non-biodegradable Styrofoam? I motor home.

I scrub the deck and hoist *One That Got Away* in the dock house. After I fillet the flounders, I head back to the house.

I take a quick shower, crank up the vintage RCA, and start cleaning. Rostropovich is performing the "Six Unaccompanied Cello Suites" by J.S. Bach, my fave. Funny how dust bunnies and dead insects love to die in hard-to-get-to corners. Ahh, the Fifth Cello Suite tuned scordatura. I love it.

I envision my house full of free-spirit-six-sensor-escapees-from-government-institutions who believe we can collectively balance Mother Earth to be love-based by 2020.

I switch the CD to Suites II, IV, and VI, set the table, and finish prepping supper.

Guide says, "Isis is pleased with the creation of Wilmington Island School. Dive deeper in your imagination. Be free. Fly."

I see Marshall's green Packard pull up the avenue of oaks and walk out to meet them.

We go inside before Flambé and Juicy go nuts.

FOUR

"I LOVE THE ECLECTIC ART TUCKED IN EVERY NOOK AND CRANNY," Rosemarie says.

"Art collected by three generations of painters, sculptors, pirates, smugglers, and world travelers," Marshall says.

Crew serves us generous pours of French Cabernet Sauvignon.

"To loving the earth and the sun and the animals," Marshall says. We clink.

"Wine, to strengthen friendship and light the flame of love," Crew says.

"To loving understanding," I say.

Small talk brings us to Professor Lowe.

"Marshall doesn't fit my parents' programmed life for me. I was raised in a barrage of CNN. They used fear tactics to make me be a straight 'A' student, appear optimistic, and parade proper etiquette," Rosemarie says.

"My parents were solitary artists. Marshall's folks raised Crew and me," I say.

"As animists," Marshall says.

"As Shaman Warriors," I laugh.

"My father has a sour disposition and a passion for Cuban cigars and Kentucky bourbon," Crew says. "And my mother is the worst type of society-snob."

"What do they do?" Rosemarie asks.

"I come from a lineage of physicians. When I refused to be a Big Pharma puppet and dropped out of pre-med, my folks attempted to cut me off from my Grandmother's trust. So, I got online and learned that what they were planning was illegal," Crew laughs. "And that's why I'm the only police chief who lives on deep water and drives a new Roadster."

"You crack me up," I laugh.

"Crew, why police work?" Rosemarie asks.

"Thunderbolt Village Police Department, the poster boy of unfair and partial enforcement, seemed like a good starting point for an up-and-coming peace activist."

"Where are your parents now?" Rosemarie asks.

"My career choice caused them so much social embarrassment that they hightailed it to Lexington, Kentucky," Crew says.

"Where they remain bitter about everything," Marshall says.

Rosemarie asks us about a picture of Marshall's parents performing as the Wanderlust Duo.

"Mr. Portunus played the accordion, and Mrs. Portunus had a low alto voice," Crew says.

"They sang South American love songs," I say. "They were beautiful people who gave soulful performances."

"Their fave was taking us to hear the Thunderbolt AME Church Hammond C3 organist, lead soprano, and gospel choir," Marshall says.

"Marshall and I are still regulars," Crew says.

"Good people, good music, and the best church supper anywhere," Marshall says. "Hey, Mary, how about a garden tour?"

"Absolutely," I say.

We refill our wine glasses and go outside.

"The Speckled Butterpea lima beans just sprouted."

"I love how the garden constantly changes," Marshall says.

"The alchemy of sun, rain, seeds, and soil," I say.

I show them the three-foot okra stalks flowering with creamy white petals that have magenta centers, eggplant bushes loaded with purple flowers, and heirloom tomatoes in every shade of green, yellow, and pale orange.

"Mary grows food where she used to mow the lawn," Crew says.

I snap off fennel for everybody to taste.

"Yum, licorice. This would be fantastic with roasted vegetables," Marshall says.

We harvest enough fennel and cilantro seed heads for everyone to take home. Joy. Gratitude.

"Hey, what's this Marshall tells us about the Mary Howard School taking over the May Howard School?" Crew asks.

"The irony," I crackup. "Wilmington Island School is the love-based takeover plan taking shape."

"WIS is the root of wisdom," Rosemarie says.

"That never dawned on me," I say.

"Wisdom, the combination of knowledge and experience," Marshall says.

"I believe the Universe will bring us artists, activists, meditators, intellects, and intuits. I'm hoping all of you will join me."

"Count me in. I'll happily teach Spiritual Yoga at WIS," Rosemarie says.

"Rosemarie, what did you study at Emory?" Crew asks.

"I was labeled the town-crier-barn-burner because I staged protests against the Textbook Industry for blatantly omitting current information on climate change and GMOs in New Edition bundles.

I was banned from Environmental Science, Biology, Physics and eventually the whole Science Department because they could not convince me to roll with the punches," Rosemarie says. "After six years, I left without a degree."

"Thankfully Diseart was textbook and rule free," I say. "On the other hand, telling people I have a Master's Degree in Fairy Magic is like saying I came here from Mars on a spaceship."

"Crew, will you teach Peace and Preservation classes?"

"I'd join the faculty in order to expand the Peace and Preservation Program if it is legal to house a school in a private residence," Crew says.

"No worries. WIS is degree-free and unaffiliated," I say. "Are you in Marshall?"

"*My Thoughts, My Things and My Soul, My Intuition* are custom made for WIS."

"Yippee!"

We walk out on the dock at sunset. The tide is high, and the river is choppy. I marvel at this place where we will serve Humanity and the personal sacrifices we will endure in order to achieve Unity. The time is now. We are worthy of the fruits of our labor. We will protect Mother Earth for the next seven generations.

"Here comes Ouida!" Crew says.

Ouida lands on the dock. She flaps her expansive wings, cuts her eyes at us, and preens. Crew tosses her the squeaky fish toy; Ouida catches it and tosses it back.

"Good girl," he says, and throws it back.

"Squeak, squeak," she catches it, throws it back, and flies to her piling.

"That's it, she won't play anymore," Crew cracks up.

"She's a two-hit wonder," I say.

We say goodnight to Ouida and head back to the house.

"How's it going with the Krispy Kreme and Coke ban?" Rosemarie asks.

"They act like sullen brats," Crew says.

"What's up?" Marshall asks.

"Chopper and Lardus decided to swap Krispy Kreme for Carry Hilliard fried seafood take outs. The station stinks."

"How do you keep your composure?" Rosemarie asks.

"Crew's a good-natured spirit. He can calm others down in times of crisis," I say.

"Not this time. I added fried food to the Krispy Kreme and Coke ban," Crew says.

"A Brown Food Ban in Savannah?" Marshall asks. "How did that fly?"

"Lardus called me a control freak and stormed out crying," Crew says.

"What did you do?" I ask.

"He's a grown man. I let him go in peace. The department knows I mean business and that I am prepared to enforce these bans," Crew says. "What I believe is that changes in my small department will lead to changes in bigger departments."

"We are what we eat," Rosemarie says.

"They'll be fine after twenty-one days," I say.

"That's hard to believe, so I kicked it up a notch with two J16 race sailboats I purchased on eBay. I'm taking TVPD out on the river."

"Two J16s sight unseen?" Marshall asks.

"That's what trust fund babies do. We take virtual tours and have big political dreams," Crew jokes.

"J16s fly," Rosemarie says.

"It's a positive distraction while they get off junk food," Crew says. "Training is everything. Mark Twain said, 'The peach was once a bitter almond; cauliflower is nothing but cabbage with a college education.'"

We get back to the house and crank up Nancy Wilson and Cannonball Adderley. Marshall refills our wine, and we tour the art room.

Crew, Marshall, and Rosemarie give me kind compliments. They love my new paintings, but strangely, nobody comments on *Movie Star Man*.

We sit down at the dining room table, and I say a simple blessing to honor Mother Earth before we pass pineapple, tangerine, pink grapefruit, strawberry, coconut flakes, and raisin fruit salad. Rosemarie thanks me for serving the fruit first. Music to my ears that someone else knows about proper food combination.

Next, I bring out the main course.

"Wow, aromatic," Rosemarie says.

"The flounder is tender perfection," Crew says.

"Fresh caught at sunrise," I say.

"What's in the stuffing?" Crew asks.

"Oven roasted zucchini, ginger, dill, and lemon."

"This is the best rice casserole, ever," Rosemarie says. "What's your secret?"

"Sprouting. When the grains and beans become a living vegetable, it not only tastes sweeter but cooks in fifteen minutes and digests the same as a vegetable."

"A sweet and nutty combination," Marshall says.

"I'm going to learn how to sprout," Rosemarie says.

"Soul Sisters," Crew says.

We open another bottle of red wine and linger at the table before moving the party out to the dock house.

The half-moon is rising, and the river is choppy. We watch eels and garfish picking at the barnacles on the dock piling under the dock lamp that illuminates the iridescent river.

The conversation drifts to banana plantations, slave labor, and toxic work environments. Marshall explains the wasted carbon footprint, massive blight, and over hybridization. We fill Crew in on our Dole and Chiquita Cavendish banana boycott.

"Bananas are better than New World Bakery, right?" Crew asks.

"Crew, everything isn't 'A' or 'F.' When we figure out a green smoothie replacement, you can jump on the Savannah banana-ban-band-wagon with us," I say.

"That's one more example of new edition textbook bundles systematically and historically omitting Resource Depletion, Deforestation, and Genetic Engineering from public school and university textbooks," Rosemarie says.

"Environmental crime is too lucrative to leak the truth to free spirits," I say. "That's why they don't teach common sense, the knack of seeing things as they are, and doing things as they ought to be done."

"So Marshall tells me your neighbor is a Primitive Calvinist," Rosemary says. "And responsible for your expulsion when you were seventeen."

"Warriors have no regrets," I say. "The sting of being expelled for immoral conduct by a Right Wing Christian Judge and a Primitive Calvinist was my ticket to escape from Mr. Nicopane's torture chamber."

"I remember when Mary started talking about Native American genocide and West Virginia Turkey Farm investigations during her God and Country Thanksgiving Speech," Crew says.

"Mr. Nicopane was clipping his toenails," Marshall says. "And, when Mary said pilgrims were envious, angry, greedy, gluttonous, lusty sloths, he went off," Marshall says.

"That's when he told me to get my 'scrawny unbaptized behind' out of his class one too many times, and I mooned him," I say.

"Then she mooned the rest of us," Crew says.

Rosemary gets the giggles, and we all start laughing.

Crew looks at his watch, stands up, and stretches. He wakes up every day at four thirty. I'm amazed he still parties.

"Words out that Mayor Archibald Doolittle has plans to sneak a vote in at the City Council meeting next month," Crew says. "The mayor is attempting to obtain illegal permits for Doolittle Development, Inc., to backfill pristine Pigeon Island. Cecil Lloyd is leading a *pro bono* team of attorneys he calls the Georgia Barrier Island Preservation Coalition. We're going to pack the courtroom with environmental activists at five o'clock on August twenty-ninth," Crew says.

"Inconvenient for nine to fivers," Rosemarie says.

"Government disparities," Crew says. "Look, we all need to speak. Doolittle is gung-ho about his latest scheme to build a billionaire fantasy island.'"

"The third generation of incompetent Doolittles that over-indulge on cornbread oysters, filet mignon, Coke-Cola cake, and Cutty Sark before warming themselves by the fire at The Olde Pink House," I say.

"The Doolittle legacy," Rosemarie says. "The epoxy greasing Savannah's wheel of progress since my Great, Great Grandparents."

"Let's get this young and rich thing going on y'all," Crew says.

"Rosemarie, we've been speaking at City Council meetings since we were fifteen," I say. "Our day-of routine is lunch at Mrs. Wilkes, cocktails at Pinkie Master's Lounge, and a buzzed march to City Hall."

"We focus on the desired outcome," Marshall says.

"Speaking of desired outcomes, I have some great news," Crew says. "When I spoke to Cecil Lloyd earlier today he said Earth, Wind & Fire have started contract negotiations."

"Visualize a signed contract," Marshall says.

"And Cecil really surprised me when he invited all of us to take a cruise to Cumberland on his new Chris Craft motor yacht to speak at the Georgia Barrier Island Preservation Coalition annual meeting," Crew says. "I told him yes. Y'all are in, right?"

Marshall and Rosemarie say yes.

How bad could it be spending the weekend with my attorney? Why should it bother me that Cecil Lloyd has seen me moon Mr. Nicopane hundreds of times on the big screen? It was a courtroom, not real life. My soul begs me to say yes. She pleads with me to let go of past shame and stop discriminating against lawyers.

I say I'd love to go.

FIVE

The next morning the phone wakes me. I say "love, love, love," and pick up.

"Patrick here, your friendly Dublin Art Agent."

"Patrick, how are you?"

"I miss you, love. And I miss your Mum horribly. I did the cliché look-in-the-mirror thing…" His voice quivers.

I envision Bonaventure Cemetery when the rain let loose, everybody left, and Patrick and I held each other and sobbed beside Mama's muddy grave.

"All we can do is keep moving forward," I say.

"Speaking of which, I had a wondrous vision of a Mary Howard Solo Show at the Dublin Art Institute," Patrick says.

"Really? When?" I ask.

"The first of November," Patrick says.

"This November?" I ask.

"Correct, November 1, 2009," Patrick says. "What are the chances that you would be ready?"

Is this really happening to me?

"I'm ready, I have hundreds of finished paintings in Savannah and Dingle."

"Done, done, done."

"Thank you, Patrick."

Mary, I'm asking you to step into a big space so keep painting."

"Will do."

"I'll send a contract to Cecil Lloyd, e-mail you the itinerary, and have my staff contact you to arrange packing and shipping."

"I'm joyous," I say.

"Ditto, Mary Howard," Patrick says. "I have a feeling this is going to be big. Love, I have to take another call," Patrick says.

"Cheers, Patrick," I say.

"I'll be in contact, love."

I dance a jig all the way down to the dock and kiss Ouida.

I get comfortable, and Spiritfly-meditate, but monkey brain micromanages every minute. Hush monkey brain and allow me to transcend. Please.

I transcend one-quarter of a minute and then float my eyes open. I slip out of my sundress and dive into the river. The tide is high, and the water is as smooth as glass. I swim until the current gets too strong and then sun-dry on the floating dock.

Okay, lots to do today. I go inside to make lunch. The fridge is bare. A trip downtown is inevitable. I make an ALT sandwich with the last of the hot mustard, avocado, romaine lettuce, and heirloom Brandywine tomato on the last two pieces of sprouted flourless bread.

I visualize world peace and let plant-based food lifeforce energy nourish my energy body. I take a quick shower and tie my hair in a knot on top of my head. I put on my go-to orange yoga skirt, white sleeveless Irish linen top, and vortex-powered Sedona cowboy boots.

The silver Honda takes three tries to start. I guess that's normal after sitting for weeks. I roll my window down and air out the stench of Boones Farm and Mexican weed that colonized in the upholstery during high school.

I cruise down the avenue of oaks and tune in WZAT 102.1. "Carry on Wayward Son*"* is playing so I crank it up and sing along. When I pass the Oglethorpe Inn, I blow Mama a kiss. Today, I'm feeling better about her dramatic exit plan.

"Way of the World" plays next, and I get a clear hit that EWF will sign the Cucurbit Pepo Contract when they read about my love-based take-over plan.

I drive down palm-lined Victory Drive thinking about all of the energy and money I wasted attending ridiculous board meetings last spring. I dive deeper in my imagination to think of ways to quash antiquated systems so that free spirits will soar.

I take a right on Abercorn. What a vicious cycle of fear-based rule followers making fear-based rules with fear-based consequences that kill free spirits. I pull into the parking lot in Forsyth Park and cast sadness away.

I grab a cart and head to the produce department. The shelves are stocked. Score. I'm in heaven. I fill my cart with local organic produce and the only case of organic Georgia peaches in town. I visualize Dole and Chiquita crumbling. I stock up on organic bulk dried fruits, seeds, and nuts. I am ready for my Daufuskie camp-out should the storm line up with the full moon.

I'm stashing my groceries in the cooler when it starts to drizzle. I grab my umbrella and take a walk through Forsyth Park. Savannah is one of the most picturesque cities in the world.

I take my time imagination-painting rain droplets hitting the lace and folds on the curly wrought iron around the main fountain.

When the rain stops, a double rainbow inspires me to walk to River Street. When I'm passing the Savannah School District Administration Building, my blood boils. Imagine Mr. Nicopane, a Primitive Calvinist, sitting in his posh office choosing puritanical lies that suck the life out of our natural love of learning. Unreal. I'm fuming.

I feel Mr. Nicopane's evil spirit smirking at me. I need closure. I cross the street, run up the marble stairs, and enter the foyer.

I catch a glimpse of the cantankerous front desk secretary. She's in the break room eating sheet cake. When she turns to pour herself a cup of coffee, I dash upstairs and race down the hall.

Mr. Nicopane is as toned as a barracuda. The only thing on his oversized mahogany desk is a box of Krispy Kreme Donuts marked 'fundraiser/free samples' and a Grande Krispy Kreme Kafe Latte with whip cream and sprinkles. Sprinkles?

"A donut fundraiser when there is a childhood obesity epidemic? Are you joking?"

"Your denial is final; go away," he puffs up, takes a bite out of his powdered sugar donut, and raspberry filling runs down his chin.

I get a surge of unbending intent to free children of puritanical values.

"Hey, let go of my collar, you brat," he squeals.

Whoa, Mr. Nicopane's stomach is the size of a Florida pomelo. Unworldly powers bellow up through my Sedona boots.

I take him down.

"Hey, get your boot off my throat."

I hold him against his plush plum Berber carpet. I use dead weight to push my right knee against his pomelo-sized-stomach and keep my left foot hovering over his Adam's apple. "The devil can cite scripture for his purpose. I accept your belief system: minister, rabbi, priest, pundit, monk, chaplain, guru, Swami, nun, atheist, and beyond, but you must accept mine as Goddess of Ancient Wisdom. God is nonjudgmental and believes I am moral."

"You heathen, I relish in the ruin of your dark soul perishing in the ring of fire."

"I am loved by a heavenly host of angels. I have gratitude that you set me free from the prison you call public schools," I say.

Mr. Nicopane thrusts his muscular body. I balance my chakras and slowly pour his Kafe Latte, whip cream, and sprinkles on the crotch of his lavish navy blue designer pants.

"Oh no, Mr. Nicopane. You peed yourself. The ring of fire is officially dowsed. What will your colleagues think when they see that you've wet yourself?"

"Vile whoremonger wicked sinner," he squeals.

"Be gone with your evil spirit, Mr. Nicopane! I am a change-agent, and I have unbending intent to create a parallel system where kids aren't bullied by evil spirited people like you."

I let go and race out of the building. My heart is pounding. Is this the woman I have become? I jog through Forsyth Park. How unsophisticated. I get back to the silver Honda. Adrenaline pulses my veins.

I peel out around the squares and speed down President Street. When I get to the Island Expressway, I get a hit to drive to the ocean. When I approach the Bull River, I open the window, slow way down, and take it all in. And when I'm driving past Fort Pulaski, I ask the *Gambas,* the tortured spirits of dead soldiers, to remove Mr. Nicopane's evil spirit.

North Beach is packed. I nonchalantly walk out to the surf, strip down to my underwear, and swim out to deep water. Strong southeast winds make the perfect waves for bodysurfing. I gain speed, catch the crest of an incoming wave, and fly diagonally across the face of the break. Exuberating. I am a change-agent. Please, let me be receptive to my soul desire.

I soak up the ocean's negative ions and swim back to shore just before shark feeding time.

I get home at dark thirty. Mr. Nicopane's flickering TV gives me the creeps. It's none of my business to know what he's thinking so I keep monkey brain from going there. No need to make myself crazy.

Why is there a box by my door? Flambé and Juicy come around the corner and unnerve me. Oh, I forgot to pick up my CSA today and Roy Day dropped it off for me.

I unload groceries and my massive box of Roy Day organic produce, raw goat cheese, and farm fresh brown eggs. I shower, Spiritfly-meditate, and visualize humanity being loved-based. Please let us be the generation that ends the separatism meme.

I'm famished. I head to the kitchen. I fry an egg, add onions, spinach, portabellos and raw goat cheese and then I make a sprouted tortilla wrap. Oh man, this is the ticket.

I steep mint tea and head to the art room.

Monkey brain goes nonstop. What will Mr. Nicopane do? What? Should I go next door tomorrow morning and apologize? At three A.M., I stop to let the paint dry. Wired, I toss and turn endlessly. When I finally drift off to sleep, I slip right into my recurring nightmare.

I am turning twelve years old today. To celebrate my birthday, Daddy is taking me deep sea fishing. We motor three hours past Wassaw Sound and throw the anchor where we see pelicans fishing.

We bait our hooks with Spanish mackerel and cast. Bonitos hit right away. We reel them in. Daddy explains that bonitos are throwbacks. Too bloody to eat. We reel in and release a half dozen more bonitos before Daddy decides to pull the anchor and motor to a new spot.

Again, bonitos hit. But this time a barracuda hits the hooked bonito. More barracuda appear. It's a bloody feeding frenzy. A barracuda jerks the rod and reel out of my hand, and I watch it disappear in deep water.

Daddy reels in a four-foot barracuda. He cuts the line, the barracuda thrusts its muscular body, lunges, and clamps its mouthful of jagged teeth around Daddy's neck.

The nightmare becomes lucid. I'm in a dream within a dream. I grab the gaff and hysterically stab the barracuda until I manage to throw the beast overboard.

I'm too late. A host of angels ascend with Daddy's spirit. I lift buckets of river water and scrub blood, slime, and ciguatera toxin stench off the deck until my arms ache.

I wake up in a cold sweat, sit up, and breathe deeply to balance my chakras. Love, love, love; be gone nightmare. I tell my subconscious to please release me from experiencing Daddy's bloody exit plan again and again.

I walk to the dock at dawn, greet Ouida, and Spiritfly-meditate. I am loved. My mind is a still river. The wrath of Mr. Nicopane stops me from transcending.

I dive into the river and sculpt my muscles against the racing tide. I am a change-agent. I am love-based. I will be of service to free spirits.

I head back to the house an hour later. Lots to do today.

I shower, slip on my orange yoga skirt, and tie my hair in a knot on top of my head. After I make a green smoothie, I head to the office to make volunteer sign-up sheets for this year's Cucurbit Pepo Pageant, and We Saw Wassaw camp-out.

I finalize today's agenda, organize my tote, and walk to the Flower Power Meeting.

Between Dublin Institute of Art, the Barracuda nightmare, and Mr. Nicopane, I'm a wreck, so I stop by Marshall's house.

"Hey there, it's me," I say.

"What a pleasant surprise. Coffee?" Marshall asks.

"I'm boycotting coffee."

"This is organic, Fairtrade, and shade grown," he says.

"No thanks. Not only is coffee the second largest commodity in the world, but caffeine makes people too frantic to meditate."

"You and Rosemarie are so much alike."

"I've got good news," I say. "Funny, we were just talking about Patrick the other night at the dinner party and then this morning he phones me."

"What's the buzz in Dublin?"

"Me! I'm giving a solo show at the Dublin Art Institute this November," I say.

"I know our folks are dancing a jig on the other side right now," Marshall gives me a hug.

"Thanks, man. I'm super amped. Marshall, I also came by to make a confession."

"I'm no priest, but I'll do my best."

"I was downtown yesterday. I needed closure and stopped by the Savannah School District Administration Building to talk to Mr. Nicopane. He was eating a donut, and when the raspberry filling ran down his chin, I freaked out."

"What do you mean?"

"I pushed him down and said I had unbending intent to create a parallel love-based universe."

"Pushed him down?" Marshall refills his coffee mug. "Your like one hundred and five pounds and Mr. Nicopane weighs one-eighty and lives at the gym. Is this Grandmama Sharon's ring of power deal? Regardless, tell me you called Cecil Lloyd."

"Yuck, how embarrassing. I do not want Cecil Lloyd to know I am still quibbling with Mr. Nicopane."

"Mary, this is bigger than a quibble."

My throat gets tight. My breathing feels constricted.

"Thanks for listening," I say. "But I'm banking on Mr. Nicopane letting this one go. And I'm visualizing that Cecil Lloyd never knows this happened."

We hug goodbye. I hear Marshall, at a soul level, pleading with me to call Cecil Lloyd. Yuck.

When I get to Wise Hoe Woo Marina, Ship Store, Live Bait, and Exotic Seeds, Wise Hoe Woo is out front watering his raised bed gardens. When he sees me, he turns off the spigot and winds the hose in a neat figure eight.

We bow.

"Wise Hoe Woo, you inspire people to grow their own," I say.

"Judge not the harvest one reaps but the seeds one sows," he says. "And always consider the water source."

"I have exciting news. On the first of November, I will be giving my first solo oil-on-canvas show at the prestigious Dublin Art Institute."

"A journey of a thousand miles begins with a single step," Wise Hoe Woo says. "Congratulations, this is an honor that you have earned."

"Thanks for always being here for me, Wise Hoe Woo," I say. "You've always understood my solitary lifestyle."

He holds my hand, and we walk into the Ship Store. I browse the new exotic seeds packages and buy several varieties for the fall garden.

A van full of eco-tourists fills up the Ship Store. Wise Hoe Woo gives them the safety talk and hands out PFDs. Before he escorts the group to the dock, he asks me to check my cubby.

I reluctantly pull out my manila folder containing one meticulously clipped article from today's *Savannah Morning News*.

> *'Cool School Apps:'*
> *"The Savannah School District has placed a restraining order against Mary Howard due to her hysterical outburst threatening Savannah School District Administration.*

I gasp. I break out in a cold sweat. Underarm odor. Yuck.

> *Superintendent Dr. Cross said, "Mary Howard's immoral conduct expulsion seven years ago alongside the situation yesterday proves she is unstable. Savannah School District is an A+ Blue Ribbon District with State Champion Football."*

Wise Hoe Woo comes back. I roll my eyes.

"No wonder my family has banned the *Savannah Morning News* for three generations. Public schools poison kids with chemicals, GMOs, and antibiotics, and they have the nerve to call me crazy for saying there is a better way."

"Have you phoned Cecil Lloyd?"

"Cecil Lloyd is too famous for this lame case. Besides, the Savannah School District Administration won't see me back on Bull Street again."

"Your mother sponsored Cecil Lloyd through Law School and set up a trust to retain him as your attorney because Mr. Nicopane is vindictive."

I muster a half-smile and start moving chairs. I set out yellow number-two pencils and crisp sign-up sheets. I move the long table to overlook Turner Creek and set up the French Cabernet Sauvignon, coffee mugs, and corkscrew.

When another group of tourists crowds into the Ship Store, I leave ten bucks on the register and grab the last two quarts of Roy Day Raw Heavy Goat Cream. I cross Wilmington River Road, sneak across the May Howard School playground, enter the maritime forest, and pass through the portal.

SIX

I find my long-time Grogoch fairy friend, Mossy Snelbaad, asleep in a tangled bed of kudzu vines hanging from a magnolia tree. Scarlatti and O, his pet possums, are sleeping next to him. Deer Helen, his miniature white tail deer, is resting on a soft pile of onion grass.

Mossy half-whistles and snores.

Scarlatti, O, and Deer Helen wake up. I coax them over, and they lap up the cream. Adorable.

"Well knock me down and steal muh teeth, Mary Howard," Mossy Snellbaad says.

I hand him a quart of cream, and he drinks it with gusto in one long swallow.

"It don't take much: cccream, meditation, and muses, life's wee lil pleasures. Hey, what's with the low spirit, Carthead?"

"I snapped. I knocked Mr. Nicopane down, and the Tongue reported it this morning. I don't know if I can face Flower Power."

His stocky body moves quicker than the eye can see.

"Flower Power is rooting for ya' and don't ya' know Mr. Nico is 'shamed letting a wee lil peanut like yous whoop his arse."

"Embarrassed, ha."

"Keep your power Carthead."

"I am. That's why I'm starting Wilmington Island School, WIS, like Wisdom."

"What the world needs now is love, sweet love. Lord, we don't need another scho-ol."

"Grogochs know Bacharach?"

"Jah, jah." He stokes the small smoldering fire, packs his long crooked pipe with weed, lights up, and rifles around his woodsy world blowing smoke rings, scratching off pesky chiggers from behind his pointed ears, and vanishing in thin air.

When I consider leaving, he materializes and blows a perfect smoke ring.

"Wisdom Seeker!" He shouts.

"I love it!"

"Knock me down and steal muh' teeth."

He transcends to eggshell colored mist with iridescent dark green stripes. The next time he materializes, he takes a shot of poteen.

"Big ethereal news," Mossy Snellbaad says. "A gang of impish leprechauns from Glocca Morra are nestin' in Thunderbolt Village."

"Mossy, are you part leprechaun?"

He stops, scratches his long gold beard, and pops a ready roll rutabaga collard wrap.

"Why cause eh' hairy and unkempt?"

"No, because of your dark green pigmentation."

"Carthead, it's not 'bout pigmentation ccolor, it's 'bout ccore beliefs; rrrealistic emotions; ccold or hot, full or hungry, sleepy or awake, hunting or rrresting. Leprechauns gots prodigious appetites that create mayhem just to satisfy their shadow sides, and they ain't what you'd cccall, positive thinkers."

"I'll tell Crew."

"Subjectivity and Crew will have to brew in its own sweet tea time."

"Agreed."

"Hey, Carthead, yous best gits to Flower Power."

"Wow, look at the time. I feel better just being around you. Thanks, Mossy."

"Mossy Snellbaad, at your woodsy service."

I walk across the playground just as Crew drives by in his black and white patrol car. He sees me. Busted. I keep a sense of humor about charting this earth journey with subjective skeptics.

My heart races. What if Mr. Nicopane pressed charges? Is Crew here to arrest me? I take a deep breath. I am loved. Public Schools are a false belief system. I cross Wilmington River Road.

Crew lifts me up, swings me around, and presses me against his 5'10" hard body.

"Mary, thanks for your culinary magic and festive dinner party the other night."

"My pleasure. Sharp haircut man."

He looks super-hot in his tight blue uniform, holstered black pistol, and shiny black boots. I can tell by his mood that he hasn't read *Cool School Apps*. We tour the raised beds.

"I love the exotic varieties," he says.

There's a sign that says 'free samples' in front of Sungold cherry tomatoes.

"So much flavor," Crew says.

"Who knew being banned from island produce departments would lead Wise Hoe Woo and me into the magical world of compost and exotic vegetable seeds?" I ask.

Crew wraps his bear arm around me, and we walk to the Ship Store.

"Hey, you seem shaky lil sistah, are you okay?"

"I'm the newly elected Prez of Flower Power, man. Pedal to the metal."

I elude his psychic vibe. "How is the Krispy Kreme, Coke, and Brown Food Ban going?"

"Today is day nine, and I do believe they have turned the corner."

"How so?" I ask.

"It's random, but I've noticed the cops being more responsive to kindness," Crew says.

"To try to do better is to be better," I say.

Wise Hoe Woo and Crew hug.

Crew reads the article that Wise Hoe Woo clipped from this morning's Tongue while I uncork wine bottles. I look out across Turner Creek and spiral into worst case scenarios. Why did Superintendent Cross have to mention my immoral conduct expulsion from seven years ago? And now a restraining order. Yuck.

"The Tongue is arrogant," Crew says. "This reporter neglected to interview me or review my online public records."

"No scandal, no paid advertisers," Wise Hoe Woo says.

I read the article. This same reporter continues to attack Crew because unlike sellout politicians and mainstream media, Crew doesn't accept kickbacks from private prisons for locking up our brothers and sisters for smoking flowers.

"Unreal, they use the same 'privileged white male on Wilmington Island does not respect the law of the land' false flag every time. And now the same reporter is so bold as to frame you for embezzling taxpayer dollars to purchase the sailboats?" I ask.

"Precisely," Crew says.

"It will be a happy day when these liars get caught," Wise Hoe Woo says.

"Cecil Lloyd is representing me in a nationwide lawsuit to fight media CEOs," Crew says with his elfin grin. "I'm thinking this is blatant enough to be the ace in the hole."

"Crumble Savannah Tongue," I say.

"I saw the cops tooling around on the new J16s yesterday," Wise Hoe Woo says. "They looked good."

"After a big learning curve, we had a great time. The guys blew me away with how quickly they picked up sailing."

"Mitzi and Glenn are here," Wise Hoe Woo says.

We go outside and greet our guests as they arrive. Gardeners swarm the raised bed. It's a challenge, but I coax them inside. We find our way to the wine and fill our mugs. When the bird clock chirps at two p.m., I stand in front of the room, clear my throat, and ask everyone to be seated.

I take a deep breath, ask my soul to rest on my heart, and focus blending my energy with this will-to-do-good group.

"Welcome and thank you for being here. First, I'd like to invite Chief Crew Potalis to speak," I say.

"I wanted to thank Flower Power members personally for implementing the After-school Square Foot Gardening Club. Since you started volunteering, the Peace and Preservation members have helped their neighbors install dozens of backyard, balcony, and window sill gardens," Crew says.

Cookie, Miss Pudding, Minnie, Burnette, and Miss Claiborne swoon over Crew's southern charm, six pack abs, and muscular legs from years of long distance running.

"I also wanted to invite all of you to speak at City Council," Crew hands out flyers. "Mayor Archibald Doolittle III is requesting permits for Doolittle Development, Inc. to backfill wetlands on Pigeon Island. They plan to develop a playground for the elite. What they are attempting to do is illegal and unethical."

It takes the rowdies a few minute to settle down before I can resume the meeting.

"I will write a two-minute speech and be there," I say. "Thanks, Crew. I'd like to invite Wise Hoe Woo to speak next."

Miss Pudding fills our wine mugs.

"First of all, did you know that Mary is showing her paintings at the esteemed Dublin Art Institute the first of November?"

They give me a standing ovation, and I curtsey.

"She has to make hay and repair the roof while the sun shines so volunteer extra for this year's Cucurbit Pepo Pageant," Wise Hoe Woo says. "I was asked to speak about my thirty-five-year-old woody plants I've raised since I was a child. My grandfather said, 'to raise bonsai one must focus the mind on a longer time frame because they are the world unto themselves.'"

Wise Hoe Woo goes into detail about several bonsais that I've admired my whole life. I invite Rosemarie to speak next.

"I've lined up four food vendors for the Cucurbit Pepo Pageant food court. They are all one hundred percent US Organic Certified, Beyond-Sustainable Certified, and non-GMO Project Verified. We're sending a clear message to Monsanto by kissing their Kettle corn and Coke good-bye."

"Go, Mother Earth!" Miss Pudding cheers and caps off her wine mug, again.

Marshall speaks next.

"I questioned the Cucurbit Pepo Pageant being fried-chicken-pulled-pork-mac-and-cheese-cream-pie-free. But fear not, necrovores; we are not talking meager dinner salads here!

"This year features the all-new Mayor's Mud-Slinging Oyster Roast, Frogmore Stew cook-off, which Chief Crew will most likely win, and locally caught Fish Fry," Marshall breakdances across the room. "The time is now to put cream pies aside for the health of our people, animals, and the planet!"

Flower Power does the wave.

"Thank you. Next, a report on the 'Organic Yard Campaign,'" I say.

"We've come up with a dog and pony show," Mitzi says. "First, we explain the Government's *Better Life with Chemicals and the Hundred Year Lie,* and then we give them the facts that herbicides, fertilizers, and pesticides cause cancer, congenital disabilities, reproductive problems, neurotoxicity, hormonal disruption, and liver and kidney failure."

"At that point," Miss Pudding inserts, "folks usually drop the f-bomb and slam the door in our face."

"Only a handful of people believe Roundup is toxic," Glenn says.

"We haven't had any luck meeting with May Howard School to discuss a nation-wide ban on industrial-strength toxicity in schools," Mitzi says.

"That's a hard nut to crack," I say.

The air gets thick. Flower Power members did read *Cool School Apps* with their Danish and coffee this morning. Yuck.

Mitzi holds up a 'Yeah Mary' sign, and Glenn holds up a 'Boo school district' sign.

I thank everyone for their support and move on.

"I've made sign-up sheets in hopes to solicit your help organizing the celebrity chef pumpkin-off, Mai Howard Bethesda Boy's Orphanage Auction, and Portunus Soul Foundation AME Church Green Award. Is there any other business before we adjourn?"

"This announcement is early, but it looks like Earth, Wind & Fire will be our entertainment this year," Crew says.

We dance our way outside singing "Way of the World."

When Wise Hoe Woo hugs me goodbye, his soul tells my soul to call Cecil Lloyd. On the walk home, I bite the bullet and make an appointment for Monday morning at ten o'clock.

Stymied by a Flower Power wine buzz and a heavy dose of summer heat, I fall into my Yucatan hammock as soon as I get home. What should I disclose to Cecil Lloyd? The donut? The Vortex powered boots? The whole incident flashes in front of me. I'll tell the truth.

I wake up at dusk and take in the petrichor of blending plant oils, bacterial spores, and ozone after last night's downpour.

I walk out to the dock. Boom, the zinnias have popped open, and the speckled butterpea lima beans have doubled in size. Ouida is still away.

I get comfortable and Spiritfly-meditate. Monkey brain spirals into worst case scenarios about Cecil Lloyd, Savannah's most famous attorney, questioning me about Mr. Nicopane's crotch. Lizard brain spits. I open my eyes. Love, love, love. Lots to do today.

I figure out how to change the name on the blog post from Wilmington Island School to Wisdom Seeker. Thank you, Mossy Snellbaad. Hallelujah, no more school. I check Underground Weather. All is calm in the tropics.

I shower, throw on my orange yoga skirt and white linen shirt, and tie my hair in a knot on top of my head.

The silver Honda starts the second try. I fight traffic to get downtown, find parking, and race down East York Street with only minutes to spare. I'm sweating. Yuck.

I turn the corner and rush up the opulent marble stairs. I ring the bell and enter the mahogany glass wrought iron, heavy lead glass doors of my attorney's Victorian mansion.

"Mary Howard?" The secretary asks.

"Yes, that's me," I say, taking in her hip glasses and sophisticated figure.

"Welcome, Mr. Lloyd will only be a minute. Please make yourself comfortable."

The place is dripping with antique chandeliers and over-the-top original paintings, including two enormous Mai Howard originals.

A raspy alto voice coming from Cecil's office has me captivated. And when the door flies open, the most dazzling, sinuous, women struts out. She has lush raven hair and million dollar legs. She's wearing a LBD and black stilettos.

"Mary, it's a pleasure."

Cecil kisses me on each cheek. It dawns on me that I'm wearing the same outfit I wore seven years ago. I'm horrified.

"I spoke with Crew this morning. I'm glad to hear you are joining us for the Cumberland trip."

"Who could resist the Georgia Barrier Island's magical scenery?"

I follow him to the parlor. We sit in the comfortable chairs near the oversized window overlooking Columbia Square. Every detail is exactly the same as seven years ago. A heavy dose of *déjà vu* hits me when my expulsion trail projects itself on my inner silver screen. Horrific.

"Mary, can I get something off of my chest?"

"Sure, shoot." Shoot? I never say shoot. I sound like a violent person. Panic attack. I am loved. My mind is a still river.

"Your mother, peace be with her, was more than generous. She believed in me, and it made all the difference in the world. I wanted to tell you that I have gratitude for the gift Mai Howard bestowed on me."

"Thanks, Cecil. She was a great humanitarian."

"I also wanted to take a moment to congratulate you on your Solo Show at the Dublin Institute of Art."

"Thanks, I'm amped."

"Patrick is confident you will be all the buzz."

"He's the most optimistic person I know."

"That's grand, Mary," Cecil pauses. "Okay, I want to explain what's happening with your case."

"Sure."

"Mary, I've made an appeal based on illegal bidding between Gold Star Security Systems and Savannah School District. I also discovered that the owner of Gold Star is the brother-in-law of the assistant superintendent, George Georges."

"Good."

"The Gold Star Security System that Savannah School District recently purchased for a small fortune allowed you undetected entry. If that went viral, it would evoke public fear, and after the gun incident last week, Savannah School District does not need negative publicity. I'm confident they will agree to our out-of-court settlement."

"Touché."

"On the other hand," Cecil looks at me over his reading glasses, "Mr. Nicopane's private team of attorneys isn't budging."

"Mr. Nicopane, let go for once in your lifetime."

"This is bound to be a lengthy process. All I can do at this stage of the game is keep you posted. Do you have any questions for me?"

"Do you think I should apologize to Mr. Nicopane?"

"Absolutely and inequitably, the answer is a resounding no. Mr. Nicopane's team of attorneys are notorious tricksters who will use anything and everything against you in the court of law."

"Got it."

"Now, how about some good news?"

"Sure."

"Earth, Wind & Fire signed the contract last night."

"That's fantastic!" I scream.

"Crew told me Marshall's parents took you to EWF shows."

"Yes, I think our first show was when we were ten. We boogied down. It was a love fest. Life changing."

My mind runs wild.

"Mary, I'd like to invite you to the upcoming August City Hall meeting."

"I'll be there. I've already started writing my three-minute speech."

"Great. I believe that we will pack the courtroom with preservation activists," he says.

He adds my name to the last page of his yellow legal pad, looks at his Rolex, and walks me to the door exactly thirty minutes after I arrived.

SEVEN

I DRIVE HOME THINKING ABOUT THE MURKY GREEN AURA OF THE lady in black. Her persona fills my imagination. Cecil's got his hands full with that one.

At Johnny Mercer Drive, I'm drawn to the Atlantic Ocean. I need to soak up her negative ions again, always, forever. I park at North Beach. The ocean is flat. I walk out to the water, nonchalantly strip down to my underwear, and swim out twenty or thirty feet.

"King of Gods, Ra, energize my soul and set me free."

After I cast Mr. Nicopane's evil spirit out to sea and imagine the earth shifting to love-based, I swim back to shore.

The silver Honda starts on the second try, and the causeway at high tide gives me validity that I have charted this incarnation in the right place. When I get home, I make a green smoothie and head to the dock to fish the incoming tide.

I cast for live bait, decorate my Shimano, and wet my hook in a sweet spot that is calling my name. Before long, I reel in a half dozen striped bass and one nice size spot tail. Thank you, Great Spirit.

I finish cleaning the fish by sunset. A marsh owl hoots from across the red, orange, and purple river. I get a hit that the owl is

Wisdom Seeker's animal spirit. I watch a school of dolphin strand feeding when I walk back to the house.

I crank up Yes and "Magnification" makes my spirit soar. I stock the freezer with fish fillets and pan fry the spot tail for supper. I make salsa with Brandywine tomatoes, avocados, lemon, evo, cilantro, and garlic and sprinkle Roy Day raw goat cheese on top.

Please let my generation master food distribution. Please let me discover the solutions that will end world famine.

Wow, clean food is so simple and satisfying.

After I clean the kitchen, I put on "Going for the One" and head to the art room.

That night, I use Mama's tiniest brush to work on tedious details. "Steady hand," I hear Mama coaching me when I'm past the point of exhaustion. My teacher's voices pop into my head, "enjoy the process." I slip into the time-is-an-illusion realm. Just before dawn breaks, I thank my muses and collapse in the hammock.

During August, I make several trips to Cecil Lloyd's office for updates and reviews on depositions. Mr. Nicopane's case is bogged down, and we still don't know if it will go to trial. I stay grounded in the garden. I harvest tomatoes, eggplant, okra, basil, and zinnias for me, Marshall, Rosemarie, and Crew.

I walk to the floating dock, close my eyes, and transcend deep into the light and cosmic love. I am the soul. I am receptive to evolutionary codes and symbols.

Guide says, "Purge."

I float my eyes open and see Ouida flying home. Poof, I'm back in the physical world.

"Whewsuu, Whewsuu," I whistle.

Ouida flaps her expansive wings and swoops down for me to pet her luxurious feathers.

"Ouida, have you been fishing?" She nuzzles against me.

"You wild bird. The wind is fifteen knots, the outgoing tide is racing, and you're out fishing," I sing-song in baby talk.

Monkey brain starts reeling commentary. Wait a minute! What was the word? I struggle. Oh, purge. I get a hit that the universe is symbolically asking me to make room for Wisdom Seeker.

I head to the liquor store, stock up on Dogfish Double IPA, and then go dumpster dive for boxes. When I get home, I blend organic frozen peaches, blueberries, celery, and fresh spinach into a creamy green smoothie.

I go upstairs and head down the hall to my parents' room. Have I been in this part of the house since I've been home? I am not my emotions. I am soul. Get to work. These material belongings no longer serve me.

I start trying on some of Mama's glamorous apparel. If we were the same size, I'd never have to shop for the rest of my life. I slip on her strapless sequined cocktail dresses, glittery gowns from strawberry ice to chartreuse, sheik zig-zag pants in lace and leather, and her standard backless animal print jumpers. Everything looks ridiculous on me. Why did I get Daddy's uninteresting body instead of Mama's buxom, tiny waist, all-woman hips, and long legged one? Let go. Let go. Nothing is my style anyway. I keep a few flouncy blouses and pack the rest up in boxes. Hours later, I start hauling clothes, shoes, purses, and hats to the garage.

I break for lunch and surprise myself when I create sensational romaine lettuce leaf tacos stuffed with leftover brown basmati rice, fava beans, cilantro, jalapeños, Kalamata olives, and goat cheese.

I clean the kitchen and head back upstairs to tackle Mama's dressers when a family photo of us in Dingle unravels me. I sit down on the bed, the floodgates open, and tears pour down.

Finally, I get myself outside, kneel down my hands and knees, and allow Mother Earth to ground me.

I stop giving self-pity power and get back to work. I focus on beauty, art, and nature. I am a Spiritual Goddess Warrior. I empty the last chest of drawers and stuff everything in the silver Honda.

When I get back to the house, I already feel the energy field is clearer. By late afternoon, black clouds are racing through the sky. I grab my Shimano and head to the dock. Ouida is away. I cast the shrimp net and pull up a dozen jumbo shrimp. I decorate my hook, cast towards the marsh grass, and fish the incoming tide.

I'm reeling in my second nice size whiting when it starts to drizzle. I barely make it to the verandah before the sky lets loose and it downpours.

That night, I stay up until 3:00 in the morning painting bark on an oak tree. I lull myself to sleep imagining that I'm on the phone with Cecil Lloyd and he is telling me good news. Please, Cecil Lloyd, call me.

I sleep late, meditate, and start cleaning Daddy's walk-in closet and meditation room. By early afternoon, I squeeze the last box of Daddy's belongings into the trunk of the silver Honda.

Moments later, torrential rains let loose. I go upstairs to my parents' master bath and fill the claw foot tub with hot water and Epsom salt.

I get used to the temperature and slip in. I have no regrets. I am a warrior. Yes, I begged Daddy to take me deep sea fishing for my birthday, but the barracuda was Daddy's karma, not mine. Daddy lusted after thousand pound blocks of marble. I do not. I stop myself from feeling guilt. I did not incarnate to feel guilt or shame. Guilt is a puritanical false belief system.

I soak in the deep tub. I am loved. When I'm completely wrinkled, I pull myself out. After a brief Spiritfly-meditation, I head downstairs.

I pour a Dogfish Double IPA in a frosty mug and make organic popcorn with coconut oil, sea salt, nutritional yeast, smoked paprika, and coconut sugar. Organic Kettle corn. No glyphosates. Alright.

I dig out *Monty Python and the Holy Grail*, find the remote, and snuggle deep into the tapestry sofa. Have I sat down on this sofa once since I've been home from Ireland? Life is grand.

I've memorized every nuance of the movie and still, I belly laugh for ninety minutes. At the end of the movie, I face the fact that I am sleep deprived and go to sleep for nine solid hours.

Thursday afternoon, I drive the jam-packed silver Honda to Marshall's house. He's locking up when I get there. When he looks in the back seat, he gives me a hug.

"It's the Shaman Way to let go and be free," he says.

I hold back tears. "I'm moving on," I say.

Marshall squeezes his long legs into the cramped front seat, and we leave.

"Crew's meeting us at Mrs. Wilkes,'" Marshall says. "And Rosemarie is meeting us at Pinkie Masters."

"Rosemarie is smart; I'm right there with her next time."

"Remember, ten percent debauchery."

"Why is ingesting animal agriculture suffering, nitrites, preservatives, flavor chemicals, bleached flour, refined sugar, GMO corn, and glyphosates celebratory?"

"Mary, you eat such a small portion. There's no reason to be fear-based."

"I'm not fear-based, Marshall. "I'm using discernment," I sigh.

"Please don't sigh during lunch," Marshall says.

"When is FDA chemical poisoning fun? The Standard American Diet is SAD because it diseases humanity and the planet that supports humanity."

I stop when Marshall tunes out. When will I have a voice?

I pull into Old Savannah City Mission. We load all of my dead parents' belongings into deep bins and drive downtown in silence.

I find parking, and we stroll down Jones Street.

"Mrs. Wilkes' Boarding House Restaurant has been the bomb since we were little kids," Marshall says.

"That was before the Food Revolution," I say. "There's Crew."

"Good to see you," Crew gives us hugs.

"This is the Last Supper for Apostle Mary," Marshall says.

"I love eating Mrs. Wilkes' fried chicken with you," Crew says.

We weave through the tourists, slip into the side courtyard, and enter the basement of the brick three-story house. We're surprised to see Tyrone, a We Saw Wassaw activist.

"How long have you been working here?" Marshall asks.

"About five months," Tyrone says.

"What's been happening?" Crew asks.

"I've got good news; I'll be graduating from the Culinary Arts at Culinard this spring," Tyrone says.

"Way to go, Tyrone," I say.

We give Tyrone the order for the first night of the We Saw Wassaw camp-out: fried chicken, squash casserole, collards, and cornbread for fifteen. I catch a glimpse of the ingredient label on a sack of flour; carbon dioxide, bromine, corn sweetener, and artificial flavors. Yuck.

We sit at one of the seven ten-seater tables in the second dining room. Mrs. Wilkes' granddaughter rings a little bell and says grace before the family and staff serve heaping platters of fried chicken, barbecue chicken, beef stew, brisket, pork sausage, baked ham, collard greens in fatback, snap beans with ham hocks, black-eyed peas with lard, squash casserole, white rice with giblet gravy, gumbo with shrimp and bacon, twice smashed cheddar potatoes in sour cream, candied yams topped with marshmallows and pecans, pickled sweet beets, and macaroni and cheese boarding house style.

"Delicious," Crew says.

"I savor every melting morsel of my beloved Southern cuisine," Marshall says.

Servers bring out fresh bowls of butter beans and white rice with giblet gravy. Marshall and Crew load up on seconds. I pick the pieces of ham hock out of my collards.

When servers pass trays of Boston cream pie, caramel custard, peach cobbler, ice cream, and pecan pie, I understand why Jesus knocked over the money table. I deep breathe. I have incarnated to learn patience. I center my chakras and allow disgust to pass by me like the wind.

When we're waiting to pay the tab, a half dozen little kids, covered head to toe in black and white striped bodysuits, storm the dining room.

"Don't eat that, trans-fat veins, butter brains/ don't eat that, lard butts, rotten guts/ don't eat that, low blood kills, our brothers/ don't eat that!" They race outside.

"Stand clear!" Crew shouts.

Crew is in police mode. By the time we get outside, Crew has already been around the block.

"No trace," Crew admits.

"Crew, look the other way. Those are the good guys," I say.

We walk to Drayton Street and pile into Pinkie Master's Lounge. Rosemarie is feeding the eclectic jukebox.

"Long Distance Runaround," Crew says.

I imagination-paint Marshall and Rosemarie's kiss.

We belly up to the bar and order Goslings with pineapple juice. After the second round, we head outside into the late September afternoon with a nice buzz. We walk to City Hall, head up the marble stairs, and enter the polished granite and limestone twenty-three-karat gold leaf foyer.

We walk across the rotunda and find a seat just in time.

"All rise, for the honorable Mayor Archibald Doolittle III," the bailiff says in a voice heard by all.

The bailiff, whose job is to ensure the courtroom, spectator area, and deliberation room for court members are neat and orderly, has packed on the pounds to the point of having to trade in his one hundred percent polyester navy blue *elastiques* for sweatpants.

Mayor Archibald Doolittle III waddles to his chair. He has a puckered brow and deep frown. He's wearing a gray and pink pin-striped seersucker suit, a hot pink bow tie, a tight eel skin belt squeezed around his girth, and a white straw hat that screams Dixiecrat.

In total disrespect for separation of Church and State, we're asked to recite the Lord's Prayer. Word. The bailiff flops down in his oversized mahogany chair. The meeting comes to order.

"Today I address you not as the Mayor of Savannah but as the CEO of Doolittle Development, Inc."

We gasp. Does he believe his own lies?

"Many of you say clear-cutting and backfilling Pigeon Island is wrong, but look, my company and my attorneys go for the jugular. Stop with your loopholes already and skedaddle home hippies; you endanger the economy. Your time is up; your few weeks are over. Pigeon Island Paradise Park is the shot in the arm Savannah needs! I'll be frank. I like country music, chop houses, meringue pies, Texas toast with butter-flavored Crisco just like the rest of you, but we need to act fast, so nobody steals our ideas or knows what we're doing. Got it? I don't want to hear any more far-fetched conspiracy theories. Pigeon Island Paradise Park is a done deal. Doolittle Development, Inc. is moving forward in our blithe high-spirited manner."

The Mayor opens the floor for public comments. Marshall is first to speak.

"Marshall Portunus, Wilmington Island, and I am speaking for preserving Pigeon Island. Good afternoon. Mayor Doolittle, City Council, the time is now to shift the political focus from profit to preservation."

Marshall goes on to explain the shift from quantitative economic growth to quality of life, food, water, and air. He spins a thread explaining how peace, non-violence, human rights, and the environment are a seamless whole and ends with his vision of government existing to represent citizens.

Crew takes the mic next.

"Good afternoon. I'm Chief Crew Potalis, Wilmington Island, and I am speaking for preserving Pigeon Island. Mayor, Council, and citizens we have united with the Georgia Barrier Island Preservation Coalition, and we are the far-fetched conspiracy theory you have never imagined in your wildest dreams."

The audience erupts in cheers.

The Mayor slams his Great Grandfather's gavel. "Respect me!" He slams the gavel. "If this audience is not silent, this meeting will be adjourned!"

Boos erupt.

"Stop it! I'll have you arrested," the Mayor swings his gavel. "I demand respect. Respect me!"

"Mayor Archibald Doolittle III and Doolittle Development, Inc., you have underestimated your adversaries," Crew says.

Applause erupts. The bailiff hoists himself up. The Mayor keeps screaming, "Silence. Respect me."

Hoot, hoot. This is the first time this courtroom has ever seen civil disobedience. When Crew speaks we quiet down.

"The Georgia Barrier Island Preservation Coalition is organized, and we have financial backing and staying power. And our mission is clear; we intend to stop the Doolittle Trail of Destruction."

Crew has to wait for cheers. Mayor Archibald and his beloved gavel have lost authoritarian control. Yippee.

"Savannah is asking some serious questions about how you are running this city. And our consensus is that we will no longer tolerate a handful of decision-makers who are alienating and deceiving the public."

I'm in the cue. My heart is pounding. I am a warrior.

"Mary Howard, Wilmington Island, and I am speaking for preserving Pigeon Island. Mayor, Council members, we have entered the Age of Aquarius. The universe is now shining the love-wisdom light on humanity. We are creating the Brotherhood of One Love," I speak slowly. "And the time is now for greedy, gluttonous, voracious, and self-indulgent land developers, corporations, and politicians to crumble in their sea of lies. We have united to take back our power. We have unbending intent to protect our sacred islands, rivers, creeks, marshlands, and maritime forests," I pause and give all of them the eye, "So, I entreat you to act in good karma."

Rosemarie walks to the podium.

"Good afternoon. Rosemarie Lowe, Isle of Hope. I am speaking for preserving Pigeon Island." Rosemarie says. She is poised. "Mayor and CEO Doolittle, I have a late-breaking news flash for you, Mother Nature is not your toxic dumping ground. Mayor, Council, are you aware that one-third of the world does not have running water? Yes, poverty exists. As a matter of fact, 24,000 people will die of starvation today. Meanwhile, it is a fact that lifting the Social Security cap for billionaires would raise enough revenue to end world famine today. So what I'm asking you to do is to evolve past your shameful delusions and get your dump trucks, bulldozers, earth-graders, and cement mixers off of Pigeon Island."

Assertive. Cecil is next.

"Good afternoon, Mayor, Council, and citizens. My name is Cecil Lloyd, and I lead the group of *pro bono* attorneys representing the Georgia Barrier Coast Coalition for Preservation. Our mission is to seek truth above all else."

Cecil sing-songs numbers, facts, statistics, and legalities. I lose myself listening to his charismatic voice.

Guide says, "The tide has changed. Pigeon Island will remain preserved."

The line of environmental activists is out the door. Attorneys, physicians, engineers, farmers, hippies, baseball players, taxi drivers, school teachers, business people, and soccer moms speak out against Doolittle corruption.

The meeting adjourns, and we walk outside. Marshall walks Rosemarie to her car. Crew shakes hands with folks while I imagination-paint their features. When the crowd thins, Crew and I catch Marshall and Rosemarie kissing.

"Fireworks," I say when Marshall joins us.

"Agreed, that was some kiss," Crew says.

"She told me she wants to spend the night tonight," Marshall says.

"What did you say?" I ask.

"I said I want to spend the rest of my life with her."

My heart sings. Love transforms me.

EIGHT

Friday morning I wake up an hour before sunrise and walk to the dock. Ouida is away fishing. I Spiritfly-meditate until Crew arrives in *Bottom Line*.

"Yippee, We Saw Wassaw camp-out!" I say.

Crew ties off and gives me a hug. We grab his cooler and head to the house. I sense something is off, and it turns out I'm right.

"I had a break-up with the woman I've been dating for at least a month," he shrugs his shoulders.

"Sorry." I'm speechless; Crew has a history of falling for two-timers.

"I feel betrayed," Crew pours his heart out. "I really thought I had someone special this time."

What can anybody say about two-timers that hasn't been said before?

Crew beats three dozen eggs, stirs in a pound of spinach, two sliced red peppers, a bunch of chopped scallions, a package of portabellas, organic chickpea flour, and one pound of Roy Day raw goat cheese.

"Thanks for ditching the all-purpose flour and sausage," I say.

"Thanks for noticing. That wasn't easy for a recipe follower like me," Crew jokes.

I grease two thirteen-by-nine-inch glass baking dishes with coconut oil, and Crew divides the batter. I pop his award-winning breakfast casserole in the oven and set the timer for fifty minutes.

We peel and slice three Crenshaw melons, two cantaloupes, and one honeydew melon. At that point, I flip on the floodlights and we take a trip to the compost pile.

"The raccoons frequently dine here. So far, the black gold has eluded me."

Marshall and Rosemarie knock on the back door just as dawn breaks.

Their love chemistry knocks me out. I crank up "Magnification."

"How's the Krispy Kreme, Coke, and Brown Food ban going?" Rosemarie asks.

"Gandhi said, "At first they ignore you, and then they laugh at you, then they fight you, and then you win. Mary was right, twenty-one days later the TVPD cops are amped with will-to-do-good."

The timer goes off, and Crew pulls the casseroles out of the oven.

"Extra-sensory," Marshall says.

We set the dining room table and place pitchers of fresh squeezed orange juice and grapefruit juice on the buffet.

"I hear the van pulling up," I say.

"Perfect timing. Let's go out and greet our guests," Crew says.

Twelve happy kids pour out of the van.

"Good morning," Crew says. "You know Miss Mary and Mr. Marshall from Flower Power Club, and this is our friend, Miss Rosemarie."

We hug. These kids are pure good energy.

"Come on in," I say.

"I hope you like to have fun," Marshall says.

Latisha and I walk inside together. She's a sixteen-year-old gifted watercolor artist with a heart of gold.

We serve our plates, get seated, and I bless the food.

"We honor you, Great Spirit and Mother Nature. We appreciate the time to be with our friends. We ask to be receptive to solutions that will cause world peace."

"We play hard so fuel up," Crew says.

"You fixed the table pretty, Miss Mary," Latisha says.

"Thanks, it's sweet of you to say so," I say.

"These wraps taste better than donuts," Tremaine says. "I'm amazed."

Tremaine is thirteen, thin, and wears horn-rimmed glasses. His IQ scores are genius level.

"Ingredients, please," Tremaine says.

"Ezekial wraps, coconut mana, honey, cinnamon, pecans, raisins, and coconut flakes," I say. "So simple."

The group is quiet the first morning. We clear the dishes and Crew gives the safety talk.

"May I add a few words?" Rosemarie asks.

"Of course," Crew says.

"Four kids in each group; Shaniqua, Tyrone, Tremaine, and Latisha are group leaders. Watch out for each other."

She organizes groups and chores.

"Sign up for something you love," she says.

Rosemarie is a welcome addition to our team. She's super organized and a natural around kids.

The kids come to life when we step on the dock. We stop to watch the fiddler crabs scurry across the pluff mud. I imagination-paint our brand of peace warriors in the dawn Rembrandtesque hue.

We fit all size and shapes into PFD's and board our three

Boston Whalers. As we approach the mouth of Wassaw Sound, we spot strand feeding dolphins. We kill our engines. The dolphins throw their massive bodies in the pluff mud, gobble up a school of whiting, shimmy back into the water, and swim off into deep water.

We fire up our engines. Marshall leads the way in *Driftwood*. I follow in *One That Got Away*. Crew brings up the rear in *Bottom Line*.

The river is as smooth as glass. We speed around the curves and bends of Odingsell River to a sweet fishing spot and throw our anchors.

The kids get the hang of casting the shrimp net. They practice tying off and baiting their hooks.

"Dang, Miss Mary and Miss Rosemarie have already caught more fish than the rest of us combined," Shaniqua says.

"Experience," I say.

We catch enough for the fish fry tomorrow night, load up the boats, and motor to Green Island to hunt shark's teeth.

Crew finds a baby tiger shark tooth right away.

"Sharks are born with a complete set of teeth so they can fend for themselves as soon as they're born," Rosemarie says.

"Sharks don't get cavities," Marshall says.

When Ben finds a 65,000-year-old shark tooth, that is bigger than his hand; the hunt gets more exciting. We find a dozen fossils before hunger calls.

We motor back to Little Wassaw, organize the camp kitchen, and pull coolers. This is the first year that Marshall and Crew have agreed to go deli meat and cheese free.

We serve my pre-made ALT sandwiches I made with spicy mustard, avocados, butter crunch lettuce, and homegrown tomatoes on organic sprouted flourless rye bread with organic blue chips and Crew's homemade salsa. Everyone loves their lunch and, like I keep saying, clean food equals high vibes.

We finish up kitchen patrol and start unloading camping gear, setting up the privy, and pitching tents. Rosemarie's plan keeps kids engaged. Camp is set up in record time.

When the work is finished, I jump in the river.

"Join me. The water is warm. At least, eighty degrees," I say.

Marshall dives in next. One by one they slip on PFDs and join us.

We float. We relax. We bond.

An hour later we change into dry clothes, explore the maritime forest, and collect firewood to carry back to camp.

We get back to camp in time to start the bonfire and catch the sunset. We unload Mrs. Wilke's takeout from the coolers and set up a self-serve buffet.

We fix ourselves a plate and get comfortable around the fire.

"Latisha, would you bless the food?" I ask.

"Yes, Ma'am. Thank you for nourishing us with this good fried chicken, in the name of Jesus Christ, Amen."

"Beautiful Latisha," Marshall says.

"Plenty for everybody," Crew says.

"Miss Mary and Miss Rosemarie, don't you like fried chicken?" Jerome asks.

"We're pescetarians," we say at the same time.

"Why?" Ben asks.

My soul longs to tell him about avian flu, bovine leukemia virus, that chickens are fearful birds and we eat their fear, and that sentient beings deserve to live, but I know it would not be cool right now.

"We prefer to fill up on the tasty side dishes," Rosemarie says.

"Hey, the half-moon is rising," Marshall says.

After supper, we stoke the bonfire and start the round robin.

"I believe we learn our unique purpose in life when we spend time in nature," Marshall starts.

"I believe we become a united brother/sisterhood when we help others gain better health," Crew says.

"I started Health Food Junkies at my school. We're trying to ban junk food from our campus," Ben says.

"Way to go, brother-man," Crew says.

"It's been amazingly popular," Shaniqua says.

Tyrone has started the same program at his high school. Yippee.

"I believe we are here to help others develop inner peace, self-awareness, and compassion," I say when it's my turn.

"I've been writing Pearson Prentice Hall requesting that they give equal word count to peace as war in new Social Studies editions," Latisha says.

"Latisha, you are amazing," Rosemarie says.

"What's happening with that, Latisha?" Crew asks.

"Still no response. I get that Peace Warriors are supposed to learn patience, but right now, it hurts my feelings," Latisha says.

"Remember: be positive, tell the truth, and stay positive," Marshall says.

"And stay focused on the next seven generations," I say.

We throw hundreds of dreams out into the Universe. When Ben falls asleep sitting up, we go to bed. The next morning we sleep late.

After breakfast, we motor to Cockspur Island and everyone takes turns climbing the wooden ladder to the top room of the lighthouse. The rest of the day we island hop, picnic, and swim. By the time we get back to camp, we feel like family. We collect firewood and clean and fillet yesterday's catch.

Rosemarie and I have replaced spaghetti and meatball night with freshly caught fish. Yes, I was right. Ground beef is contaminated with feces. Finally, we're moving on.

We serve everyone a plate of hot crispy pan-fried fish fillets, homemade coleslaw, and Mrs. Wilke's cornbread. Super fresh. Crumble Grocery Manufacturers Association. Crumble Animal Agriculture. We will never turn back.

We stoke the bonfire and start the second Think Tank.

We agree that being of service is the number one way to cause peace. We soul search ideas to help migrant workers, end famine, and house the homeless. Change seems light years away.

I give gratitude for our small band of peace warriors. My heart knows that we are one light and we will shift the meme to positive. Time is an illusion.

We retire to our tents around midnight and laze around camp the next morning. After lunch, we load up the boats and explore Bull River, Lazaretto Creek, and Little Tybee Beach.

We get back to camp, change, and collect firewood. Crew fires up the propane cooker. He brings the water to a boil and works his magic adding red potatoes, Vidalia onions, garlic, red peppers, and shrimp at just the right time to create his award-winning Frogmore Stew. Perfection.

The final Think Tank is about ways we can sneak-teach difficult people to see with their hearts. When everybody goes to bed, I slip away to the beach and star gaze. Please help me guide others to find their unique ways to be of service.

The final morning in paradise is always bittersweet. We finish the Frogmore Stew leftovers for breakfast, teardown camp, and take a long swim in the river.

Midmorning, we load up the boats and motor back to Wilmington Island. The van is waiting for us when we get home.

"I'll see you Wednesday at the Peace and Preservation new member orientation," Crew says.

We hug goodbye and hand out certificates.

"Please call if you need anything," I say.

"Keep in touch," Marshall says.

"Love and peace," Rosemarie says.

They head back to Forsyth Park to be reunited with their loving 'rents.

"Did we earn a cold beer?" I ask.

"You don't have to twist my arm," Crew says.

We go inside, pour ourselves frosty mugs of Dogfish Double IPA, and head back to the dock.

"Look, Ouida's back," Rosemarie says.

"Good girl," I say.

Crew throws her the squeaky fish toy, she catches it and throws it back.

"We started We Saw Wassaw with two kids, nine years ago," Crew says.

Marshall twists one up, and we alter our psychoactivity.

"Rosemarie, I came home from Ireland every year for this camp-out."

"Kids have unlimited potential," Marshall says.

"I'm optimistic these kids will create positive change in their communities," Rosemarie says.

"Agreed," I say.

We head back to the house and plate up leftovers. After we finish another round of high gravity beers, Crew, Marshall, and Rosemarie head home.

I head to the office and fire up the computer. I've been curious about the weather all weekend. And the full moon is less than a week away.

A storm is developing in the far reaches of the Atlantic Ocean. It's about 5,000 miles east/southeast of the U.S. mainland, forming a westward low pressure easterly wave.

I paint and keep an eye on the weather the rest of the day. Am I ready to accept the third ring of power? Will this separate me even more from the masses? Do I have to go to Daufuskie and survive a hurricane to get where I need to be? Should I tell Marshall and Crew?

The next two days, the tropical depression continues to gain rotational speed and increase in wind velocity. By day three, NOAA upgrades the system to a tropical storm.

I jump when my phone rings. It's Marshall.

"Hey, Mary. I just got off the phone with Crew. He's watching a tropical storm in the Atlantic that is predicted to bring high winds and flooding this way."

"I might as well let you know," I say. "I'm going solo camping on Daufuskie. I intend to paint the storm."

Dead silence followed by a nervous laugh.

"Grandmama Sharon predicts I'll be safe," I say.

"Mary, Grandmama Sharon is ninety-two years old, lives three thousand miles away, and has never owned a computer or TV. Please don't go."

"I have an invitation from Isis to raise my vibration. I have to go."

"Okay, I respect you," he says. "How long will you stay?"

"Storm energy, full moons, tides, unpredictable wind, vibrational shifts, rings of power; I'm dealing with the unknown."

"Be safe, Mary."

"I will. Thanks for understanding."

The next morning the Tropical Storm is upgraded to Hurricane Marguerite. She slams her way through the Leeward and the Windward Islands and is headed for the US Virgin Islands.

I load a cooler with veggies, fresh fruit, frozen green smoothies, dried fruit, nuts, and seeds. I pack the grill, fat lighter, and my Shimano rod and reel. I get the hand truck from the tool shed and haul the first load down to the boat.

When Ouida sees me load the cooler, she stays perched on the bow of *One That Got Away*.

I go back to the house. The storm has been stalled over the Atlantic for hours. I go upstairs, pack my slicker, a travel towel, and change of clothes and haul another load to the dock.

I head to the art room and organize canvases, sketch pads, charcoal, brushes, and my oil paints. Thankfully, I remember the kerosene lamp when I pass by the tool shed.

I tie down gear, check the levels, and I'm good to go. I walk back to the house and take a long hot shower. I dress in what I'll be wearing for the next few days or weeks, turn off all the lights and head downstairs to check the weather one last time.

Yes, the storm is starting to move again.

I get a whim to tell Mossy Snellbaad I'll be on Daufuskie Island during the storm. I jog down the avenue of oaks, across the golf course and into the woods. I find Mossy Snellbaad dancing to a fast jig he's playing on a tin whistle.

"Well knock me over and steal muh' teeth, it don't take much but a wee lil' bit 'o Mary Ccontrary."

He stretches his 3'5" stocky frame, takes a shot of poteen, lights his pipe, and blows perfectly round smoke rings.

"What brings 'eh to my woodsy world?" He rubs his gold beard.

"I've been invited to Daufuskie Island to receive my next ring of power."

"Good, girrl cccarthaead! Remember to sets up the lean-to low likes I showed yous and call me if yous needs help."

He vanishes in a green vapor. I hear his voice from the top of an oak tree. "Winds a' pickin' up, you best git, ccarthead."

I blow him a kiss and take off.

Ouida nestles against me as soon as I board *One That Got*

Away. I untie the lines and drift away from the dock. The water is choppy, winds are from the southwest with gusts up to seventeen knots so it's slow go. Half way to Daufuskie, winds pick up to twenty-five knots and wave height increases to four meters, so I slow down again.

The course I chart from Wilmington Island to Daufuskie Island is engrained in my neurons from past lifetimes traveling with my father's fathers, Indigenous Guides, ancient river saints, mermaids, goddesses, wisdom seekers, river fairies, and witnesses.

I release the shame I felt when I wouldn't conform and take USkidpsychmeds™. I'm not a zombie they can standardize through PISA tests. When Mama said I was being bullied, Superintendent Dr. Cross told her to grow a pair. How Neanderthal! How they can schizophrenically push a trillion-dollar War on Drug epic failure and simultaneously shun Mother Nature's plethora of healing medicinal and psychoactive plants and herbs is beyond comprehension?

A school of dolphins plays off the bow.

I imagination-paint holistic people leading us on the path to love-based. Gale force wind gusts and white caps intensify. The last leg of the journey slows down to a crawl.

Maybe I've reincarnated at the wrong time. Maybe my voice won't be heard in a society that seeks wisdom inside brick and mortar institutions. It seems unlikely that one solitary change-agent can shift the Deep South to love-based. I stop myself. Warriors never ask how. Unbending intent. Word.

I approach Daufuskie at high tide. I maroon *One That Got Away* and machete a campsite under a canopy of privet at the edge of the maritime forest.

NINE

I sketch Daufuskie swaying to the prelude of Hurricane Marguerite. Massive energy bends the palm trees and crashes the surf. I study the sharp contrasting shadows cast on the beach by the low clouds racing across the black sky. By late afternoon, strong wind and lightning send me inside the tent. I coax Ouida to join me, but she prefers to stand guard under the awning.

I organize my tiny space and fumble with the wick of the lantern until the lighting is just right. Ah, home sweet home. Fueled by storm energy, I sketch from my mind's eye. After several hours, I put the lantern out and fall asleep. When I wake up, dawn is breaking.

"Good morning, did you stay dry last night?"

I throw on my slicker and run to the privy. The wind died down, but the rain continues to be torrential. Let's hope it lets up soon, or I'll be flooded.

"Whewsuu, Whewsuu," I coax Ouida to come inside, but she prefers looking out over the river. I hang up my slicker and crawl inside my sacred place.

I Spiritfly-meditate. My Healing Angels take me to a new room. They spin my chakras with Universal Truth and when I open my eyes after what seems to be twenty minutes, two hours have passed.

I stretch my back out, assemble my table-top easel, and sketch storm energy, the wind, and torrential rain.

The rest of the day, I fall into a comfortable pattern of work and sleep. Every moment in Spiritfly-meditation is pristine, present, peaceful, and clear.

The next morning, I suit up in my slicker and dig trenches around the camp. The rain is torrential the rest of the day, that night, and through the next day.

On the third night, at midnight, the rain stops. Ouida flies down the river, and I go for a walk on the beach.

I discover a covered cove, get comfortable, and Spiritfly-meditate. My Guides give me light. I raise my vibration. I transcend across worlds. Voices are speaking in an unrecognizable language. I stop myself from over-analyzing.

They show me world peace and fill my heart with unconditional love. I attempt to imagination-paint the dazzle when everything goes blank.

I come out of meditation just as the full harvest moon rises. I have validity that we exist in two worlds. I evoke a cry to the House of Shamballa for humanity to join me in our evolutionary plight to heal Mother Earth's condition and use the power of good to shift to love-based by 2020.

My nervous system jacks up to a higher frequency. I'm uncomfortable. In pain. I stand up. My chakras spin faster and faster. I freak. I'll come undone.

A voice I don't recognize as my own says, "I accept my next ring of power," and I am airborne. What? Relax.

I catch a wind current and body surf across the starry sky. I start to fall. I allow fear to pass by me like wind. I catch a strong current with my right side and again I am soaring over the pearl-colored beach.

I struggle to stay present when I feel myself falling faster and faster, but fear consumes me and I crash. Am I alive? I must be. I stand up and start walking. If anyone saw that, I'd be burned for heresy.

I'm completely disoriented. I bushwhack my way through the maritime forest the rest of the night.

Just before daybreak, I hear Ouida squawking.

"Whewsuu, Whewsuu!"

I follow her strange tune back to camp.

Everything is as I left it. I kiss the beach. Gratitude, Great Spirit. The sky is azure, the natural light is aglow, and the air is crisp.

I prepare my palette with titanium white, raw umber, ivory, and black. I focus on a single vantage point at the breach between the beach and maritime forest.

I break to let the paint dry and lunch on dried figs and cashews.

Just before sunset, I clean my brushes, grab my Shimano, and hike to the side creek. I nab a fiddler crab, bait my hook, and cast toward an oyster bed. Before long, I get a nibble. After the first pass, I keep my tip low and my line tight. When I get the next hit, I set the hook. After a long run, I reel in a big sheepshead. I take out the barbless hook, the sheepshead smiles at me with its hauntingly human-like teeth, and I get big-time shivers.

Thank you, Great Spirit, for providing me with the gift of divination.

I make a small fire, clean the fish, and fry the fillets in hot coconut oil. When the fish is resting, I use the hot skillet to stir-fry garden veggies. I fix a plate, open a Dogfish double IPA, and walk to the beach.

Please let everybody experience heaven on earth.

I stargaze half the night.

On the twelfth night, Guide nudges me to go home and start Wisdom Seeker. I fall asleep dreaming of a shower and my bed. The next morning, I get up at dawn and drag *One That Got Away* into the river.

Ouida stays perched on the bow watching me break down camp. I make one last sweep.

Am I sleep deprived? Is that a person running through the forest?

A girl runs towards me and throws herself at my feet. What in the world does she want with me?

"I mean no harm," she says with a soft-spoken voice.

"Please, stand up," I say.

She is tall and thin. Her almond-shaped eyes radiate light. She has a diamond nose piercing that glistens from the sand and sun, and she wears strands of black and white beads on her long slender neck, wrists, and ankles.

"My father is the Supreme Chief of the Voodoo Nation. I am with child. The father of my baby is not the man I am to marry tonight. Will you help me?"

Lizard brain spits and Monkey brain warns against getting involved with Voodoo.

Guide says, "Service and sharing."

"What can *I* do?" I ask.

"Take me with you," she pleads.

Her indigo aura fills my heart with love. Suddenly, Mr. Nicopane pops into my head.

"I'd like to help, but I have an intolerant neighbor."

"One neighbor can't be as bad as an entire tribe."

A voice that is not my own says, "I will help you."

"Tenke, tenke; meet me at Bloody Point in ten minutes."

She disappears into the maritime forest. I approach Bloody

Point as she is running out of the forest. I have no idea how I'll get close enough to the rocky shore. She motions for me to stop, leaps across boulders, and jumps aboard.

I whistle, Ouida nestles beside me, and I open throttle. My heart is pounding. I kill the engine when we're a good distance from Daufuskie.

"I'm Mary Howard. Nice to meet you."

She delicately shakes my hand.

"I'm Princess Pearle Isle, tenke, tenke."

"This is Ouida."

"Well, hello there. How do you spell her name?"

"O-u-i-d-a."

"Ouidah ending with 'h' is where my people are from in Benin, West Africa."

"Who knew?"

"Why did you choose Ouida as her name?"

"She sang her name to me when she was a sick newborn."

We say 'no coincidences' at the same time.

"Is this your art?"

"Yes, I painted Daufuskie during the storm."

"I love the energy and movement. Stunning, Mary Howard."

"Thank you."

I open throttle. Pearle, Pearle. I repeat her name. My heart sings. Mr. Nicopane pops into my head. I slow down.

"Pearle, my next-door-neighbor, Mr. Nicopane, is a racist hate monger."

"Love has united us. In divine time, Jim Crow will step off the bus and Mary Howard and Princes Pearle will get on."

"Meanwhile, my Grandmama Sharon is a spiritual midwife. She lives in a small village in Ireland. We could stay with her this winter, and she could deliver your baby."

"Ireland sounds picturesque, but the medicinal roots in my backpack aren't used as legal tender yet."

"No worries. I'd be happy to buy you a plane ticket."

"I don't have a passport."

"We can expedite your passport."

"I don't know what to say."

"Say yes. Ireland is every shade of green."

"Yes," Pearle says.

"Good, you will love Grandmama Sharon."

I get a signal and call Marshall. I act like I'm alone.

"Mary, your timing is unbelievable. Cecil Lloyd just phoned this morning. Savannah School District has dropped the charges and Mr. Nicopane has agreed to settle out-of-court."

"Big relief!"

"Crew's been worried about you. I'll let him know you're safe."

"Thank you. My batteries are low. We'll catch up soon."

Five minutes later I get a text from Crew: 'I'm happy you survived. I'm looking forward to our cruise to Cumberland.'

'Ha, me too.' I press *send*.

Ouida flies to her piling.

"Pearle, that's us. The tide is racing. Can you manage?"

"Yes Mary, I know tides."

She swings her athletic body to the dock and secures the lines.

"That was much easier with your help."

"My pleasure."

I check to see if Mr. Nicopane is home. The coast looks clear. We haul everything out of *One That Got Away* and head to the house.

"Wow, the Speckled Butterpea Lima Beans are full of flowers," I say.

"Look, a tiny lima bean! This small plot is bountiful," Pearle says.

"I've only been gardening for one year. Everything is organic."

Pearle tastes the soil. "Sweet and fertile. The medicinal roots I brought from Daufuskie will grow well here."

We harvest giant cucumbers, the last of the tomatoes, a few eggplants, and a handful of okra.

"Beautiful food," Pearle says.

"A miracle. Come on in, welcome!"

"Gorgeous, Mary. The sculptures are magnificent."

"Thanks, Victor Howard, my Dad, was a brilliant artist."

Pearle's favorite room is the library.

"Floor to ceiling collections; heaven on Earth," she says browsing.

"Three generations of eclectic thinkers interested in everything from fairy magic, botany, ancient wisdom, and the arts, to quantum physics."

We make stacks of books that we want to read.

"I'm starved. Are you hungry?" I ask.

"This is the first time I've had an appetite since I can remember," Pearle says.

"Let's figure out what's for dinner."

"I brought pink crowder peas, Daufuskie rice, and wild saffron."

"How thoughtful, Pearle."

Pearle rinses the rice and peas and cooks them at a low simmer. We talk about organic gardening and saving seeds. I steam squash, eggplant, and okra. She says she has been foraging for chanterelles, oyster mushrooms, and medicinal roots her whole life. I make a salad with layered tomatoes, basil, and Roy Day raw goat cheese. We sit at the kitchen table.

"May I say grace?" I ask.

"Yes, I'm happy you are spiritual," she says with a smile that is pure joy.

"Pearle is a blessing to me. Thank you, Law of Attraction, for bringing us together. Please allow us to see the truth, connect with spirit and nature, see miracles where others see danger and be receptive to the solutions to balance nature. One love."

"Mary, your prayer sounds like Voodoo."

"Pearle, is Voodoo a religion or spirituality or what?"

"Voodoo is an indigenous and earth-based religion, but more so it is a phenomenological approach to mystical origins. The word 'voodoo' means to 'view you' because we believe that we are mirrors of each other's souls. Each thing affects something else. In *Fon, Gbe* means 'life', and it also means 'universe'," Pearle says.

"Wow, I was raised in the Shaman tradition, and I'm amazed at the similarities."

"This food smells heavenly," Pearle says.

"*Bon appétite*," I say. "Wow, the saffron is the ticket."

"*Délicieuse*! I love the garden veggies and fresh cheese."

"I have a CSA with Roy Day Goat Farm."

"What is a CSA?"

"Community Shared Agriculture. I buy shares to support his farm, and he delivers eggs, cheese, and produce each week."

Pearle tells me about her Voodoo Chieftaincy like it's no big deal.

"We studied from traveling healers who gave lectures, demonstrations, and guided prayers. They left us with exercises to practice. We have an expression, *hunkpamé* that means discipline and tenacity are essential to make the mind, heart, and body work together. All *Vodun* children are trained in personal healing, spiritual transformation, healing our hearts, filling our hearts with love, and becoming instruments of love," she says. "The teachers were strict. We were raised to believe, *E-gblé-ma-kú*, may-I-die-if-it-goes-wrong. In our tribe, laziness is worse than the plague."

"Similar to the unbending intent of the Shaman Warrior," I say.

"Did you learn Shamanism at the schools on Wilmington Island?"

"Marshall's folks raised us as Shamans. I attended May Howard School right here on Wilmington Island. They stifled my love of learning. The drill was mindless memorization about the pros of colonization. Multiple choice tests measured student's success." I say.

"That sounds more like a prison than a school."

"I am no conformist, so they labeled me uncooperative since first grade. I was incapable of doing any good in the eyes of the May Howard School. Anyhow, I endured authoritarian badgering until they kicked me out."

"Sorry, Mary," she squeezes my hand.

"Thanks, it's all good. Shaman Warriors have no regrets. Lessons ignite our Goddess power. And if not for public schools, I would not have had the unbending intent to start Wisdom Seeker. Someone has to say 'no' to standardization."

"School for me was completely different. We learned to use our energy to see the truth with the power that our eyes possess. When we weren't in class, we explored the forest and foraged medicinal roots. Doc is one of the most powerful root doctors in the world. Many internationally renowned root doctors studied with Doc."

"What's Doc like?"

"When Doc takes off his purple-blue sunglasses, every human, animal, and crop better watch out," she says. "Most people miss his extra-dry sense of humor, but the two of us are close. Doc practically raised me."

"That's how I feel about Mr. Portunus, Marshall's dad."

Pearle shows me a few photos.

"This is me, my dad, Supreme Chief Isle, and Doc taken a few years ago."

"You look exactly like your father," I say.

"Thanks, I had just passed my exams for ancestral healing spells, nature spells, purification spells, and joy spells," she says.

"Pearle, have you ever considered modeling?"

She belly laughs. "Mary, I'm a healer."

"I'd like to make a confession," I say.

"Go ahead, Mary."

"I've faked casting Voodoo spells my whole life. Would Doc be mad if he knew I gave people the evil eye?" I ask.

"Absolutely not. What makes conjuring work is the belief that it works," Pearle says. "Mary, your art is unworldly. Are you a seer?"

"Well," I hesitate. Voodoo and Shamanism are one thing, but Fairy Magic is still way out there. "I see vibrations move in space, and I see the color of auras of people, animals, and nature. So, yes, I think meditation has awakened some of my sensibilities."

"Good, good, good."

I imagination-paint Pearle pouring boiling water over sea myrtle and sassafras roots. The smell is sensory. When the cuckoo clock strikes seven, we toast to the man she is not marrying right now.

I tell Pearle about Mr. Nicopane and my expulsion.

"There is nothing more dangerous than evil taking the shape of good," she says.

"Agreed."

We clear the dishes and go to the living room. I turn on the Bach Cello Suites, and we collapse on the sofa.

"Can I tell you about the father of my baby?"

"Yes, I'm here to listen."

She wells up. I squeeze her hand.

"Well, I'm ashamed that I am a statistic for unwed pregnant teenagers. I was twelve and the youngest to complete my A*gooma-yi-sogwé* that marks adolescence and initiates us into the School of Life. Joyous, I believed I was ready to face the world."

I have no idea what to say.

"From the time I was twelve, I have pleaded with my father to end the antiquated Voodoo tradition of prearranged marriages. But Daddy has always remained crystallized.

"One morning I had a bitter argument with my father about prearranged marriages. I ran out of the house and stowed away in the woods the rest of the day. At sunset, I found my boyfriend, Joseph, and told him I was leaving Daufuskie. That's when he held me tight and told me that we would leave together. Then he kissed me.

"I believed him when he said that he would always love me."

All I can do is hold her hand.

"I have studied with worldwide healers, chiefs, priests, root doctors, and elders. I find it unbelievable that not one of my mentors ever mentioned the heat of the moment. Ever.

"Fast forward to Joseph leaving on the six A.M. ferry the morning after I tell him I'm pregnant," Pearle says.

"Where did he go?"

"Macon, Georgia."

Pearle buries her head in her hands and sobs.

"He's married, and his wife is expecting."

"Pearle, I'm sorry."

I hand her a box of tissues.

"When I started showing and the prearranged wedding was looming, I was paralyzed with fear and indecision. And then today I woke up clear-headed. I understood that humankind possesses the existence of a Supreme Being. I felt as if I had the wisdom to serve *Mawu*, my Supreme God.

"At that moment, I had an epiphany. I must leave my tribe, in order to honor my fate, and to evolve past my tribe.

"I harvested roots, rice, and peas, packed my knapsack, and ran all the way to the beach."

"Wow, one minute later and we would have missed each other," I say.

"Can you imagine how I felt when I saw you? I'm one lucky nineteen-year-old."

"Pearle, you're an old soul."

"Yes, and so are you, Mary Howard," she says.

"We will amplify our will-to-do-good," I say. "Pearle, do you think your father and fiancé will be searching for you?"

"If they do, they'll have to be discreet. The Voodoo Nation does not want the public to learn about asinine practices like prearranged weddings and animal sacrifices."

At midnight, we head upstairs.

"This will be your new digs."

"The energy is magical."

"This was my parents' room. We can make a baby room in Daddy's meditation room. We tour the over-the-top bathroom.

"A claw foot tub. I'm pinching myself," Pearle says.

"Me, too. This house is too big for one person."

"Mary, where are your parents?"

"On the other side, ethereal, and three feet above."

"Oh, they are in the metaphysical world, *Yêsùnyimê*, in their original state with my mama."

We stay up late talking about Wisdom Seeker. Pearle shows me dozens of notebooks she's been compiling since she was twelve. She's been outlining a curriculum for Spiritual Healing ever since she learned that we walk for each other, and each one walks for himself to attain the fullness of life.

"I have gratitude that I've found my place in the sun," Pearle says.

"I'm pleased, too, Pearle," I say. "Let's change the meme to love-based."

"Divine time," we say at the same time.

It's three A.M. when we finally go to bed. I'm too happy to sleep. Wisdom Seeker is materializing.

TEN

I walk to the dock before dawn. I get comfortable and Spiritfly-meditate. Gratitude, Law of Attraction. Gratitude, Law of Karma. Gratitude, Pearle Isle, Voodoo Healer.

I open my eyes. Ouida flies off towards the ocean.

When I get back to the house, Pearle is in the kitchen making porridge. I love lingering over root tea. I love the camaraderie. Joy.

We head to the library. The Internet experience is totally new for Pearle.

"I avoided the electromagnetic radiation and advertisements coming into this house until last year," I explain.

I have success purchasing roundtrip tickets on the plane, train, and bus. It's tricky but I even finagle our seats so that we can sit together on our connecting flights.

The online application for an expedited passport turns into major red tape.

"We are protected by good intent," Pearle says.

"What if this is a warning signal for Supreme Chief Isle to find you?" I ask.

"Don't worry about anything," Pearle says. "And I mean anything."

After a morning of jumping through hoops, the government confirms Pearle's eligibility. We complete the application and press 'send.'

For lunch, I thaw out fish fillets, and Pearle figures out how to make biscuit batter out of chickpea flour, oat flour, flax seeds, maple syrup, salt, baking soda, baking powder, and coconut oil.

I food process cabbage, carrots, chives, celery, and dill. While I pan fry the fillets, I mix up coleslaw dressing with horseradish root, raw apple cider vinegar, and a splash of maple syrup. Everything comes together at the same time.

We steep a pot of root tea and sit down at the kitchen table. Pearle's biscuits are bite-sized, airy, flakey mouth-watering heaven. She loves my slaw. The fried spot tail fillets are crispy, flaky, perfection.

When Mr. Nicopane walks out of his front door, Pearle starts to chant. Her voice is loud and resonant. Pearle continues hand clapping, foot stomping, and chanting until Mr. Nicopane disappears in his yellow Mercedes.

"You are amazing," I say.

"*Gho* will protect us from Mr. Nicopane's invading spirits."

"Oh, how I love that you are a Voodoo Princess," I say. "Let's grab some towels and go swimming."

We dive into the river. The tide is almost high, and the water is as smooth as glass. Pearle tells me about learning prayer talk, *Fon*, and French. We both have loved swimming since we can remember.

After we dry off in the sun, we check out the tool shed.

The garden fairies instantly appear. They lavish Pearle and her baby with golden retriever puppy dog enthusiasm. One of the little guys boldly hands Pearle a tool.

"Look, a classic single prong weeding cultivator. My Granddaddy had one. I love this tool."

"That was my Granddaddy's tool," I laugh. "This is my fave, the stirrup hoe."

We throw two flat shovels, the stirrup hoe, and the cultivator into the wheelbarrow. The fairies hop aboard, and we head to the garden.

"Pearle, would this be a good time to welcome you to my world of fairy magic?" I ask.

"Haints?" Pearle asks.

"Hardly. These little ethereal beings are helpers," I laugh.

"I'm happy that you understand we are living in two worlds," Pearle says.

"My Master's degree is in Fairy Magic. When I told you I saw energy vibrations, I was talking about fairies. Right now a half dozen garden fairies are vying to help us."

"Mary Howard, we are soul tistahs," she embraces me.

I breathe a sigh of relief.

We labor to remove sod, plant Pearle's medicinal roots, and direct sow a new crop of buckwheat and red clover ground cover.

"I think we doubled the size of the garden today," I say.

When Mr. Nicopane pulls up, we run inside feeling like six-year-old kids.

The next morning I order four yards of Wise Hoe Woo's Magic Compost. Over the next week, we spread compost and sow cruciferous, rutabaga, and cos seeds.

Pearle gives the garden shed a complete makeover. I love being amidst her magical whirling dervish energy.

We spend our evenings in the library reading *Ancient Wisdom Revealed*. We're learning about expanding our narrow minds, the 'Raincloud of Knowable Things' and healing humanity of the separateness meme.

The day before the Cumberland trip I can't make up my mind about anything. Should I wear cut-offs or a sundress? Red or tie-dye bikini? Purple gown or black cocktail dress? Maybe, I'll ask Rosemarie? Yuck, no. Just pick something to wear, nut-case.

That night, Pearle and I take a pot of tea to the living room and look through my parents' photo albums. She asks a million questions. We come across a five by seven black and white glossy of Marshall, Crew, and me asleep in the playpen on Marshall's dock when we were five-months-old. Why haven't I told my lifelong friends about Pearle? Yuck.

"Pearle, I want to bag out of the cruise tomorrow. Now that Wise Hoe Woo said Supreme Chief Isle is looking for you, it's more complicated."

"Mary, I think you should go."

"What if you and the baby need something?"

"We'll be fine. Reading and relaxing are the most luxurious things I can imagine."

"I'm a straight talker. If I blow our cover, it could mean trouble with Supreme Chief Isle and the tribe. And what if Cecil Lloyd finds out we're starting Wisdom Seeker under the radar?"

"My intuition says you should go."

I consider her words.

"Intuition is always right," I say.

The next morning, I get up early and walk to the dock to Spiritfly-meditate. When I get back to the house, Pearle and I make Steel Cut Irish Oatmeal, fruit salad, and root tea.

"Mary Howard, you don't need to worry about anything at all,"

Pearle hugs me goodbye. "Good intent will protect you."

"*My Thoughts, My Things*," I say.

We hug goodbye one last time before I motor to Marshall's house.

Cecil comes around the bend in his brand new Chris Craft 45 Motor Yacht, *Fish to Fry*. He's a new captain, and the tide is racing. When he overshoots the first approach, Crew signals for him to swing around and come in from the other direction. On the second pass, he's right on.

Cecil cuts the engine and invites us aboard.

We tour the spacious main deck, galley, and helm. Everything is brand new, one-of-a-kind, and a replica of a vintage 1978 Chris Craft. We go below. Impressive. The forward stateroom is well furnished and has a queen-sized berth. The master stateroom is over the top. Mama's thirty-six by forty-eight Sunset Colored Nude hangs above Cecil's elegant king-size cherry rice carved poster bed.

We crowd into the extra-large private head and check-out the full-size shower stall. Cecil looks hot in his khaki shorts and purple Lacrosse shirt. The Lady in Black with the murky green aura pops in my head. Is she Cecil's lover?

"She's a beauty," Rosemarie says.

"Thanks, I have zero buyer remorse," Cecil says.

We load up, untie the lines, and Cecil eases up on the throttle.

"Man, Diesel 325 HP, that's the ticket. Safe and reliable," Crew says.

We pass by my dock. Cecil tells us he's been looking for riverfront property because he's over living downtown. We watch an eagle swoop down and capture a spot tail a few feet in front of the bow.

"Cecil, I caught you on Savannah Bright's *Be Here Now Show* last week," Crew says. "You busted Doolittle's chops with that conflict of interest piece."

"I thought you were brilliant," Rosemarie says.

"Savannah Bright is a stellar journalist. Unfortunately, establishment owned networks quickly undermined our interview by coining me the 'poster boy for underarm sweat reversal.'"

"Please. You're alive. You sweat," I say.

"Not to mention Savannah Bright's shiny hair and full lips heating things up," Crew says.

"They also turn off the air for the soundman," Cecil says.

"'Television; that insidious beast, a Medusa which freezes a billion people to stone every night, staring fixedly, that Siren that called and sang and promised so much and gave, after all, so little,'" Marshall quotes Ray Bradbury.

"Savannah Bright is shaking things up as host, interviewer, producer, and executive director of the *Be Here Now Show*," Rosemarie says.

"I love her progressive, philanthropic slant on issues," Crew says.

"Savannah Bright is the new spokesperson for Mad Mother's Against Monsanto," Rosemarie says. "I'm thrilled with her endorsement."

"Tell me she's not a mom?" Crew sighs.

"She has two adorable kids. Her family is one hundred percent organic," Rosemarie says.

We motor along at a leisurely pace.

"St. Catherine's Sound next," I say. "We've learned to be respectful of her unpredictable currents and sandbars."

"Tell us about your Cumberland client," Marshall says.

"She has involved me in lawsuits she's filed against the rich and famous, inlanders in shacks, tree-huggers, politicians, and government bureaucrats," Cecil says. "If she senses our message is unclear, it's doomsday. Mrs. Warbaldie is prone to run to Washington and make matters disastrous."

"We will keep that in mind," Crew says.

"Indeed. Mrs. Warbaldie is the most powerful, self-indulgent, tempestuous, stubborn woman I have ever known," Cecil says. "Normally I'd steer clear from Mrs. Warbaldie-types, but somehow she persuaded me to put my principles aside."

"Pristine scenery," Rosemarie says.

"I've always dreamed of taking a cruise down the Intracoastal Waterway," Cecil says.

"Marshall's folks believed Cumberland had magical energy," Crew says.

"They took the three of us camping on Cumberland two or three times a year," Marshall says.

"Cumberland is where we were initiated to use nature as a catalyst on our quest for power over ourselves," I say.

"We learned that nature is a gift from the spirit world. We were raised to express gratitude to minerals, plants, animals, humans, and spirits," Crew says.

"We're animists," we all say at the same time.

I keep my trap shut about West African *Vodun* people also being animists.

"Anybody up for a swim?" I ask.

Everybody is game. We throw the anchor at the next side creek and jump in the water. I have gratitude that Pearle encouraged me to be here. After a brisk dip, we climb back aboard and continue cruising down the Intracoastal Waterway.

Crew serves homemade boiled peanuts, sausage balls, cheese sticks, and Ritz crackers topped with cream cheese and Pickapeppa sauce.

"Best apps in Savannah," Marshall says.

Crew means well, but he needs to lose his Grandmother's cholesterol-laden *Southern Living* recipes.

He fumbles around in the cooler. "New World Bakery turkey and Swiss on rye," Crew says.

Really, deli meat? How many times have I pestered them about nitrites and slaughterhouses? Why don't people get that it is wrong to torture animals and eat their flesh?

Guide says, "Unity."

"No thanks, I'll stick with boiled peanuts," I say.

Rosemarie takes half of sandwich and nonchalantly hides the turkey under the iceberg lettuce. I'm not that polite.

"St. Simons and Jekyll Island up ahead," I change the topic.

We see fabulous mansions on grandiose lawns, blue herons, eagles, ospreys, and red-tailed hawks. Acrobatic dolphin race beside the bow echoing their twenty-million-year-old songs.

By early afternoon, we approach the Cumberland National Seashore.

"Just ahead is the Brickhill River," Crew says.

Cecil navigates past the northern tip of Cumberland Island. A brawny Brooklyn redhead in her mid-fifties waves us into the dock. Cecil kills the engine. Crew and Marshall jump onto the floating dock and tie us off.

"Welcome to Plum Orchard. I'm Mrs. Warbaldie."

We grab our luggage and follow her up a wide brick path. She points out varieties of camellia japonica and sasanqua, native azalea species, hostas, crinum lilies, and lady banks roses along the way. I imagine digging up the expansive lawn and growing food.

"Did Cecil tell you I'm on holiday suspension from millionaire's jail for fortuitous circumstances? I'm fighting the Forest Service, the Department of Agriculture, and any other government agency that protects the commerce of big lumber corporations. They're arrogant butchers trying to control what is wild.

"Tonight we kick it up a notch. I've invited the most influential attorneys and preservationists in Georgia. We'll stop consumer America from destroying the planet," Mrs. Warbaldie says.

I'm glad I'm not Cecil.

We approach the twenty-two hundred square foot mansion and climb the grand marble staircase. Oil paintings of Mrs. Warbaldie's lineage of Revolutionary War generals line the grand foyer walls.

"I'm the fifth generation to live in this house," she says.

Each artist has unique color effects and opaque brushwork.

After Mrs. Warbaldie takes us for a quick tour of the formal gardens and the vaults and markers of her family cemetery, she shows us to our rooms.

"Please enjoy the air-conditioned squash courts and Olympic-size pool on the basement floor," she says.

We grab towels and find our way to the pool. The basement is deserted when we get there. I dive into the crystal clear Olympic-size pool and swim the length underwater. Marshall performs a one-and-a-half flip off the high dive. He's still got it.

We hang out in the pool the rest of the afternoon. When we find our rooms, there is just enough time to take a quick shower, condition my wild red hair, and Spiritfly-meditate. I slip on my purple gown at the last minute and find the others at the east side of an endless hallway.

"Dashing," Marshall says. "Let's find the library."

The speeches are a series of negative oppositions that use lethal, slanderous language. Why do smart people give negativity so much power?

I give a short speech about preserving Cumberland Island and the Georgia Barrier Islands with grassroots caring people.

Marshall magically brings us together when he covers the speaking points of *My Thoughts, My Things,* and *My Soul, My Intuition.*

Rosemarie's speech is impeccably organized with a hook about worldwide environmental coalitions successfully beating the odds.

Cecil Lloyd moves the entire audience with his closing speech. Could he be anymore distinguished-looking in his vintage tux? By the time Cecil finishes speaking, everyone has pledged their membership to the Georgia Barrier Island Preservation Coalition.

When the double doors swing open, swarms of beautiful servers appear with trays of wine, bacon-wrapped prawns, strong cheeses, and Beluga caviar. One hour later we are escorted to dinner.

The formal dining room is twice the size of my downstairs. I find my name tag between two attorneys who are in love with the sound of their voices. I get a hit that Mrs. Warbaldie enjoys pitting them against each other.

Servers bring us she-crab soup, sweet potato soufflé, crispy fried fava beans, and a whole pheasant under glass drowned in cream sauce. The vivacious brunette who has been nursing her red wine intrigues Crew with her fireworks, moons, and stars.

Coffee. Pass. Pecan pie with heavy whipping cream. Pass.

After dinner, we're escorted to the parlor. Servers pass trays of cognac and Cuban cigars. We witness the influentially elite playing hardball. At midnight, we retire to our rooms.

I toss and turn digesting rich food. The next morning, the relentless raucous cawing of a Rhode Island Red rooster wakes me. I Spiritfly-meditate, shower, pack, and find the veranda.

I fix a plate of fruit salad from the breakfast buffet and join Mrs. Warbaldie, Marshall, and Rosemarie. Mrs. Warbaldie hits her Kool cig hard, swigs black coffee, and nibbles on a bear claw.

"Cecil Lloyd was smart to bring your group to speak. I like your optimism," Mrs. Warbaldie says.

"We've formed an impressive coalition," Marshall says.

"We'll stop the government from snatching up the maritime forest for lumber yards," Mrs. Warbaldie says.

"I admire your spirit, Mrs. Warbaldie," Rosemarie says.

"I have a parting gift for you," Marshall says.

Marshall gives Mrs. Warbaldie signed copies of both of his books.

"I'm a big fan, Marshall. Positive Thinking is the wave of the future," she says.

We say goodbye and meet the others on the dock. Crew grabs the minnow trap, and we motor up the Brickhill River.

"That went better than expected," Cecil says.

"I feel empowered bonding with like-minded people," Rosemarie says.

"Witness the shift," I say.

"Mary, what do you mean when you say 'witness the shift'?" Cecil asks.

"Humanity is shifting out of the old meme that war, hunger, and destruction are natural. We are raising our vibration and awakening to the truth that man is energy, and we can positively influence the Wobble of the Earth's axis, the orbital shape, and tilt of the Earth by shifting to a higher, truer, love-based dimension where we will co-create World Peace."

Mr. Inquisitive keeps asking questions, but I stop myself from blabbing. I don't want to deal with a mountain of legalities before I'm allowed to start Wisdom Seeker and teach free spirits critical thinking in my home.

"Time to lighten up," Marshall says.

We dock at the Ranger Station Southern Dock, cut through to River Trail, find Dungeness Road and follow the signs to the Dungeness Ruins. After we explore the ruins and cemetery, we find the one-room First African Baptist Church where John F. Kennedy, Jr. and Carolyn Bessette were married. Photos of Carolyn in her simple silk slip fill my imagination.

"This chapel is exquisite," Cecil says.

"Cumberland is magical," Rosemarie says.

We get back to the South Beach Trail and head north. A team of spirited wild horses thunder out of the dunes and gallop across the beach. I imagination-paint their lean muscular bodies playfully splashing through the surf.

We board *Fish to Fry*, motor down the river one mile, and throw the anchor. We grab our gear, wade across the surf, and hike two miles down a grassy path to our favorite fishing hole.

"I love it back here," I say.

"We always catch fish here," Marshall says.

I bait my hook and cast.

"Gotcha!" I say. I reel in a nice-sized red drum.

Rosemarie gets the next bite, and they dance. I throw my catch in the cooler, bait my hook, and cast again. Rosemarie reels in a six or seven-pound whopper red drum. From nowhere, a thirteen-foot gator appears and snags Rosemarie's catch.

A shotgun fires.

"Get down!" Crew shouts.

The gator races to the bush.

"Always keep your guard in these waters. Giant reptiles have up to eighty sharp teeth used to stab, pierce, and grip prey using vertical crushing power."

The stranger with the shotgun slogs through the swamp towards us. He's Marshall's height, fifteen pounds slimmer, and around Pearle's age.

ELEVEN

"Ancestral crocodilian fossils date back over 200 million years. They have the right to evolve. I'm happy she swam off safely."

He flashes us a charismatic smile, slings his shotgun over his shoulder, and shakes Marshall's hand.

"Alligator, Alligator, chomp, chomp, chomp. We're happy you didn't shoot us. Marshall Portunus, nice to meet you."

"Ha! I mean peace. My name is Fletcher Melville; it's a pleasure. Hey, you wouldn't happen to be the overnight philosophical sensation dude, would you?" Fletcher asks.

"That's me," Marshall says.

"Dude, awesomeness. This scenario is unreal. I love both of your books. Hey, did you write those books tripping on peyote?"

"Yes, visions came to me during a Shamanic Spiritual Ritual involving peyote," Marshall says.

"Alright! I knew that was true. Too cool, dude. Both books are one-hundred-twenty-three pages, and for so many reasons that's my favorite number. I love your anti-intellectualism."

"Nice, thanks," Marshall says.

Fletcher's smile rocks.

"Are you a student?" Cecil asks.

"I'm a surfer. My rents teach math and science at Emory. I love my folks, and I love math, but academia, dude, is way too stifling."

I imagine Fletcher teaching Wisdom Seeker how to hang ten on a longboard.

"Agreed. Institutions are a distorted illusion," Marshall says.

"We happily exist outside the ivory tower," Rosemarie says.

"How did you get to Cumberland?" I ask.

"I took the Dog from Atlanta to Savannah and found work as a striker on a shrimp boat trawler on Tybee Island. When we fished Cumberland, I fell in love with her, and stayed."

"What do you do when there are no waves?" Cecil asks.

"I'm an Endangered Species Protector. Every raccoon and redneck poacher have to deal with me. I'm here to stop extinction and make sure sacred species continue to evolve."

"Are you part of the Forest Service?" Crew asks.

"Oh no, no, no. We don't see eye to eye on anything. I'm sustainable. I feel good about what I do. You can't get that with government jobs."

I imagine Fletcher teaching marine critter care at Wisdom Seeker.

"What do you do to entertain yourself?" Marshall asks.

"I'm a born analyzer; I study random topics. I'm a reader. What do y'all do for fun?" Fletcher asks.

"Cecil Lloyd, I'm an environmental attorney."

"Crew Potalis, Police Chief, Thunderbolt Village."

"Whoa, a good lawyer, nice cop, and cool philosopher. Comical changeup."

Fletcher's laugh is contagious.

"Hey, I'm Mary Howard, oil-on-canvas artist. Nice to meet you, Fletcher."

"And I'm Rosemarie. I am a Spiritual Yoga Practitioner."

"Dudes after my own heart. What brings you lovely people to Cumberland?" Fletcher asks.

"We're preservationists," Cecil says.

"One love," Fletcher says.

"Do you want to join us for lunch?" Rosemarie asks.

"For real?" He asks.

"It doesn't appear you have a personal chef hiding in the bushes," Marshall says.

"True that," Fletcher laughs. "I'm going on day 183 of eating shrimp, fish, conch, wild yams, dandelion greens, and chanterelles."

"How does turkey and Swiss on rye sound?" Crew asks.

"Dude, I dream about deli meat. Y'all are too kind."

We hike back to *Fish to Fry*. Fletcher wears his baggies low on his hips. His tan line looks like he doesn't own a shirt. His see-through blue eyes radiate truth, honesty, and love.

"I want people to protect this coast and realize it is the spawning and nursery of menhaden, drums, crab, shrimp, gopher tortoises, sea turtles, frogs, lizards, alligators, snakes, egrets, kingfishers, red-winged blackbirds, owls, hawks, storks, piping plovers, and bobolinks," Fletcher says. "To name a few."

"Where do you live?" I ask.

"I've been moving between Backcountry Campsite and Wilderness Campsite every two weeks, to avoid eviction, but the fees killed me. So for the past few months, I've been solo camping under the stars."

"Where do you get clean water?" Marshall asks.

"I use a Berkey Filtration System," Fletcher says.

We board *Fish to Fry* and serve lunch. I'm astounded that Fletcher can eat twice as much as Marshall and Crew combined.

After lunch, Crew stands up and looks at his watch and Marshall asks 'what now?' the question that made him famous.

"I'm waiting for a sign," Fletcher says.

"Anything so far?" Rosemarie asks.

"Zilch," he says.

"I'm starting Wisdom Seeker on Wilmington Island for passionate people who believe they can make the world a better place. I offer room, board, and a teaching stipend."

Crew and Marshall are disappointed. Cecil is puzzled.

"Dude, yes, yes, yes. I have so much to offer," Fletcher says.

He gives us bear hugs and sloppy kisses.

"Thank you, Mother Earth; thank you, Universe. I have gratitude," he says. "Can I bring my stuff?"

"Yes, can we help?" Rosemarie asks.

"It's a three-mile hike," Fletcher says.

"We're up for it," I say.

Fletcher jumps off *Fish to Fry*, falls to his knees, smears sand on his forehead and chest, and kisses the beach. We follow him across the maritime forest and bushwhack through bramble, scrub oak, and palmettos.

"Mary, have you started the paperwork for school certification?" Cecil asks.

"Wisdom Seeker is unaffiliated and degree free," I say.

"Where will classes be held?" Cecil asks.

"In the Wilmington River at high tide," I joke.

"I'd like to meet with you before you leave for Ireland. Schools are tricky. Fletcher, your parents, need to sign waivers," he says.

"Dude, they're really supportive like that," Fletcher says.

"Good. Mary doesn't need kidnapping charges. Until papers are drawn up, Fletcher should stay with Marshall or Crew," Cecil says.

I panic. Is taking Pearle to Ireland an international felony?

"We have plenty of room," Rosemarie says.

"Dude, I can sleep outside. It's all good," Fletcher says.

"I don't see what's wrong with offering free spirits a haven," I say.

"Government and State regulations," Cecil says.

"Will you be the Wisdom Seeker attorney?" I ask.

"Yes, Mary, I'm your man, but I'll be honest; starting a school will be the most tedious legal challenge to date," Cecil says.

"In my home?" I ask.

"You live in a residential neighborhood and have an intolerant neighbor. We have to proceed with caution."

"Rule followers should confine themselves to institutions and leave me alone to do my soul's work in peace," I say.

"Almost there," Fletcher says.

We get to Fletcher's camp and help him tear down. I wonder how he's survived the mosquitoes, sand gnats, and no-see-ums that are feasting on us right now. Fletcher fits his tarp, clothes, sleeping bag, thermorest, mag light, and water filter in his backpack. He slings the backpack on his shoulders and hoists his yellow longboard on top of his head. The rest of us grab crates of books.

When we get back to the beach, the incoming tide is racing. We have to carry the books on our heads. We struggle against the waist-deep water and manage to board Fish to Fry. Crew pulls the anchor, and Cecil is underway.

"Let's celebrate your first teaching job with a cold IPA," I say.

"Craft beer! Gratitude!" Fletcher says. "Hey, dudes, this is like the coolest gig ever. Just to let you know, I love to chef."

"What's your specialty?" Crew asks.

"Pecan pie, three-layer coconut cake, and crispy oven-fried chicken," Fletcher says.

"Nice roommate skills," Marshall laughs.

Crew, Marshall, and Fletcher go off on unhealthy recipes. I allow disgust to pass by me like the wind. I focus on unity. When I get back from Ireland, I'll show Fletcher undercover Youtube videos of slaughterhouses, and I know that he will get why Wisdom Seeker boycotts Animal Agriculture.

I walk to the bow and stretch out in a chaise. I shut my eyes, breathe deeply, and balance my chakras. I am grateful that Wisdom Seeker is materializing. I think about spending the winter with Grandmama Sharon in Dingle, Kerry County. There's no place I'd rather be to organize Wisdom Seeker and greet Pearle's baby. After ten or fifteen minutes, I head back to the wheel room.

"Crew, you're a cool dude. Why a cop?" Fletcher asks.

"Gandhi, Chavez, and King inspired me. I think shifting my small remote department to be a peace center will inspire bigger departments to do the same."

"Good enough," Fletcher laughs.

Fletcher talks nonstop about humanity and evolution. My soul rests in my heart. Fletcher is good because good is all he knows: which is the best type of good. Love, love, love.

We get back to Marshall's house and clean coolers. When Cecil shoves off, I motor home.

"Whewsuu, Whewsuu."

Ouida flies to the bow when she sees me. I pet her luxurious feathers. I love you. The tide is racing. I kill the engine, leap to the dock, and tie off. Ouida flies to her piling. I run all the way back to the house.

"Hey there! I'm home."

Pearle runs down the stairs, and we hug.

"How was the trip?" she asks.

"You were right; I was supposed to go. Big news, we have a new Wisdom Seeker! Fletcher Melville; he's your age."

"Where is he?" she asks.

"He's staying with Marshall and Rosemarie until we leave for Dublin."

"What's he like?"

"He's passionate, spiritual, and energetic. Wisdom Seeker is materializing."

"Amen, tistah."

"Did you relax?" I ask.

"Mary, I'm renewed. Hey, look what I made for the baby."

I follow her upstairs. Pearle used my Grandmother's scraps of silk, denim, felt, and wool to sew stuffed toys in the shapes of pigs, chicks, stars, moons, and hoops. She's even made swaddling blankets, bibs, cloth diapers, and a padded sling.

"I'm blown away," I say.

That afternoon, during a torrential downpour, we watch surfing YouTube videos to learn about Fletcher's world.

The next morning, I greet Ouida and Spiritfly-meditate. Monkey brain makes lists. When I come out of meditation Ouida is gone. I go back to the house, careful not to wake Pearle, and slip into the baby room.

I put the finishing touches on the surfer girl's black bikini and finish the white caps. Done. I hear Pearle stirring.

"Hey, good morning. I'm in the baby room," I say.

"Good morning, Mary. How beautiful." Pearle gives me a kiss. "When did you finish?"

"Just now."

"I love the surfer," Pearle says. "Ahh, Mama and baby dolphin kissing goodnight. So sweet."

We're beyond excited getting this far with the baby room.

After breakfast, I head downtown to Alex Raskin Antiques on Bull Street. I buy an artisan rocking chair, dresser, and a nightstand they will deliver Friday morning. The next stop is Mary Jane

Children's Boutique. I buy an infant car seat and confirm the crib delivery. Now we only need to find Swedish organic KRAV baby clothes in Dublin secondhand stores.

I drive back to Wilmington Island and pull into Wise Hoe Woo Marina parking lot. I grab my agenda and a case of wine and head inside. Between Pearle, the baby, and Dublin Institute of Art, I hope I'm ready for the Cucurbit Pepo Pageant this year.

I set out French red wine on the table overlooking Turner Creek and arrange the fold up chairs in a semi-circle. Everyone arrives on time. We serve ourselves mugs of wine and socialize before finding our seats. I'm happy to be the President of this positive tribe.

I start by making sure that all of the pieces of the event fit together smoothly. We make small touch-ups to the event program and wrap up parking, promo, security, and first aid. After we confirm set-up and tear-down teams, we paint dozens of signs and banners. When we've covered all of the bases, I adjourn the meeting.

Friday night I sleep well, wake up at dawn, and walk to the dock. Before I Spiritfly-meditate, I take my time loving on Ouida. When I come out of meditation, I pray to my Indigenous Guides to help Pearle and me get to Dublin safely.

"Stay at Marshall's dock this winter. I'm going to Ireland. I'll be back this spring." Ouida fills my heart with sacred animal spirit when I kiss her goodbye.

The garden fairies salute me and promise to help Marshall, Rosemarie, and Fletcher tend the fall garden.

I get back to the house, make us breakfast, and get ready to leave. When we hug goodbye, the baby kicks. Lifeforce energy. Wow.

I grab my straw hat and walk down the avenue of oaks. I take the shortcut through the woods and cut across to the May Howard School Playground.

The equipment truck ends up arriving two hours late. The rest of the day we play catch-up setting up the stage, dance floor, and the big tent.

I get a text. Earth, Wind & Fire is stuck in Atlanta International Airport due to engine problems. My mind spirals to the worst case scenarios. I am a warrior. I am loved. My mind is a still river.

What in the world? Is that Pearle's people in the Wise Hoe Woo Marina parking lot? Yuck, it is. Good heavens, they are crossing Wilmington River Road and coming this way. It's Pearle's father, Supreme Chief Isle, and Doc. I recognize them from Pearle's photos. Supreme Chief Isle is six-four, pure muscle, and regal. Doc is menacing. I break out in a cold sweat when they approach me. Please don't let Doc take off those purple shades and give me the evil eye for faking Voodoo vexes my whole life.

Supreme Chief Isle shows me a photograph of Pearle. His hands are gigantic. His voice is rumbly and deep. He asks me if I have any information on Pearle's whereabouts. I keep my gaze askance, think soil, soil, soil, and tell him no.

Next, they approach Marshall and Crew. What a nightmare.

Rosemarie texts, "giraffe snappy."

I head to the petting zoo and sit with the giraffe until she unwinds. EWF text. They've left Atlanta. Thank you, Universe.

I grab the twelve-foot extension ladder and prop it against the grand oak. I climb to the top rung, shimmy across the branch, and balance myself. On top of the world, I hang dozens of Daddy's handcrafted circa 1700 Cockspur Lighthouse glass lanterns.

Daddy marveled that pumpkins and gourds have the power to evoke Unity Consciousness whereas religion and politics perpetuate separatism.

TWELVE

Earth, Wind & Fire equipment trucks arrive. We greet the production and stage managers. The next bus arrives with the monitor engineer and the sound and lighting crew. They work quickly. Everyone is kind, calm, and super flexible. This is really happening.

The tour manager texts that EWF has landed in Savannah. Thank you, Universe.

One hour later a shiny bus called the "Living Room" arrives. Fourteen musicians immerse us in love wisdom energy. Within the hour, they take the stage for the sound check and a quick rehearsal. Wow, pros.

We head to the cafeteria and pop open bottles of 1986 Chateau Mouton Rothschild. Wow, a backstage rider requirement with undeniable taste thrills and the sophistication worthy of twenty Grammies and fifty Gold Records.

Rosemarie, Crew, Marshall, Fletcher, and I have prepared fresh-caught crispy oven-fried flounder, grits, baked tempeh, red rice, kale and shitake stir-fry, and stoneground pan-fried hushpuppies. We walk through the buffet and sit down family style. EWF. High vibe Unity Consciousness.

I excuse myself to make the final rounds. The vendors are set. The energy is electrifying. We open the gates when "Magnification" starts on the house sound system.

Hundreds of Unity partygoers pile into the school grounds.

Marshall and I make our way to the stage.

"Ladies and gentlemen, I am Grand Marshal, Marshall Portunus, and we would like to welcome you to the 2009 Twentieth Annual Cucurbit Pepo Pageant in Celebration of Unity."

He waits for applause.

"Thank you for being here! Without further ado, I'd like to introduce the powerful All AME Gospel Songbirds."

The Hammond C-3 wails a soulful intro. The soprano steps out to the mic and sings "Oh, Happy Day." They are well-rehearsed and having fun.

"Give it up for the All AME Gospel Songbirds. I'm Mary Howard, and I welcome you to the twentieth Victor Howard Cucurbit Pepo Pageant, or for folks that prefer, the Pumpkin Peace Party. I have a few announcements. The giraffe is snappy, so please stand back a neck's length. All proceeds from the silent auction benefit the Mai Howard Bethesda Scholarship Fund, so please bid generously. Enjoy food vendors serving local, sustainable, one hundred percent organic, and animal agriculture-free healthy cuisine."

The tide has turned. The crowd is cheering for clean food choices. My heart sings.

"Enjoy Moon River Brewery and cast your vote on Best Celeb-Chef-Pumpkin-off. Then, at 8:00 P.M., "Boogie Fever" because Earth, Wind & Fire is in the house y'all! And we will cap off this magical night with Wise Hoe Woo's spectacular silent firework show. Now, back to Marshall Portunus, Savannah's one and only Positive Thinking Guru."

Marshall takes the mic.

"It is my pleasure to announce this year's winner of the Portunus Green-Up-AME-Sunday-School Campaign and recipient of a vintage mint condition 1965 Hammond C-3 organ, with Leslie 427 cabinets. The winner is Reverend Saw, Talahi Island AME Church."

The crowd cheers. Reverend Saw comes up to the stage and takes the mic.

"I'd like to thank Mr. Portunus for our beautiful Hammond C-3 organ and for helping me help my community. The past year has been an eye-opener. We banned Krispy Kreme, coca-cola, ice cream, sheet cakes, cookies, chips, Ritz crackers, pork, and beef from church socials and donated the money we saved, $2,950.00, to assist West African villages with garden start-up costs. Our congregation has lost four hundred and ninety pounds and, best of all, we feel empowered to help other folks be happier," Reverend Saw says.

The All AME Gospel Songbirds sing "We Shall over Come," *a cappella*.

Next, I introduce Crew. He takes the stage and invites a dozen We Saw Wassaw alumni to join him. They cue the sound man and perform an original called "Clean Up Yo' Own Mess Baby," an environmental rap that brings down the house.

"Crew is full of surprises, dude," Fletcher says.

"He's got the moves," Rosemarie says.

"Folks meet the Potalis Peace and Preservation Program alumni. Peace is our goal. Talk to us at our booth and pledge to give peace a chance."

Crew gives me the mic.

"Give it up for Chief Crew and the We Saw Wassaw Rappers. And now, the one and only permit giver, Mayor Archibald Doolittle III."

Black vultures land on the stage when I hand him the mic. I keep my spirit high. Tonight is for Unity Consciousness, not his eel skin lies. I exit backstage, slip away into the woods, cross the golf course, and jog down the avenue of oaks.

When I open the garage, Pearle comes right out.

"Doc and your dad showed up. They about scared me to death. Maybe I should come back and get you after the show."

"Remember Mary, I have power, too. Daddy and Doc won't stop me from hearing Philip Bailey and Maurice White sing tonight."

"Okay, if you say so."

We stow our luggage and a cooler in the trunk. The Honda starts the second try. When we get back to the school, I cut off the headlights and park by the woods in the bus parking lot.

"Are you sure you will be okay? I ask.

"Don't worry about anything, Mary."

Pearle heads to the woods, and I go back to the playground. Supreme Chief Isle and Doc are still questioning quests in the teacher's parking lot. My nerves are on edge.

Time drags until Earth, Wind & Fire, in shimmering costumes, take the stage. I squeeze between Marshall, Rosemarie, Crew, and Fletcher and we dance for ninety minutes to pure Spiritual, Universal, and Egyptology funk. They treat us to three encores. The last one, "That's the Way," is our fave.

When Wise Hoe Woo starts the silent firework show, I hug everybody goodbye and take off.

Pearle is hiding in the backseat when I get there.

"Stay low," I say. "Supreme Chief Isle and Doc are still here." I drive past the school.

"Coast is clear! Hotlanta-bound, girlfriend!"

Pearle jumps in the front seat.

"Are you okay?" I ask.

"This was the most fun night of my life. I danced in the woods all night. I'll never forget this," she says.

"Hot times for Unity Consciousness in the old town tonight," I say.

I take out a stack of EWF CDs, and we blast them all the way to LaGrange, where we stop to gas up and use the bathroom. Pearle goes inside while I pump gas. When I go inside, she's combing the aisles of brightly packaged junk food.

"John Robbins said never eat at a gas station."

"Baby-brain-cravings," she says. "I want salt, fat, and sugar."

"But you do not want junk food in your placenta."

"Lead me not into temptation. Thank you, John Robbins."

"Let's break out the ALT sandwiches and keep driving."

After we eat, Pearle falls asleep. Monkey brain chatters about international kidnapping charges. I cringe thinking about police arresting us as soon as we walk inside the terminal.

Guide says, "Visualize being in Grandmama Sharon's loving arms."

Pearle wakes up when we hit Atlanta traffic.

We pull into Atlanta International and leave the car in long-term parking. We catch the shuttle. Relax. No one notices us. Relax.

When we get to the gate, they announce our flight is delayed due to engine problems.

"What do they mean engine problems?" Pearle asks.

"Stay calm. They know how to fix engines."

"Voodoo pantheon of Mami Wata spirits," Pearle chants softly. "*Jo*, the *Vodun* of the air, *Agê*, the *Vodun* of the animals, birds, agriculture, and the forests, *Sakpata*, the *Vodun* of the earth and mountains and *Xêviso* the *Vodun* originally from the sea that ended up in the sky, protect us."

Pearle closes her eyes and sways until she enters *Sangh Yang* trance. I smile at the old lady who is staring at us.

"Horse of the Spirit, please allow the pure universal energy of good to enter my diamond nose piercing. Damballah!" Pearle startles the old lady. "Damballah," she repeats with a stern expression.

They announce that our flight to JFK is now boarding.

"Let's board before they run us off on broomsticks," I say.

We request extra pillows and blankets. The plane is empty. We make nests and fall asleep.

I wake up when we're circling JFK.

"Hey, Pearle. Wake up."

"Wow, the big city," she says.

"I considered moving here but who could give up Wilmington Island for New York City?"

The plane jolts to a stop, and Pearle gives thanks to each one of her deities. We grab our carry-ons and head to the International Terminal.

"Follow the smell of rancid grease to the food court."

"I'm craving fish," Pearle says.

"Airports have industrial factory-farmed fish raised in China on pig feces."

"That's shameful!"

"Institutional fish sandwiches contain sixty-one artificial ingredients."

"Poison," Pearle says.

"When Wisdom Seeker makes edible education popular, the FDA will crumble."

"So what do you recommend until then?"

"Steamed vegetables have the least chemicals."

We eat at Hibachi Grill and then take a quick walk around JFK before it's time to board our flight to Dublin.

"Lucky us, we have the whole row to ourselves again," I say.

We order extra blankets and pillows and prepare for take-off. At the last second, a dozen glamorous twenty-somethings shuffle on board and go to the back of the plane.

"Yippee, we're safe," I squeal.

"I believe this is my seat," a man says.

I audibly sigh. We make adjustments, and he crawls over us to the window seat.

"Omar Victor, filmmaker, it's a pleasure to meet you," he says.

I gasp in disbelief. Am I dreaming? It's like *Movie Star Man* just materialized right in front of my eyes. His shoulders and Hollywood dimples are an exact likeness. And his last name is Daddy's first name. I spiral away.

"Pearle Isle. Nice to make your acquaintance."

Pearle snaps her finger.

"Hey, um, Mary Howard, nice to see you."

The plane takes off. I open *Quantum Mechanics of Many-Body Systems* and pretend to reread the introduction. Unable to resist my urge, I sneak a peek at *Movie Star Man*.

"May I take your beverage order?" The server asks.

I jump. Yuck, busted.

"Cutty Sark on ice," he laughs.

"Bottled water, please," Pearle says.

"Jameson straight up, thanks," I say.

When Pearle starts reading, I strike up a conversation.

"Do you live in the city?" I whisper.

"I was in New York on business. My home is in Cairo, but I also have a flat in Dublin. Where is your home?" He asks with a soft-spoken baritone voice.

"Savannah, Georgia, USA."

"Ahh, taking a holiday in the Deep South has always been on my bucket list."

"Are you kidding?"

"I kid you not. My parents raised me on *Gone with the Wind*."

My brain scuttles about looking for another topic of conversation.

"Victor was my father's name."

"Victor Howard, the sculptor?"

"Yes."

"My dear, fate brings us together. Victor Howard's 1976 marble *Acrobatic Dolphin* graces the fountains of my family villa in Cairo."

"That was his most ambitious work."

"The sculpture is enormous, graceful, and evocative. Victor Howard will always be loved as an artist and humanitarian. I'm sorry for your loss."

"Thank you."

"What do you do for a living?"

"I followed in the family footsteps. I'm giving a show at the Dublin Art Institute Friday night."

"What medium?"

"Oil-on-canvas."

"Good grief, you're so young."

Having a conversation with the subject of my quantum-Newtonian painting is surreal. He orders us another round.

"Are your parents filmmakers?" I ask.

"Hardly, they are scientists. My mother researches opiate for pain relief and sleep aids, and my father is an organologist."

"Organologist?" I ask.

"He studies the structure and functions of organs."

I stop myself from criticizing Big Pharma.

"I'm the black sheep of the family. My parents have always criticized me for being too forward-thinking and emotional," Omar says.

"In the New Age scientists will collaborate with intuits to balance nature. And culture will no longer be allowed to ignore quantum physics once we shift to love-based," I say.

"My argument has always been that science counts what already exists," he says.

I stop myself from talking about the banana blight, FDA food flavoring chemicals, GMOs, and glyphosate poisoning.

Pearle senses I'm in trouble. She puts down her book and leads the conversation to the safe waters of meditation and the Law of Attraction. That's when Omar tells us he recently read *My Soul, My Intuition* and *My Thoughts, My Things* and I get points that Marshall is my lifelong friend.

"What do filmmakers actually do?" Pearle asks.

"I write, direct, and produce films ranging from political figures legislating policies that stop the cattle, pork, and poultry industries from ruining the planet to altruism that is shifting the economy from commodity to trust and sharing."

We tell Omar about Wisdom Seeker.

"Again, serendipity. In Egyptian, there is no word for philosophy, as we left that to the Greeks. What Egyptian children are taught is to obey the laws of order, *ma'at*, that allow us to gain Wisdom," he says.

"How?" Pearle and I ask at the same time.

"Our instruction is called *Se Bayt*. It teaches children to be at peace, cultivate happiness through spiritual development, and to understand that our ability to know is unlimited."

I tell him about my plot to co-create peace with collective creativity and unbending intent. Pearle and I talk about practicing meditation as a way to raise our vibration in order to shift humanity to love-based perfect vision by 2020.

"That's important to me as a filmmaker," Omar says.

"World leaders have conditioned us to accept that war is a reality, and world peace is an illusion," I say.

"As we connect with like-minded people, we will continue to expand our narrow minds," Pearle says.

"Normally I avoid using the word fate, but I've always dreamed of creating a film institute to support a pantheon of visionary filmmakers, with a Fellini, Frances Ford Coppola-type originality, to document the good we are doing with our twenty-first-century power."

"Help and be helped," Pearle says.

Omar tells us he's in postproduction on a documentary about recreational marijuana and Colorado fly fishing that exposes drug war and privatized prison corruption. And he's also directing a documentary he is filming about indigenous Africans who are reclaiming their ancestral lands from the US beef industry.

"Lights, camera, action," I say.

When the plane lands, I still don't have the guts to tell him that Grandmama Sharon said he would be my first husband or that I've already painted him.

"Production is grueling, but I hope to make it to your show this weekend."

He crawls over us, hands us our luggage, and rushes off with his glamorous entourage. I look for him at the luggage carousel and outside, but he has vanished.

I hail a taxi, and we peel out into bustling traffic.

"I can't believe we're in Dublin!" Pearle says.

"I can't believe *Movie Star Man* materialized. I told Marshall I'd call him when we landed."

"Remember, don't say 'we.'"

"Got it."

Marshall picks up on the third ring. His voice sounds like home.

"Hey, Marshall, I'm in Dublin, headed to the hotel."

"Thanks for keeping us posted. Congratulations on the best Cucurbit Pepo Pageant ever," he says.

"A good time was had by all."

"How was the flight?"

"Interesting. I sat next to a filmmaker who documents what good we are doing with our twenty-first-century power."

"Fantastic."

"His family owns Victor Howard sculptures. And he says he's interested in purchasing the *Merman and Mermaid*."

"That would boost your trust."

"Plus make room in the garage."

"What's his name?"

"Omar Victor; he's Egyptian."

"How Freudian is that? By any chance is he your type?"

"He's young and gorgeous if that's what you mean."

"He's a movie star. That's always been important, right?"

"Yes, I know, I know."

"Mary, you have a history of closing the door before a guy gets a chance to knock."

"Hey, I know my history, but I'm purdeesho I left the door open." Marshall tells me Fletcher is settled in at my house, and he loves the library. He says the *Kama Sutra* and *Isis Sex Magic* have been more valuable than a $250,000.00 college education."

"I agree. Hey, the taxi just pulled up to the Shelbourne Dublin."

"Take care and have a great show."

"Thanks, keep your fingers crossed that people will attend."

The bellman fetches our luggage. Emotions flood me the minute I step foot inside the lobby. I transgress to our Mother-Daughter Show at the Dublin Art Institute when I was seventeen. We sell out, Ireland coins me a prodigy, and when I get home, the Savannah Tongue snubs me, my school banishes me, and then the car crash.

Pearle and I find our suite, call room service, and go to sleep by midnight.

THIRTEEN

The next morning we hit the streets of Dublin. We comb neighborhood thrift stores and score on organic KRAV baby clothes. After shopping, we head to Bram's Café for organic porridge and stewed apples. By mid-morning, the fog has lifted.

We take a walk through St. Stephen's Green, visit the Long Room of the Old Library at Trinity College Art Department, and then lose ourselves in Chapters Book Store.

When hunger strikes, we walk to Poolbeg Street, find the John Mulligan Pub, and sit down at the two-hundred-year-old bar. We order pasta with roasted vegetables, and I order a pint of the dark stuff.

"This city is mighty," Pearle says.

"I've considered being an expatriate, but I keep going back to Save-Anna," I say.

"Tonight's the big night," Pearle says.

"I hope people will attend."

"Mary, the gray horse appeared in my dream last night. No worries."

"Let's hope Mami Wata comes through. I love the beer in

Ireland, much better than the American stuff."

I order another pint. Five stars.

After a relaxed lunch, we head out in the bright Irish sunshine and taxi back to the hotel.

I sleep off the beer buzz, shower, Spiritfly-meditate, tie my hair in a knot on top of my head, and slip on my purple gown.

"Tah, dah."

"Mary that dress was made for your cute little figure."

"This was my tenth-grade prom dress."

Pearle cracks up.

"What's up with the *Women River Saints*?" I ask.

"It's about the innate feminine power in all women. You share many of the same traits as Mother Mary."

"I'm no Puritan."

"Mother Mary is the archetype of the loving mother."

"Ha, loving mother meet Mother Earth lover."

The front desk rings. My limo is waiting. Pearle and I hug goodbye.

I climb in the back of the limo, and we take off. When we pull up to the Dublin Institute of Art, I snap a photo of 'Mary Howard, oil-on-canvas, Solo Show' lit up on the marquee.

Patrick opens my door, and we embrace.

"Mary, it's fabulous to see you," he says.

"Thank you, it is a joy to be in Dublin."

"Look, patrons are already wrapped around the corner waiting for us to open."

We slip into the alley and enter the back door of the green room. Patrick and I walk down the long familiar corridor. When he leads me into the Main Gallery, I know why Mama called him a genius of light and space.

"I have gratitude for your vision, Patrick," I say.

"You like?" He asks.

"Yes. Every detail sings good *feng shui*," I say.

When doors open, I'm immediately walled in with patrons. I ask my soul to rest in my heart. I power up and talk about the glow in nature, sharp breaks in shadows, and night skies. Kind people offer their respect. Critics ask tough questions. I surreally dance between a dream come true and claustrophobia.

Omar Victor enters the gallery with his entourage. Next, the paparazzi storm in and pack the gallery. My heart is pounding. Patrick works his way to me.

"Excuse us, loyal patrons, Miss Howard is scheduled for a short break."

Omar leaves. I'm crushed. I follow Patrick to the Green Room.

"Oh, you little rascal, I met your ultra-beautiful boyfriend, hot-hot," Patrick laughs. "I was hoping he was hitting on me, but then he asked me to give you this note, you naughty girl."

"I'm speechless."

Patrick gets serious.

"Mary, tonight is the biggest night of our careers. Omar Victor just purchased the entire Daufuskie series plus the Victor Howard *Merman and Mermaid* sculpture."

"I don't know what to say."

Patrick's phone rings.

"I have to take this, love. Patrice will take care of you."

"Hello, I'm your server, Patrice. Sauvignon Blanc? Prawns wrapped in bacon?"

I imagination-paint his long face, thin cheeks, half smile, dark circles, and bright green eyes.

"Who could resist?" I ask.

I'm shaky, opening Omar's letter.

"Yippee, he asked me out!" I tell Patrice. "He loves my art."

I call Pearle.

"It's Mary. I'm on break. How are you?"
"Good, good. How's the show?"
"Packed. Omar showed up."
"Get out. What happened?"
"He asked me out after the show," I squeal.
"Go celebrate. I'm glued to *Women River Saints*."
"Who are these women?"
"Whores, housewives, mothers, sisters, outcasts, seductresses, nuns, and herbalists. You name it, they all had divine visions."

Patrick opens the door and waves.

"Break's over, I have to go."

The next hour passes quickly. At nine P.M., Patrick locks the doors and turns off the gallery lights. Thank you, muses. When we get back to the Green Room, we collapse on the sofa, and Patrice serves us champagne in crystal flutes. We joyfully reminisce about Mai Howard's art shows without shedding a single tear.

"Tonight is for romance," Patrick says. "I'll walk you to the limo."

We kiss goodnight, and I head to O'Donoghue's Pub. I take a deep breath, walk across the room, and sit next to Omar.

"Congratulations! The show was brilliant. Your paintings are alive, moving, and energetic."

"You are kind," I say.

The bartender's name is Nick McBride. He has a mop of wiry red hair and a genuine smile. Omar orders us a Guinness and a Teeling Small Batch Irish Whiskey served neat in a snifter.

"Oh good Lord, protect us! It's a wee wizen monkey fairy, the size of a hare," Nick says.

"Where?" I ask.

"In the dark shadows of the ceiling beams. They come from the Old Jameson Distillery. They carry wee lanterns and whistle sharp ringing sounds. Be careful what promises you make tonight," Nick

McBride says. "They are the infallible harbingers of ill omen."

I relax my facial expressions.

"I brought you a gift," he hands me *The Goddess Ishtar*. "She was a Sumerian goddess. The Babylonians called her Inanna, goddess of sex, love, and war. She is the most prominent female deity of ancient Mesopotamia. It is told that Ishtar went to Hell for the many men that she seduced and destroyed, but now she is back."

"Wow, thanks." I skim the inside jacket: esoterica, nefarious apples, and Inanna's breasts that represent war and peace. I stick the dog-eared paperback into my purse.

"How's your Irish dancing?" I ask.

"Not bad for an Egyptian."

We head to the crowded dance floor. The band is top notch. The musicians perform jigs and reels that get faster and faster. Omar can cut a rug.

I fantasize about Omar energizing my *Ka* body. I coax him, at a soul level, to grab my waist, hold me tight, and kiss me hard, but when he doesn't respond, I spin into worst case scenarios. Maybe my shoulders are too muscular from years of open-water swimming. Maybe my scrawny behind is too unwomanly. Or is my solitary personality a turn-off? I stop right there.

Please, Universe, coax Omar to knock on my proverbial door.

Soon after Nick announces the last call, we walk outside. Omar hails a taxi. What? Was that brush across my forehead a kiss? Why is this man treating me like I'm his great aunt?

Omar opens the door for me and I crawl into the backseat. Then Omar shuts the door behind me. What? The taxi pulls out into traffic.

My sacred sex drive dies a hundred deaths. By the time I get back to the hotel, my head is pounding from rejection and my bladder is about to burst.

The next morning is crushingly bright and hectic. We taxi to the bus depot and board the eight o'clock train to Dingle.

"Mary, what do you think went wrong?"

"I wish I knew. It was fun until that bizarre kiss and the taxi surprise."

I shut my eyes to meditate but fall into a deep sleep. I wake up when the driver announces we're in Limerick.

"Good nap?" Pearle asks.

"I was out. Let's head to Platform Five Bar and Restaurant. We've got an hour break."

I order soda crackers with cheddars and a Guinness, a blonde in the black skirt. Pearle orders fish and crisps and lemon water. After lunch, we board the bus to Tralee. I sketch the rolling hills dotted with medieval castles and monasteries. By early afternoon, racing dark clouds erupt into a torrential downpour.

The rain stops by the time the train pulls into the Tralee station. Pearle and I take the shortcut to Brogue Maker's Lane and hike out to the jagged coastal cliffs to catch the panoramic view of the North Atlantic. When we get back to the bus depot, it's time to board the last bus to Dingle.

We arrive in Dingle at dusk, collect our luggage, and head to the village. We make our way through the cobblestone streets and a labyrinth of whitewashed thatched roof cottages.

"Dingle is another world altogether," Pearle says.

"Yes. There's Grandmama Sharon's straw bale cottage with the bright yellow trim," I say.

I tap on her low wooden door.

"Come in, children."

I fall into Grandmama Sharon's loving arms.

"This is my friend, Princess Pearle Isle."

"Pearle, I recognize your indigo aura. I knew you in Tibet. We've been healers together for many incarnations."

They embrace like soulmates.

"Come in. Make yourself at home."

"It smells amazing in here," Pearle says.

"I've made a fresh pot of potato and leek stew. Are you ready for supper?" Grandmama Sharon asks.

"Oh jah," I say.

"Mary brags about your stew," Pearle laughs.

Setting the table with Grandmama Sharon's linen makes me nostalgic for my parents. Dingle is where we came to "escape reality."

We sit down to supper. Grandmama Sharon says grace.

"Fantastic," I say.

"Are these dandelion greens?" Pearle asks.

"Yes, I hope they aren't too bitter." Grandmama Sharon says.

"I was raised on wild bitter greens," Pearle says.

"How is Mr. Pope?" I ask.

"Mr. Pope is remarkable. The children adore him," Grandmama Sharon says.

"How long has the Dingle Orphanage been next door?" Pearle asks.

"Mary's mother, Mai, founded the orphanage forty years ago. Mai was known as an artist, but her soul's purpose was humanitarian work," Grandmama Sharon says.

"Mama has always been a major supporter of Bethesda Orphanage in Savannah, too," I say.

"Mai met Mr. Pope at the Dingle fish market when she was fifteen. They soon discovered they shared a passion for helping street children. We invited Mr. Pope over for dinner, and they started scheming.

"Mr. Pope repaired his van and took Mai to Dublin to sell her art. They ran into Patrick right off the bat. Three years later, Mai had earned enough to make a down payment on the property next door."

"The inn was in shambles," I say. "Mr. Pope and Mama remodeled everything."

"Their mission statement was a Maya Angelou quote that says, 'If you ain't got but one smile in you, give it to the people you love,'" Grandmama Sharon laughs.

We cluck like chickens, clean the dishes, and settle in the tiny den. I stoke the fire.

"Five months along?" Grandmama Sharon asks.

"Twenty-four weeks."

"Pearle, the baby needs to shift, but your energy is blocked due to sadness."

Pearle is not surprised to hear this. A tear rolls down her face.

"Tell me why you feel sad, love."

"I was the youngest in my class to achieve chieftaincy in the pedagogy of initiations. From my earliest memories, I was gifted with spirit possessions and an urge to heal others. And as the daughter of the Supreme Chief, I was privileged. Life was mystical.

"V*oodoo,* view you, teaches us that the universe is all one, and each thing affects something else. During *novitiae*, the school of life we enter at age twelve, I optimistically spoke out against animal sacrifices," she dries her tears, "and arranged marriages."

Pearle looks out the window. Grandmama Sharon takes her hand.

"Speak your mind, child," Grandmama Sharon says.

"My protests were considered a threat to the Deities and ultimately to my tribe's protection. My elders shamed me, and I tore my parents apart."

"Where did your mother stand?" Grandmama Sharon asks.

"She believed that every soul deserves eternal happiness. She fought to amend the codes and creeds of arranged marriages to include two consensual adults, under no duress, and without any psychological stress."

"Was she successful?" Grandmama Sharon asks.

"No. Daddy is crystallized."

"Have you told your mother that you are pregnant?" Grandmama Sharon asks.

"She committed suicide last year."

Pearle breaks down. I walk over to her and rub her shoulders.

"Her suicide note said, 'Perfect is the enemy of good.' Daddy was supposed to protect us, but instead he killed our spirits."

I remember Pearle teaching me the Voodoo expression, *e-gble-ma-ki*, may-I-die-if-it-goes-wrong.

"Mama's suicide completely deflated me. I was bedridden. But then on the night of the full harvest moon, I evoked a cry to the House of Shamballa to heal myself of self-pity and loneliness, and that's when it dawned on me that I would have to leave Daufuskie to evolve past my tribe."

"Like Mary, you have been asked to be guided by your Inner Mother and trust your soul intuition," Grandmama Sharon says. "Tell me about the father of your baby."

"When I told Joseph I was healed, and that I was planning on leaving Daufuskie the next morning, he held me tight and coaxed me with as many kisses and lies as there are stars in the sky. Why did I believe him when he said he loved me?"

"The universe tests us," Grandmama Sharon says. "We must learn to pardon ourselves of shame from this life and past lives in order to develop our unique goddess power."

"Pearle, there is only joy and love now," I say.

It's late when we go to our rooms. I'm grateful for Grandmama Sharon's help. The next morning, I wake up to the sun shining brightly through my lace curtains. I sit up on my cot and Spiritfly-meditate. Pearle and Grandmama Sharon are already in the kitchen when I get there.

"Humans have had babies for two thousand years. Babies survived the Stone Age," Grandmama Sharon laughs. "Babies are resilient."

"I have zero baby experience," I say. "I've never even held a baby."

I pour us mugs of strong root tea, and Pearle ladles up porridge in wooden bowls. After breakfast, Grandmama Sharon starts a series of Rolfing sessions to balance Pearle's chakras.

The baby shifts at the end of Pearle's second trimester.

FOURTEEN

Over the next few weeks, Pearle and I get to know the unique personalities of the three girls and four boys currently living at the Dingle Orphanage. The youngest is a six-year-old boy, and the oldest is an eleven-year-old girl. Mr. Pope and Grandmama Sharon are respectful of their spirited temperaments. All of these children know that they are loved unconditionally.

At least once a week, Mr. Pope, the kids, Grandmama Sharon, Pearle, and I take overnight walking excursions along the Dingle Way. A few times a week, we buy monkfish, trout, and clams fresh off the boats. Every Friday, we go to the Dingle Farmers Market for local organic fruit, veggies, artisan cheese, brown bread, and seed cakes.

Sunday afternoon, we enjoy the local buskers in the town center. We get to know the old man with a Kerry blue terrier and the gift of Blarney, potters throwing clay earthenware, and glass blowers etching crystal.

On Friday and Saturday nights, after Grandmama Sharon and Pearle go to sleep, I grab my sketchbook and charcoal and walk to An Droichead Beag Pub. I order a pint from the friendly barkeeper, Connor McCourt, and sketch the local trad bands, step dancers, and general merriment. By midnight, when it's too packed to sketch, I walk home.

A week before Thanksgiving, when I'm walking home from the pub, I get a tinge of homesickness and call Marshall.

"Mary, hello! It's good to hear your voice," Marshall says. "How are things in the old country?"

"Hello. All is good. I'm walking home from the pub right now, and I feel like anything is possible."

"That's great. Rosemarie and Fletcher are here. I'm putting you on speaker phone."

"How's Ouida?" I ask.

"She has me wrapped around her little web," Fletcher laughs.

"Big news. Mr. Nicopane listed his house for sale," Marshall says.

"Yes!" I say.

"The asking price is crazy for the smallest lot on the river," Rosemarie says. "But we have our fingers crossed."

"Please, Universe, allow me to have a kind neighbor," I say.

"Visualize a signed contract," Marshall says.

"Mary, you were featured in the Dublin Sunday Art section," Rosemarie says. Ouida's portrait is on the front page."

"How exciting! I had no idea."

"What's the word with the Egyptian film director?" Marshall asks.

"Zilch."

"Dude, he's über famous in Egypt. His cinematography is sick," Fletcher says.

"He's also a multi-billionaire," Marshall says.

"Sadly, we had no chemistry."

I wait while the shock settles.

"Mary, please don't judge this guy after one date," Marshall says.

Brother, have I heard that line before.

"I'm just being truthful," I say.

"How's Grandmama Sharon?" Rosemarie asks.

"Grandmama Sharon is ninety-three and her youthful exuberance is an inspiration. Has Cecil Lloyd made Wisdom Seeker legal yet?"

"Hardly. There are many roadblocks," Marshall says.

"Well, my soul says that Wisdom Seeker is unstoppable."

"Right on, dude," Fletcher says. "Hey, the cruciferous are taking off and the lima beans are crazed."

"We've been making Lima Beans Three Ways," Marshall says.

"We're sprouting, too," Rosemarie says.

"Too cool. Hey, I'm almost home. I'd better say goodnight."

I snuggle up in my cot and fall into a deep sleep. I'm running in my dream when Supreme Chief Isle appears. I am frozen with fear. I wake up at dawn, terrified.

Grandmama Sharon trains me to recognize my sleep states. Every night, I practice shifting gears to rewire and remake my brain during the bizarre state of REM consciousness. I make forlorn attempts to navigate my sleep states and wake up exhausted from the complex struggles of keeping us safe.

Before I fall asleep, I ask my guides to be receptive to my warrior spirit so I will be able to make Supreme Chief Isle leave us in peace and let us do our soul's work.

On Christmas day, we head to the shores of Beenbawn Strand for the polar bear plunge. The next day, we don bird costumes for La An Dreoilin, Wren Day. After the parade, we take the kids door to door to fill their backpacks with toffee, potato candy, and shortbread. We eat fish and crisps from outdoor vendors and dance to local trad bands the rest of the day.

On my twenty-fifth birthday, the twenty-eighth of December, Grandmama Sharon makes a reservation at Out of the Blue on the Waterfront for our group of eleven. The chefs are brilliant. We feast on steamed mussels, pollock in potato crust, and whole chargrilled seabass. After dinner, we catch a reggae concert at St. James Church to soak up the high-vibe acoustics.

The next day, I'm hoping to finish a painting of Grandmama Sharon adding wild bitter greens to the cast iron vat that hangs over the wood stove. I wish I could get Omar out of my head. Why do I keep thinking he's going to knock on the front door any minute?

Grandmama Sharon gives Pearle vitamin K drops and checks her blood pressure, albumin, glucose, blood iron, and weight.

By the end of February, Pearle is full term.

"The kids are here," I say.

Grandmama Sharon leaps up to greet them. We should all be so limber at ninety-three.

"Come on in, kids!" Terrance and Rory, is it already your week to fetch supper?" Grandmama Sharon asks. "Offer these to the others for a fun surprise."

She hands them a dozen homemade soft, chewy toffees. "Ah, thank you, Grandmama Sharon," Terrance says. "We will be popular."

I fill their takeaways with potato and leek stew, steamed cabbage, beetroot and carrot salad, pan seared trout, and freshly baked buttery shortbread.

On the night of the Full Worm Moon, Grandmama Sharon, Pearle, and I hike to the coast. After we meditate, we evoke a cry to the House of Shamballa to raise our vibration so that we will be receptive to better ways to co-create peace.

The next morning, I get up early and Spiritfly-meditate. When

I hear the others stirring, I join them. I stoke the wood stove, and we make porridge and scones. After the kids pick up breakfast, I set the dining room table, and we sit down to eat.

"Meditation, deep breathing, muscle relaxation, and visualization exercises have been a Godsend," Pearle says. "You have helped me to look inside and become a better healer."

"You are a Godsend, Pearle. Sanghyang has cleansed my energy field and restored my spiritual balance," Grandmama Sharon says.

"I love Voodoo. Stomping my right foot for good luck and making wishes on the new moons is effective," I say.

Pearle doubles over and wails. "This is a lot heavier than anything so far."

Pearle has three contractions on top of the other. We help her to her bed. Grandmama Sharon asks me to make a pot of anise and thistle tea and keep Pearle hydrated.

Grandmama Sharon is calm. Pearle is noble. I slip into my pain body. Time passes slowly.

"Pearle, I can say first hand, during my life as a spiritual midwife, and I've had the good fortune to witness hundreds of joyful births, that every woman has a unique way of bringing her baby into the world."

As the day turns to night, Pearle's contractions get more intense.

"Pearle, you have to relax long enough to have the baby," Grandmama Sharon says. "Is there anything you need to say right now? Do tell me, love."

"I'm weak. What if I'm too exhausted to push?" Pearle asks.

"Love-energy will birth your baby," Grandmama Sharon says. "Tell the universe that you are ready to take responsibility for another life and visualize the baby entering the world."

I massage Pearle's lower back. I never knew it would be this bad or take this long.

Several hours later, Pearle is fully dilated.

"Okay, focus on your breathing and pay attention to the expansions, not the contractions," Grandma Sharon says. "Push with your abdominal muscles. That's it, love. You are doing a fine job. Okay, push the baby through your pelvic bone; go slow, Pearle, you have control, no need for tearing. Relax, love, and remember to grunt."

"Good, the baby is crowning," Grandmama Sharon says.

"The baby turned, Pearle. Keep pushing. Well done, love. Here comes the body."

The baby emerges.

"She's breathing," Grandmama Sharon says. "She's a healthy, intelligent, spiritual girl, capable of being God and blessed with free will."

"Born on the third of March at twelve P.M.," I say.

Grandmama Sharon places the baby on Pearle's stomach.

"She's got Mama's strong pipes," I laugh.

She opens her eyes, wriggles her facial muscles, and latches on to Pearle's nipple.

"She's nursing," Pearle cries.

I take a deep breath. Love-based magnifies.

"This baby is telling me her name is Millie after my Great Aunt Millie," Pearle laughs.

"Millie Isle, I see God in your face," I say.

"Millie has Pearle's indigo aura. She has incarnated into the right family this time. Now we lay in and rest in shifts," Grandmama Sharon says.

Grandmama Sharon and Pearle rest first. I rock Millie until she falls asleep and then I Spiritfly-meditate. Love, love, love. A few hours later, Pearle and Grandmama Sharon wake up.

Laughter fills the cottage.

"Somebody will always hold you, Millie," Grandmama Sharon says. "You are safe, and you are loved."

"Will she be spoiled?" Pearle asks.

"No dear, she'll know she is loved. Love will give her strength," Grandmama Sharon says. "Babies should always be held and told they are loved, safe, and will receive help discovering their unique place in the world."

Mr. Pope and the kids come over and take turns holding Millie in the rocking chair with unsurpassed gentle kindness.

That week Pearle starts a regime of getting extra rest and increasing her intake of fresh fruit and dark leafy greens. Grandmama Sharon teaches us how to bathe Millie with warmed organic washcloths and diluted Dr. Bronner's peppermint castile soap. We learn how to give Millie baby massages, communicate using baby sign language, and make tinctures and ointments out of the wild herbs we foraged last fall.

On Millie's fourteenth day we make lunch reservations at Fenton's on Green Street. We bundle Millie up for her first venture out. We dine on Dingle Bay Wild Mussels, pan-fried monkfish in lime and ginger sauce, and roasted root vegetables. Everything is cooked to perfection. The staff and patrons shower Millie with love. Life with a baby starts to feel normal.

"Is everybody up for Cosán Na Naomh pilgrimage?" I ask.

"Yes, of course," Pearle says.

"We need to pick up the exercise routine," Grandmama Sharon says.

"More than the regular baby exercises?" Pearle asks.

"Yes, love. I'd like you to have your figure back in six months."

"Fine by me," Pearle says.

"Sign me up," I say.

We start ballet exercises the next morning. Grandmama Sharon is big on strengthening the core. We practice moving gracefully without breaking the line. Pearle and Grandmama Sharon are eloquent and then there is me and my wobble that adds an element of humor to our workout routine.

When Millie turns five-weeks-old, we're ready to walk the Saint's Road. We pack rain gear, fennel, fenugreek, and milk thistle tea, drinking water, pears, walnuts, hard cheeses, and seed bread.

The next morning, we wake up at sunrise. By eight we are headed south to Ventry Beach. We start the pilgrimage at Traight Fhiomtra. The sky is a fantastical bright blue, and the sun warms our backs. Millie's eyes radiate love and understanding into the universe.

We picnic at the House of the Stranger's Beehive and then head north on the Cosán Na Naomh.

"Why doesn't Daddy use his power to make himself less rigid?" Pearle asks.

"Change is powerful," Grandmama Sharon says. "Your father must go deep into the woods, by himself, and take the time to meditate and be receptive to the gifts the world is offering him."

After we rest at Cill na gcolm, we hike to the Rathanan Castle and onto the ancient beehive huts of Teampall na Cluanach. We explore the ancient alphabet stone and walk through the Eye of the Needle to make eternity ours.

We cross grassy rolling hills with breathtaking views of the sea crashing into the rugged cliffs. By early afternoon, low black clouds race across the sky and strong winds whistle through the silver birch trees.

When will I stop thinking about Omar?

We start the gentle climb to Baile Breacm. I am awestruck in this vibrant land.

"Millie's always smiling," Grandmama Sharon says.

"She even smiles when she's sleeping," Pearle says.

When we get to the base of Mount Brandon, there's no denying that heavy rains are fast approaching. Just before the storm lets loose, we find a quaint family inn with a panoramic view of the rugged Wild Atlantic Way.

The rain stops before midnight. We bundle up and hike to the base of Mount Brandon. The moon is new, and the darkness is soft and comforting. We set our intentions for what we wish to manifest in the new moon cycle and meditate in this safe spiritual land. It's around two when we get back to the inn.

The next morning we head to the dining room for breakfast. Padraig and Ciara Flannery, the owners, greet us and tell us that all of the food is organic and homemade from scratch. We feast on grilled Dingle Bay kippers, freshly harvested duck eggs, stewed rhubarb, and hot scones.

We check out at eleven and head south. I feel refreshed and optimistic walking back to Dingle. It's three when we get to town. On a whim, we stop by Doyle's Seafood Restaurant and splurge on their Dingle Bay Seafood Chowder and sublime shellfish risotto.

The next morning, Grandmama Sharon prepares the living room for Pearle and me to have Runestone readings. When Pearle starts her reading, I take Millie to Lidl's Dingle to buy bread, bitter greens, and cheese. When I get back, Pearle takes Millie next door.

I take the Runestones, ask my soul to rest on my heart, and throw.

"Good Lord, Mary, what are you thinking? I've not witnessed this before, love. You've thrown the stones to look almost the same as Pearle's throw. Collect the Runestones, love, and throw again."

I tell monkey brain to skedaddle, repeat 'My mind is a still river,' and throw. Grandmama Sharon is quiet. I can't read her.

"The Goddess Isis is present," she says turning over the first Runestone.

"This is your hook to Isis, who is the one who is pushing you to raise your vibration to love-based."

"In Savannah?" I ask.

"The Deep South," Grandmama Sharon says. "She has selected thousands of change-agents worldwide. The shift to love-based is well underway."

Grandmama Sharon turns over two more Runestones and tells me that Isis will instruct me via impressions.

"These seven stones symbolize Wisdom Seeker students."

She picks up the blank Runestone. "This stone represents a young woman who will complete the power pyramid with you and Pearle."

"Rosemarie?" I ask.

"No, Rosemarie is the gatekeeper. You have yet to meet the third woman."

She points to three Runestones that form a pyramid.

"This is what is identical to Pearle's throw," Grandmama Sharon says. "Supreme Chief Isle had a near-fatal crisis when Pearle's mother committed suicide, and then Pearle ran away. He has been to the woods and prayed to his deities for peace."

The third Runestone is marked 'M'.

"Millie will be the catalyst to shift Supreme Chief Isle to love-based. It is Millie who will bridge the gap that allows for the ideal partnership to develop between Wisdom Seeker and the Daufuskie Voodoo Tribe."

"Supreme Chief Isle has unworldly powers," I say. "It's too risky to take Millie to Daufuskie."

"Mary, you are a change-agent. The situation is vital. You must go."

"Supreme Chief Isle will summon deities to enter my soul, dance my body, and control my thoughts."

"Spirit possession is a common belief in Christianity, Buddhism, Wicca, Hinduism, Islam, Southeastern Asia, and Africa. Conservative Catholics even believe that angels exist as both non-corporeal, spiritual beings and fallen angels that possess you demonically and leave you morally blameless."

"But Pearle's people base their decisions on animal sacrifices and communal blood drinking."

"In the name of religious dogma, Voodoo is no guiltier of sacrificing sentient beings than the Judeo-Christian tradition," Grandmama Sharon says. "Mary, love, your soul's purpose is to quash distorted fear-based illusions. Go to Daufuskie with pure love in your heart. The truth is stronger than dogma."

"So it looks like a peace mission is our destiny."

"Yes, destiny. Questions, love?"

"Will Mr. Nicopane sell his house?" I ask.

Grandmama Sharon has me collect the stones. I hold them in my hands and imagine loving neighbors and cast. Seven Runestones pile up in potential.

"No, love, he won't sell the house. He thrives on conflict, he's ghostly attached to the property, and he won't fetch the high price he desires. Any other questions?"

"Will Omar Victor be husband number one?"

"Let's see, love. Collect the stones."

I hold the Runestones in my hands and imagine waking up and seeing Omar in my bed after a hot night of wild sex. I cast the stones.

"Here is Omar. He's on the cusp. He could go either way. If he does ask you to marry him, it won't be anytime soon."

She pauses, turns over the blank Runestone, and nods.

"A year for Omar is like a month for others. Omar is undecided about many things."

That night tricksters visit Pearle in her dreams. They distract Pearle and steal Millie. Pearle practices being forthright until she can stand up in her dream and tell them to leave.

FIFTEEN

I book two flights from Dublin to Atlanta. Our last night in Dingle, we take Mr. Pope, Grandmama Sharon, and the kids to Dick Mack's Pub. My emotions are racing from sad to fearful.

The next morning is heartfelt.

"I'll see you again this earth journey," Grandmama Sharon hugs me goodbye, and I tear up.

We get to the station and board bus 275 to Tralee. When we arrive at Tralee, we walk to the train station and board the Éireann to Limerick. I give Marshall a ring when we're walking to Luigi's Café.

"Hey there, how are you?" I ask.

"Fantastic! How was the Spiritual Pilgrimage?"

"Inspiring. Hey, I'm calling to let you know I'm in Limerick and headed home."

"Good timing. Fletcher is in Italy with his parents. He's getting back Sunday night."

"Good, I'll have time to get over jet lag. Marshall, I've been wondering if I should buy Mr. Nicopane's house. Eventually, Wisdom Seeker will need additional space."

"Mary, Crew made an offer the day it went on the market. Unfortunately, the property is already off the market. Sorry."

"Well, we're warriors, right?"

"Say *that* three times fast," he says.

"Thanks, that always makes me laugh."

Pearle and I order takeout. We picnic at People's Park. The chips are thick, and the cod fillets are crispy. We walk back to the station and board the train for Dublin.

Millie sleeps in my arms while monkey brain chats at high speed. I imagine peace talks with angry men wearing masks and war regalia.

"Maya Angelou says," Pearle reads from a book Grandmama Sharon gave her, 'If you don't like something, change it. If you can't change it, change your attitude. Don't complain.'"

"Please let me become the person that never complains," I say.

"Amen, tistah."

We pull into Dublin. It's rush hour when we taxi to the Shelbourne Dublin. When we enter the lobby, Millie is mesmerized by the Waterford hand-blown etched crystal chandeliers. We check into our suite, order room service, and turn in early.

Thunder and lightning wake us up before the alarm clock goes off. By the time we check out, torrential rain makes getting to the Dublin Airport in rush hour hectic. Millie sleeps the entire taxi ride to the airport. We find the gate, board the plane, and Millie is still sound asleep.

When we get cozy, Millie wakes up in her usual bubbly mood.

"Millie, you have the most expressive eyes," I say.

"I'm convinced she is communicating to us telepathically," Pearle says.

"I know that's right," I say.

A few hours later, we fly out of the storm. We land at JFK and make our connecting flight in plenty of time. After a full day of travel, we arrive at the Atlanta airport, collect our luggage, and head outside.

"Alright, the Deep South, my skin feels home," I say.

We get Millie situated in her new car seat. The Silver Honda starts on the second try. I exit the airport, merge onto I-75 Southbound, and maneuver across six lanes of bumper to bumper traffic.

I turn up the tunes and we make our way through Atlanta traffic. An hour outside of the city, I set the cruise control and relax.

"We have to teach ourselves self-love before we can teach others," I say.

"The same thing goes with patience, calming the mind, controlling the appetite, and being emotionally grounded," Pearle says.

"Add a complete do-over with our human family," I say.

We cross the Chatham County line, cruise through Savannah when everybody is still asleep, and finally get home.

Mr. Nicopane's yellow Mercedes is in his driveway. Deja vu. Did we ever leave this place? Stop. Let disgust pass by me like the wind.

Millie's out like a light. Pearle lifts her from her car seat, and we hurry inside. There's a note on the kitchen counter.

> Welcome home!
> We stocked your fridge with organics.
> Love, Marshall and Rosemarie

"Check it out, Pearle," I say. "They delivered our CSA."

"Remarkable," Pearle says.

We put on a pot of grits and whip up goat cheese, spinach, shrooms, spring onions, and asparagus omelets.

When we're clearing the table, we see Mr. Nicopane locking his front door.

Pearle performs the *Gho* Ritual.

"*Da gu do*! We will not accept complicity with evil. Awaken, dormant soul qualities, awaken!" Pearle resonates.

Mr. Nicopane drives away in his yellow Mercedes.

"The Peace Mission starts now," I say.

We high five, pack some fruit, water, and baby gear, and head to the dock. I hoist *One That Got Away* into the river. Fletcher has all of the levels full so we're good to go.

Temperatures are in the high seventies, winds are calm, and the river is as smooth as glass.

We get to Daufuskie at noon and secure *One That Got Away*.

Pearle holds Millie and leads the way. She moves like a deer in the maritime forest.

Three miles into the hike, several men wearing loincloths appear out of nowhere, surround us, and herd us at a fast clip. Sunlight filters through the dense canopy, creating a strobe effect that obscures my vision. I barely keep up.

An hour later we arrive at a tiny whitewashed chapel and enter through the bright red double doors. Supreme Chief Isle, Doc, and at least a dozen angry men are seated at a long rustic oak table. Pearle tells me to sit in the first pew. She crosses the bar and curtsies before her father.

"Supreme Chief and brothers of *Vodun*, I honor my *Voodusi* creed of gaining insight from otherworldly dimensions, ability to disrupt energy potential circulation between physical and spirit bodies. My spirituality is true.

"I invite you to honor my Voodoo Chieftaincy of the Mami Wata Deity in my calling to start Wisdom Seeker on Wilmington Island with Mary Howard."

The council points to me and yells *yovo, yovo!* Doc is austere. I look away, cover my solar plexus, and attempt to still my racing mind. I am loved.

Supreme Chief Isle claps his enormous hands and the tribal council reluctantly settles down.

"This is your granddaughter, Millie Isle," Pearle says. She hands Millie to Supreme Chief Isle. Millie coos. Supreme Chief Isle halfway smiles.

"Daddy, I no longer desire your approval. Millie will connect to spirit directly and use her mind to discover her unique supernatural powers," Pearle says.

The tribe erupts in hysteria and anger. I'm scared for my life.

"Order, order," Supreme Chief Isle roars.

They sit down.

"Pearle, as the Princess of our Voodoo Nation, you must understand that ours is a spirit religion. We are servants of the spirit and provide offerings that honor the spirit. We would be naïve and fallacious to disobey the doctrines of our ancestors."

"True *Vodun* is the phenomenon of magic and sorcery. Man-made dogma written by antiquated ancestors have yet to stop evil invasions, curses, demons, the angel of death, or materialism," Pearle says.

The men shout protests.

"Be seated and listen to her," Supreme Chief Isle bellows.

Doc clears his voice and adjust his glasses. My life flashes before me. Why didn't I tell Crew and Marshall that I was coming here today?

"You have allowed this tribe to replace what is sacred in our culture with what is wrong in every other religion," Pearle says. "Spiritual power as a means to control the masses with fear is misuse!"

"Order, order!" Supreme Chief Isle wails.

"Change is inevitable, Daddy," Pearle says. "Evolution forces change. First, you were a son, then you were a warrior, and then you were Supreme Chief of a self-governing body. You have the power and the wisdom to rule love-based, right now."

Supreme Chief Isle has kind eyes and ageless skin.

"The council will now convene," Supreme Chief Isle says.

Thankfully, he hands Millie back to Pearle before they exit through heavy gold and purple curtains.

Pearle explains that they will sacrifice a pig, share the blood of the sacrificed pig, and then summon the V*odun* son of *Mawu, Da Gu Do,* to decide our fate.

Hours pass. We hear the pig's heartbreaking last squeal. Holding hands, we visualize making peace. The tribe returns.

"The great serpent deity of the *Mami Wata* pantheon, *Damballah*, has spoken to me," Supreme Chief Isle says. "I have failed miserably. Pearle, will you ever forgive me?"

"Daddy, no longer do I joyfully march in rank and file."

"I've changed. I will no longer give tribal power to evil spirits and wicked witchcraft. I will no longer allow fear to consume me."

"Why should I believe you?" Pearle asks.

"I take full responsibility for your mother's suicide," Supreme Chief Isle pauses. "And for you leaving the tribe."

Pearle tears up.

"Allow me to perform *aga basa-yiyi* for Millie," he says. "Allow me to fulfill my desire to amplify your power."

"Daddy, if you've changed so much, ban animal sacrifices," Pearle says.

The tribe is outraged. I hold my vision on leaving this island alive.

"Silence!" Supreme Chief Isle demands. "Sacrifices are the propitiation of offerings, and prayers."

"Sacred violence is normal only because we have not yet asked why. You know as well as I that *Lêgba* prefers mounds of earth and tree trunk sacrifices to animal sacrifices."

"I will start the process, but there are no guarantees to the results," Supreme Chief Isle says.

"Process over perfection," Pearle cuts her eyes at her father.

"Pearle, please allow me to perform *aga basa-yiyi* for Millie."

"Only if women are allowed to drum," Pearle says.

Doc looks over his purple shades. The council goes nuts.

Trembling, I count the worn pine floorboards.

Supreme Chief Isle claps his hands three times. The council sits down.

"Pearle," Supreme Chief Isle says. "Women?"

"Yes, women."

"If you allow me to perform *Agabasa-yiyi*, for Millie's ancestral cohesion, at your new home, I will allow women to drum."

"In that case, we are honored," Pearle says.

Supreme Chief Isle and Pearle embrace.

I freak. If Mr. Nicopane sees Voodoo worshipping, it's all over. After the meeting is adjourned, two tribal members escort us back to *One That Got Away*. As soon as we shove off, the men disappear in the maritime forest.

"Why do your people run everywhere?" I ask.

"The mosquitos will eat you alive if you don't keep moving."

"Oh." I suppose some questions have their own answers.

"Mary, our power to do good has just been magnified."

"Are you kidding? I'm scared to death."

"Good intent will protect us."

"Mr. Nicopane and the Voodoo Tribe are like mixing gasoline with fire."

"Mr. Nicopane works on Mondays. The ritual takes ten minutes, and the luncheon takes one hour. The tribe will be long gone by the time Mr. Nicopane gets home. No worries, Tistah."

"You're right, Pearle. I'm being fear-based."

"Mr. Nicopane is the one who has to adjust to world peace, not us."

We get back to the dock and walk across the lawn. I feel Mr. Nicopane watching us from his bedroom window. Pearle chants in *Fon*, French, and Prayer Talk. I allow the shivers to pass by me like the wind. We go inside, shut the blinds, and head upstairs.

Pearle nurses Millie while I read W*hen Baby Animals Kiss Goodnight*. When Millie falls asleep, Pearle puts her down in her new crib.

We head downstairs and start supper.

"Do you think we should invite Marshall, Rosemarie, Crew, and Fletcher to the *Gho* Ritual?" I ask.

"Yes, please!" Pearle says.

"Okay, I'll make the calls after we eat," I say.

I thaw out fish fillets, make coleslaw and tartar sauce. Pearle makes oven-baked hushpuppies while I pan-fry the trout.

It's nine when I head to the library, make the phone calls, and drop the Voodoo bomb.

"View you, we are all mirrors of each other's souls," I say. "Voodoo people are animists like us. Who knew other animists lived in the Deep South? Right?"

Everybody is game for the luncheon, *Agabasa-yiyi* and *Gho* Ritual this Monday. Yippee.

The next morning I board *One That Got Away* and motor to Marshall's house. Ouida is perched on Crew's floating dock piling. I kill the engine.

"Whewsuu, Whewsuu," I whistle.

When she sees me, she flies across the river and back before landing on the bow. I wait for her to stretch her wings and waddle to me.

"Come here, Ouida. I missed you. Love, love, love!"

She nudges me, and we take off. I stroke her soft feathers all the way home.

When I tie off, Ouida flies to her piling, and I walk back to the house. Pearle's in the kitchen nursing Millie.

"Good morning. Did you sleep well?" I ask.

"Yes, I feel totally refreshed," Pearle says.

"Millie, gentle. Why does she tug like that?" I ask.

"The coconut oil really helps," Pearle says.

Millie pulls away completely satisfied.

"Look, Millie just signed 'all done.'"

"Now you're talking Millie. Would you like to meet Ouida?"

Pearle goes upstairs to shower, and I take Millie down to the dock. As soon as Ouida sees us, she flies down to check out the baby. Love, love, love. When I start to Spiritfly-meditate, Ouida flies back to her piling. I have a clear vision that World Peace will be a reality in my lifetime.

"Lots to do today, Millie. We've got to catch fish and rake oysters. Granddaddy Isle and the tribe are coming tomorrow."

When Pearle joins us, we load *One That Got Away* with fishing gear and coolers and drift away from the dock. It feels good to be on the river. We head to Olinger Creek and throw the anchor.

Millie takes it all in.

After we rake oysters, the sun burns off the morning haze, and we motor to my favorite fishing hole.

I nose into the marsh grass and throw anchor.

We bait our hooks and cast. Pearle reels in a nice size spot tail. Within a few hours, we've caught enough fish to feed twenty-four guests. We give gratitude to the river gods and motor home.

We unpack the new playpen that we stashed in the dock house last fall. While Pearle nurses Millie, I assemble the playpen.

Millie sleeps the whole time we gut the fish, hose down the oysters, and scrub the deck. We hoist *One That Got Away* into the boathouse. The tide is high and the river is as smooth as glass.

When Millie wakes up from her nap, we head back to the house. We fix a plate of leftovers and think about what to serve to the tribe on Monday.

"I'm in a quandary. My people use bacon grease in everything," Pearle says.

"Why is ingesting pig fat universal?"

"God only knows," Pearle says. "I keep wondering if Daddy was patronizing me about ending animal sacrifices."

"Only time will tell," I say. "For now, let's use the remainder of Fletcher's Savannah River Farms Heirloom Bacon so the Wisdom Seeker fridge will be animal-agriculture-free."

"Humanely treated," Pearle reads the package. "As if slaughtering a pig farmer when he reached a certain weight would be considered humane."

We prep the ingredients for the oyster stew, batter for the fish, salads, casseroles, corn fritters, and cheese biscuits. Pearle makes her heavenly vanilla custard with sugar, egg yolks, cream, and butter. We layer custard and frozen mixed berries into parfait glasses. We're set.

After a long soak in the tub, I crawl in bed. Exhausted, I toss and turn half of the night imagining ways to keep Wisdom Seeker animal-agriculture-free but stay rule-free.

SIXTEEN

Marshall, Rosemarie, Crew, and Fletcher pull up in the green Packard. My heart sings. We pile in the kitchen and pass Millie around like a trophy.

We walk out to the dock to greet the tribe. Supreme Chief Isle and Doc arrive in the first dory. Supreme Chief Isle is wearing a pure white gown with gold trim and a beaded headband decorated with eagle feathers, and Doc is wearing a Roman priest cassock and his dark purple shades.

The dories keep coming. The men are wearing loincloths, and the women drummers are bare-breasted.

Supreme Chief Isle lights strong incense, and the drummers start the ceremony. We walk to the lawn and form a power circle around Supreme Chief Isle, Doc, Pearle, and Millie. Supreme Chief Isle's bass-baritone voice sounds like thunder when he chants in French, *Fon*, and prayer-talk.

The tribe's hand clapping and foot stomping gets faster and more frenzied. Supreme Chief Isle falls into a trance state. I imagination-paint his 6'4" frame, bulging thighs, sculpted shoulders, ageless skin, and almond eyes when it looks like he is being electrocuted by the spirit world.

Once he has summoned *Mami Wata,* he performs the *Agbasa-yiyi,* and Millie receives access to her ancestors' living room. Next, Supreme Chief Isle performs the Rite of Integration so Millie will know her spirit protectors, grow into a woman with roots, and be linked as a true family member.

"Mary, negative energy is radiating from next door," Supreme Chief Isle says pointing to Mr. Nicopane's house. He invites me inside the power circle and puts his gigantic hand on my head. I immediately feel engulfed in love by this awe-inspiring, powerful, and intriguing man.

"*Danxomê ki tonye die emi so do alomê nu hwima e je ayi gbede o. Danxomê ki tonye die emi so do alomê nu hwima e je ayi gbede o.* I place in your left hand the dirt of *Danxomê,*" he shouts.

He directs me to squeeze the dirt in my left hand. Then he claps his hands three times, takes the dirt from me, and throws it over my right shoulder.

He sips palm wine, spits it out, pours some on the ground for the deities, and instructs me to do the same. We repeat the ritual with cheap European gin until the drummers signal the end of the ritual. I'm woozy with a sky-high vibe.

After the rituals, we tour the garden.

"Pearle, the Voodoo people have united with the changing world to help primary people know that animals have spirits and are not a commodity for sacrificing."

I imagination-paint Pearle embracing her father. Yippee, compassion wins.

We get everyone seated at the dining room table. Supreme Chief Isle blesses the food, and we serve Pearle's oyster stew. Pure creamy heaven. When everybody lines up for the buffet, I take the soup bowls to the kitchen.

What? Mr. Nicopane just pulled up in his driveway. My heart stops. Why is he here on a Monday? I'm woozy from palm wine and cheap gin. Yuck.

I head back to the buffet.

"Pearle, these corn fritters are the best I've ever tasted," Marshall says.

I get Crew's attention, and he follows me to the kitchen. I point out the window.

"Mr. Nicopane is home."

"That's not all," Crew says.

A cop car pulls up to the house. We go outside.

"You're in violation of residential noise ordinance 2587-D," the cop says.

"I'm hosting a luncheon. I've done nothing wrong," I say.

"I'll need to complete a cursory visual inspection of the property," he says.

"Crew Potalis, TVPD Police Chief. You are out of your jurisdiction and in violation of code 12785-C," Crew says.

After Crew writes down his license plate, vehicle identification number, and mileage, the cop scurries away like a wet rat in a flood tide.

When we're headed back inside, Mr. Nicopane starts his 'perish in hell' sermon over the bullhorn.

"Oh, Mr. Nicopane called the cops," Crew says.

"I vow it will be better for Millie," I say.

We go inside, turn up the stereo, fix a plate, and join the others. Doc clears his throat and grins. Everyone gets quiet.

"These roasted root vegetables are good," Doc says.

We bond with our kind, wise guests. Magically, Mr. Nicopane stops preaching around the same time we finish dessert, so we hurriedly escort the tribe to the dock, and they leave in good spirits. Love, love, love.

That summer, we make weekly trips to Daufuskie with supplies, tools, seeds, and compost. By fall, every family has a veggie plot and fruit tree. Next, Wisdom Seeker starts a Sustainability Grant Program to support Low Country and Benin, Africa Voodoo people. Over the winter, we distribute fabric, thread, yarn, sewing machines, native seeds, cultivators, and modern seeders to hundreds of families.

Millie turns one in a blink. We wake up at dawn on her birthday and prepare to cruise to Daufuskie Island.

When Marshall and Rosemarie arrive, they tell us that Crew has a situation at the TVPD and won't be joining us. Somehow I'm not surprised.

We load the boats with camping gear, veggie seeds, bare root fruit and nut trees, and fresh-picked garden veggies and head out.

We drift away from the dock. I lead the way in *One That Got Away* and Marshall and Rosemarie follow in *Driftwood*.

We arrive on Daufuskie Island mid-morning, secure the boats and hike deep into the maritime forest for at least six miles. When we arrive, the tribe goes gaga over Millie.

We tour the compound, drop off our bags, and then head to the Commons area for a lunch of wild ginger steamed sheepshead, yellow rice, red peas, bitter greens, and cornbread. Everything is simple and delicious. After lunch, Pearle attends Chieftaincy meetings while the rest of us learn the sacred cultural chants and advanced stomp and clap responses for tonight's festivities.

When the full moon rises over the tall pines, the drumming and chanting begin. Supreme Chief Isle, in all his grandeur, emerges from his private quarters wearing sensational *Vodun* regalia. Being in his presence is phenomenal. We form a power circle and perform stomp and clap responses that get more frenzied until Supreme Chief Isle falls into a trance.

Agbe, the *Vodun* that gives life, and voice of the Supreme Being *Dú*, temporarily speaks through Supreme Chief Isle to bless Millie's entry into the land of life, *Gbetomê*.

It's three in the morning when I stumble back to the sleeping quarters completely K.O.-ed with a throbbing head.

The rest of the night musk and rustling cockroaches keep me awake. And Pearle says she was privileged.

By the third night, I make peace with Bob, the bravest cockroach, and finally get some sleep. The next morning, I wake up at dawn and hike to the beach. I find the cove where I received my last initiation, get comfortable, and close my eyes.

Guide says, "Humanity is shifting to Unity, Unity is real, and Unity is happening now."

Optimistic, I hike back to camp. After a luncheon feast of fried whiting, grits, biscuits, and steamed asparagus, we load up *Driftwood* and *One That Got Away* and motor back to Wilmington Island.

We get back home by late afternoon. I take a shower, resist the urge to take a nap, and head to the art room. It's midnight before I stop to let the paint dry.

The next morning, when I come out of Spiritfly-meditation, I walk down the avenue of oaks and check the mail.

What in the world? Omar Victor? Paris, France?

> *Dear Mary,*
> *   You are cordially invited to be my guest at the Telfair Ball in downtown Savannah, Georgia, USA, on June 12, 2011. Promising a night of cocktails on the rotunda,*

al fresco dining in Telfair Square, followed by big band ballroom dancing.

I have exciting news!
Warm Regards,
Omar Victor.

When 'cordially' and 'warm regards' remind me of the bad kiss, I stop myself. My door is open. Time *is* an illusion; *Movie Star Man is* back. Thank you, Universe. Thank you, validity. The Law of Attraction is real.

I run back to the house and show Pearle and Fletcher my invite.

"Let's celebrate," Pearle says.

We change, grab some towels, and head to Tybee.

We park at North Beach Grill and walk out to the beach. Millie explores the sun-drenched tidal pools and Pearle follows her. Fletcher and I swim out twenty feet and body surf.

We spend the afternoon at the beach. Happy hour, we're on the deck at North Beach Grill. We eat an early supper and drive home when the sun is setting.

Time drags waiting for the day that Omar will arrive in Savannah. I make a shift as an artist. Techniques that previously felt like tedious lifelong struggles have become exciting and simple.

I am prolific.

After what feels like an eternity, Omar is due to arrive. I drift through Spiritfly-meditation, yoga, and green smoothie klatch. Afterward, I shower and go downstairs to wait.

Fletcher is in the library, perched in a nest of open books.

"What's new?" I ask.

"Scientists are taking forever to embrace quantum physics," Fletcher says.

"Establishment scientists need to fall out of love with the periodic table of chemical elements and get their heads around the relativity of distant spooky dream actions and waking things."

"Yes, the Uncertainty Principle changes everything we know. Science can no longer mask the puffs of probability affected by interpenetrating billiard balls and simply continue to dissect frogs."

"Publishing proof of tangible things advances scientists' academic careers. We need more visionary writers to publish books. Are you still waking up at three A.M. and writing?" I ask.

"Yes. And Marshall has been helping me organize my notes. I thought of a title early this morning; *Quest to Discover Existence Outside of Our Reality*."

"Good, Fletcher, I love it," I say. "Hey, did you finish *Psychic Intelligence* by Terry and Linda Jamison?"

"Yes, I finished it earlier this morning. It was a page-turner. They give intuition validity. Fascinating read."

"When intellect and intuition achieve Unity, World Peace will be real."

I hear a car pulling up the avenue of oaks. I run outside.

The chauffeur gets out of the stretched limo and opens Omar's door.

Poof, *Movie Star Man*. Wow. Just wow.

"A thing of beauty is a joy forever," Omar says.

"Welcome," I say.

Do I remind him of his Great Aunt? Was that even a kiss?

"Savannah is spectacular," he says.

My hormones are on a slippery slope. We head inside.

"I feel like I've just entered a national art museum. These Victor Howard sculptures are magnificent," Omar says. "Are these your paintings?"

"This series is by Mai Howard, my mom."

"Exquisite," he says.

He takes time studying my new painting.

"Sublime," he says.

"Thank you. Patrick sells them faster than I paint them."

"How old were you when you started painting?"

"Three years old. I imitated my mom painting."

"I'll show you your room."

We collect his luggage and go upstairs.

"The view is superb."

I close the door and will him to kiss me and mean it. Instead, he organizes his wardrobe.

"This is for you."

He hands me *The Standard of Ur.*

"It's one of the most iconic and beautiful works of ancient art," he says. "It was created by the Sumerians. I thought you would appreciate owning a copy. It's very rare."

"Thank you."

"And something else. I had it made in Paris."

He hands me a slinky gown.

"Wow! For me? Will it fit?"

"I'm in film. I know sizes."

I get modest and change in the walk-in closet. Wowie, look at me. Who knew an emerald batik silk gown could do this for my figure? I take a few deep breaths and model.

"Mama mia, la bella bella; perfect for paparazzi."

Uneventfully, I go back to the closet and change. I grab the twenty-five pound *Standard of Ur* and escort Omar to the library.

"Fletcher Melville, this is Omar Victor."

"It's a pleasure," Omar says.

"Dude, the pleasure is mine. Your environmental documentaries are sick."

"Thank you. Mary tells me you are an Endangered Animal Protector."

"Yes, I help critters in a culture that is unconscious to their plight."

"I'm looking forward to the turtle excursion tomorrow night," Omar says.

"Right on. Tomorrow night marks the full moon, six-month anniversary of Mama Loggerhead swimming out of the sea at high tide, crawling to the dunes, scooping out the powdery sand with her hind flippers, and laying about 200 eggs," Fletcher says. "And tomorrow night, at midnight, we will again witness the magical world of barnacle-encrusted loggerhead hatchlings unfold."

Pearle and Millie join us.

"Remember me?"

"Yes, of course," Omar says.

Millie nose dives for Omar. It's a near miss, but he catches her.

"We were just filling Omar in on the Turtle Excursion," I say.

"We're talking a big turtle. At least 350 pounds," Pearle says.

Millie gets down. She's a compulsive walker, hand clapper, and foot stomper these days.

"I'm going to take Omar out on the river," I say. "We'll be back before cocktail hour."

"Enjoy," Pearle says.

"Fletcher and I are making dinner tonight, so no need to hurry back," Pearle says.

"This garden is inspiring," Omar says.

"It's more than doubled in size since Wisdom Seeker started."

Omar asks a million questions. He wants to know about the fiddler crabs, pluff mud, and the murky water. I explain that it is the phosphorus, calcium, nitrogen, and sediments that make the Georgia Barrier Islands one of the richest estuaries and spawning ground for marine life.

"Careful, the floating dock ramp is steep at low tide."

I give Omar a hand aboard *One That Got Away* and we head to Wassaw Sound. A male dolphin surfaces. I kill the engine. Soon a female surfaces. She is in full pink moon. And then the male dolphin shows his enormous erection, and we watch their brutal mating ritual. They disappear into deep water five minutes later.

"Why didn't I bring my cameras? Has that ever been documented?" Omar asks.

"Not that I know of," I say.

I open throttle.

"Look, dolphins are keeping up with us," Omar says.

"They move at mystical speeds that are physically impossible," I say.

We wind around Halfmoon Creek's twists and turns. At Little Wassaw Island, I throw the anchor, and we wade to shore.

"Magnificently pristine," Omar says.

"Little Wassaw Island is uninhabited," I tease.

Omar takes off his shirt. Wow, he's a rippling hard body.

I take off my shorts and tank. When Omar goes to the edge of the maritime forest to take a leak, I slip out of my bikini and dive into the river.

"Come swimming with me. The water's great."

Omar hesitates.

"It's warm, probably twenty-two Celsius," I say.

"I can't see the bottom," he says.

I'm speechless.

"I can't swim without seeing what's swimming with me," Omar says.

"No worries." I fake smile.

"I'm going to catch some rays," he says.

My first date in years and he's a scaredy cat. I stop myself. Door open. I'm shriveled by the time I get the nerve to crawl out of the river.

SEVENTEEN

I STRUGGLE TO PUT ON MY BIKINI OVER MY WET BODY ONLY TO discover Omar is passed out. An hour later, frustrated beyond belief, I fake wake up with him.

"I think this is the most relaxed I've ever been," Omar says.

"Rest, the river's negative ions, and the sand's mineral energy are healing," I say.

"Mary, after we met, I went to the home of Om Seti and spoke with my psychic advisor to ask her why you were visiting me in my dreams," Omar says.

"Me?"

"Yes. And that's when I learned that we have agreed to be partners this incarnation."

"Partners?"

"Yes, and I have a stop-me-in-my-tracks-surprise."

Swimming alone seems moot when my mind races ahead to waking up in the morning next to this hunk.

"I purchased the Oglethorpe Inn for the Omar Victor International Film Institute. I came here to invite Wisdom Seeker to partner with me."

"Omar, the dilapidated Oglethorpe Inn where Turner Creek and Wilmington River meet?"

"Yes," Omar says. "Isn't it marvelous? The property has been tied up in litigations with one deal breaker after the next. Finally, I retained Savannah's 'Most Famous Attorney' and he managed to bring the PGA, EPA, and Sicilian mafia to the table to nail down a deal."

"Did you buy the pool, lounge, and golf course, too?"

"The PGA Golf Course wasn't part of the deal. Cecil Lloyd, my hotshot attorney, said the EPA and PGA were more hardcore than the Sicilian Mafia."

"Cecil Lloyd?" I ask.

"Yes, do you know him?"

"He's my attorney and the attorney for Wisdom Seeker."

"Mary, this is meant to be."

My mind spins. Monkey brain chatters away.

"It's a done deal?" I ask.

"We closed at the end of last month. It's a dream come true."

"I'm speechless."

I watch the surf hit the shore. I regress to being seventeen, sensing something is wrong, running all the way to the entrance of the Oglethorpe Inn, and watching the wrecking truck untangle Mama's green Jaguar from the grand oak tree.

"I hope they specialize in condemned buildings."

"Mary, we're only here for a speck of time. The worst crime I can commit is to die rich. Please allow me to help Wisdom Seeker shift humanity to love-based."

"Omar, do you love me?"

"Yes, we are kindred souls. I came thousands of miles to be with you."

"Omar, I'm asking about romantic love?"

"Aren't you and Pearle together?"

"What in the world?" I gasp. "Pearle is my Tistah. How could you assume such a thing?"

"I'll fast forward to act two."

"Roll film," I say.

"When two roads diverged in the woods, I took the one less traveled, and it made all the difference in the world; Mary, I'm bisexual."

"What's bisexual? Omar, I'm sheltered and clueless."

"Bisexuals get crushes on both sexes. We're hated more than homosexuals and considered to be the worst type of promiscuous," Omar says.

"I'm sorry. I pray love will win." My head is reeling in circles.

"I brought you a copy of John Irving's, *In One Person*. The novel is a coming of age story set in the 1950s. The lead is a bisexual male and deals with the same lack of compassion that persists today."

He holds my hand. I feel love.

"I'm glad you're being honest," I say.

"I've been in a loving relationship with my two partners for nine years. We meet on the down low because we wish to stay at peace with our elders and maintain proper conduct toward the magistrates."

"At least, I know where I stand now."

"This would have been easy if you and Pearle were a couple."

"Ha."

"That brings me to act three."

"Seriously?"

"Yes. I've devised a plan to dance into the hearts of Savannah's elite and rocket launch your love-based takeover plot."

"Omar, are you aware of the Deep South's resistance to change?"

"That's why I'm proposing that we upgrade our status to husband and wife."

I'm not sure I can take much more.

"What in the world?"

"I know, I know, just hear me out."

"I'm all ears."

"When the 'Savannah Tongue,' as you call it, is offered an exclusive to cover 'Local immoral conduct expulsion and restraining order artist, engaged to Egyptian multi-billionaire filmmaker,' I guarantee they will bite the hook."

"How did you know that about me?"

"Easy. It's all over Facebook."

"Yuck. Gag."

"Mary, will you fake-marry me?"

"I'm a lousy fake."

"I've got your back."

"You pique my curiosity. What exactly is the responsibility of a fake wife?"

"Fake blowjobs."

"Very funny."

"Seriously, I intend to lavish you with gowns and jewelry and take you to galas. I am no swinger; I will remain faithful to my life partners. You, of course, are free to follow your own moral conduct as long as you are discreet."

"I've developed giving puritans zero power to a fine art, but why me?"

"Because you are a beautiful dreamer who has the unbending intent to shift humanity to be love-based by 2020," Omar says.

"The Oglethorpe Inn is too materialistic."

"The Oglethorpe Inn is 70,000 square feet. It's just the right fit. The Film Institute requires screening rooms, audio post suites, edit labs, design production, and a state-of-the-art cinema. Wisdom Seeker will house art studios, a gallery, classrooms, and a concert hall. Meanwhile, the cottages will serve as accommodations for guest speakers and resident artists."

"Unreal."

He goes into details about Foley rooms and automated dialogue replacement studios. His words are a blur. My head is spinning.

"Mary, *will* you fake-marry me?"

A distant voice I don't recognize says yes.

Omar plants a platinum ring with a humongous rock on my finger and shows me a picture of my beaded wedding gown on his smartphone.

"Let's load up," I say. "Cocktail hour is starting somewhere right now."

We motor home in silence. Is this it? Is this the woman I have become?

Ouida is on the floating dock when we get back.

"Ouida, Omar, Omar, Ouida."

Ouida opens her mouth, stretches her wings, throws back a croaker, and flies to her piling.

We get back to the house in time to shower before we greet Marshall, Rosemarie, and Crew. Introducing Omar is awkward. Who is this man?

We take the pitcher of Gosling and pineapple punch to the verandah, and Omar wins us over with his kindness and quick wit. His Egyptian allegorical sense of humor is funny as the dickens.

When the no-see-ums get thick, we head inside for dinner.

"Crew, your grilled sheepshead has always been my fave," I say.

"Tender, flaky perfection," Rosemarie says.

"Pearle's bite-sized cheese biscuits are the bomb," Fletcher says.

"I've done my share of worldwide fine dining, and I'd rank this meal higher than any five stars I've sampled," Omar says.

"Good to know," Crew says.

After dinner, we refill our wine glasses and head to the dock. The half-moon is rising, the river is choppy, and a strong warm breeze is coming off the Sound.

I chug the rest of my wine and take a deep breath.

"Can I have everybody's attention? Omar and I have an announcement to make."

I smile and prepare to burst their bubbles.

I focus on keeping my brows relaxed.

"Omar just purchased the Oglethorpe Inn and will be renovating it for the future home of the Omar Victor International Film Institute."

They congratulate him.

"And I accepted Omar's invitation to house Wisdom Seeker in the West Wing."

Everybody claps. I clear my throat.

"And there's more! Um, Omar has asked me to fake-marry him and guess what? I said yes!"

"Fake?" Crew asks.

"Yes, fake because, well, um, Omar is bisexual. He already has life partners in Cairo."

Marshall's and Crew's nasal-labial folds say 'what the?'

Rosemarie looks compassionate, Pearle rubs her chin, and Fletcher has a surprised look.

"I know it's strange," I say.

"We can handle more," Marshall says.

"Well, we believe this façade is the best way to create a parallel universe in the Deep South," I say.

"We are writing a new story to create the New Age," Omar says.

Crew gets in Omar's face. He's a good four inches shorter than Omar.

"You should have told Mary your intentions before you came here," Crew says.

"My intent is to magnify Mary's love-based takeover plot by utilizing the power of film," Omar says.

"Why did you wait to tell Mary about your sexual preferences?" Crew asks.

"I assumed Mary and Pearle were being discreet in a sexually intolerant world," Omar says.

Crew's wound up tight, but he doesn't have a comeback.

"Dude, film and social media create powerful changes," Fletcher says.

"Win/win," Rosemarie says.

Everybody gives me a hug, and I show them my ring.

"I hope you can lift your paintbrush," Marshall says.

We head back to the house and pop the cork on a bottle of 1988 Krug Burt Champagne that Omar brought from Paris. Vintage.

The next morning we jump in the limo, swing by to pick up Crew, Marshall, and Rosemarie, and head to the Oglethorpe Inn.

I haven't been back here in years. The pool is cracked and slimy green. Disheartening.

Omar is all business. He's already shaking hands with the foreman before I can blink. Nothing stops him.

"Good afternoon, Omar Victor," he says.

"Mr. Brew, foreman, Green Dream Building Team."

"It's a pleasure."

Mr. Brew opens his briefcase and shuffles papers. We wait.

"We finished inspection this morning," Mr. Brew says.

After a pregnant pause, Mr. Brew tells Omar the Oglethorpe Inn has busted pipes, flooding, rot, black mold, lead paint, and asbestos.

"I mean," Mr. Brew takes another pregnant pause. "You name it; you got it."

"What do you suggest?" Omar asks.

"Hire a hazardous waste team."

"How long will it take?"

"Depending on your optimism anywhere from nine to nineteen months. When the project is underway, I can give you a more accurate timeline."

Omar gives Mr. Brew the go-ahead, signs liability documents and writes a check for two point seven mil on the spot.

We head to North Beach Grill on Tybee, find seating on the outside deck, and order pitchers of Goslings and pineapple juice.

"Toast to collective creativity," Pearle says.

"Here's to 2020, perfect vision, and World Peace," Crew says.

"May we be skillful in speech, know that words are braver than fighting, have character without exaggerating it, and understand that idleness is not for the sensible man," Omar says.

We dine on grilled triggerfish and pasta primavera. By the time we head to the beach, I'm good and rum buzzed. The sky is azure and warm winds are out of the southwest.

I dive in first. Omar tells Crew, Marshall, and Fletcher that he's scared. Yuck.

"Shuffle your feet to let stingrays know you're coming," Fletcher says.

"Are there sharks?" Omar asks.

"Thirty or forty species of sharks thrive in this rich estuary," Fletcher says. "But no worries, dude, they consider human meat dry. Just avoid flutter kicking at twilight and you're cool."

Omar opts for a walk on the beach with Pearle, Rosemarie, and Millie. The rest of us swim out twenty or thirty feet and body surf. At the end of the day, we've all had fun.

We head back to Wilmington and drop Marshall, Crew, and Rosemarie off on our way home. We shower and meet back in the kitchen.

I pour us all frosty mugs of Dogfish Double IPA. We throw together a kale Caesar salad and corn fritters. We haul everything to the dock just before Crew, Marshall, and Rosemarie arrive on *Bottom Line*.

We set the table in the dock house and sit down for supper. Omar blesses the food in Bedouin Arabic. Our combined culinary skill is magic.

After supper, Omar directs us in a game of charades until turtle time. Crew hands out PFDs and we board *Bottom Line*. The full moon rising over the Wilmington River is mystical. We anchor off Little Tybee, wade to shore, and wait with the no-see-ums.

Exactly six months after the last time we were here, baby loggerhead hatchlings claw their way out of the sand and scurry into the surf toward the stars hovering over the sea's horizon.

We are awestruck by this spiritual experience. After we safeguard hundreds of one-inch hatchlings' journey back to the sea, we motor home under a bright full moon that illuminates the purple sky.

EIGHTEEN

The limo arrives at eight the next morning. Omar and I head out for meetings with architects, publicists, and sponsors. At noon, we race to The Bohemian Hotel Savannah Riverfront to attend a luncheon in Omar's honor. We barely make it back to Wilmington before we have to leave again.

I shower and slip on my glam gown. Tonight, Cinderella. Tomorrow, Mary Howard. Yuck. Pearle checks in on me.

"I'm practicing."

"One more time. Try not to break the line," Pearle says.

"I walk like a comedian," I say.

We crack up.

The limo arrives, Pearle helps me put my hair up, and we hurry downstairs.

Wow, Omar in a tux. Pearle snaps our photo.

We crawl in the back seat of the limo, Omar pops the cork on a vintage bottle of Dom Pérignon 2000 Rosé Vintage Champagne, and we head downtown sipping bubbly from crystal flutes.

We arrive at the Telfair Museum and walk down the red carpet. Omar was right. Local press took the bait. Hordes of photographers and news videographers surround us. I'm ready. I show off my gown and engagement ring exactly as directed.

I have a clear vision of our love-based take-over scheme happening by 2020.

After a meal that tastes and looks like cardboard, I wane. Who knew that playing charades on the dock was infinitely more entertaining than high society soirees? We head to the ballroom. The jazz band plays funeral music. Old men grope women in slinky gowns and furs. Furs? Lizard brain spits. Is this the twenty-first century?

Love-based slips light years away from my imagination. I drown in the elite's pretentious desire of luxury. After what seems to be forever, we slip out through a side exit, jump in our limo, and head to the Savannah Airport.

The last ten days feel like a dream.

"Mary, I've never been this relaxed," Omar says.

"You look good with a tan," I say.

"Together we will help humanity raise the collective vibration," Omar says.

We awkwardly hug goodbye.

Driving back to Wilmington, I imagine Omar back in Paris surrounded by his lovely, creative staff. I stop myself. I am young, and humanity is young.

Everybody is sleeping when I get home. My usual positive affirmations don't stop loneliness from engulfing me. I toss and turn half the night before dozing off.

The next morning, Millie and I head to the dock. After we greet Ouida, we Spiritfly-meditate. Just before I open my eyes it dawns on me; I am engaged to Wisdom Seeker, and we will live at the Oglethorpe Inn once we are married.

Pearle joins Millie and me on the dock. I fill her in on the Telfair Ball while she nurses Millie.

"Pearle, it was discouraging," I say. "Unity Consciousness seems lifetimes away."

"The fastest path to Unity is keeping our spirits soaring," Pearle says.

Millie pulls away completely satisfied.

"Ready to go swimming, Millie?"

I jump into the river, Pearle hands me Millie, and then Pearle dives in and joins us. Millie loves being in the water. We play until the tide changes directions. When Pearle takes Millie back to the house, I jump into *One That Got Away* and motor to Marshall and Rosemarie's house.

"Hey, it's me," I say.

"Hello, Mary. Come on in," Rosemarie says.

"How was the Telfair Ball?" Marshall asks.

"Pretentious. I'm looking forward to getting back to painting today," I say.

"Join us for brunch," Rosemarie says.

"Are you sure you have enough?" I ask.

"Of course," Marshall and Rosemarie say at the same time.

Crew shows up with a copy of the *Tongue*. Wow, I'm on the front page of the Society section.

"Go, Love-based," I say.

I describe the Telfair Ball without talking trash about rich old people or giving loneliness power.

We set the kitchen table and sit down for lunch. Marshall asks the Hierarchy, Masters, Angels, Elementals, and Aspirants to bless Mother Nature, the animals, and the people.

Wow, Rosemarie's portabello mushroom slammers, homemade onion rolls, coleslaw, and sweet potato fries rock.

"I lost sleep worrying about you, Mary," Crew says.

"Don't worry about lil' sistah," Marshall says.

"Omar is asking a lot of Mary, and I'll be forthright: bisexual men have different boundaries," Crew says.

I wish Crew understood that drinking coffee fuels fear-based. I center myself in compassion. My parents died, Crew's parents abandoned him.

"Crew, allow truth to move in a figure eight from your mind to your heart," I say.

"Mary, I know how to see with my heart but what about discernment? What about AIDS?"

"Omar is faithful to his life partners," I say.

"Life partners in Cairo and a fake wife in Savannah don't add up. This situation has the potential to be dangerous."

"Relax brother-man. Omar is cool," Marshall says.

"Let's trust Mary on this one," Rosemarie says.

"I believe Omar is good-hearted," I say.

"Let's face it; Mary snagged a multi-billionaire to back Wisdom Seeker," Rosemarie says.

"We need big budget publicity to shift humanity to love-based," I say.

"Well, I am aware that my parents raised me to discriminate," Crew says.

"We're all evolving," Marshall says.

"I need time to separate Wisdom Seekers from being single, too."

Crew is struggling, but he relaxes his stance.

"I'm glad we talked," Crew says. "Mary, I don't want you to get hurt."

"Thanks, man," I say.

"Mary knows we will always be here for her," Marshall says.

"We are all expanding our narrow minds," I say.

"Right on," Marshall says.

"Well, the tribe's arrival tomorrow will be a positive distraction," Rosemarie says.

"When Fletcher gets home from surfing, we're going to do some major yard work," I say.

"Do you need help?" Marshall asks.

"Hardly. Wisdom Seeker prospers with help," I say.

"Win-win," Crew says.

I thank Rosemarie for lunch and hug everyone goodbye. Feeling healed, I motor home.

When Fletcher gets back, we crank up surf music and kick yard work up to high gear. We weed the garden, plant out dozens of cos seedlings, and rake oak leaves to use as mulch around the garden beds.

We head inside before the sun sets, make fried egg sandwiches, and spend the rest of the evening deep cleaning and finishing kitchen prep. By midnight, we crash.

The next morning Millie and I walk to the dock. We greet Ouida and Spiritfly-meditate. We get back to the house at the same time Fletcher is getting home from his morning surf session.

"Are you ready to party with Granddaddy and the tribe?" He asks.

Millie gives him two thumbs up.

"The last time they were here you hadn't started talking," Pearle says.

Millie is perched in her high chair, drumming on her stainless steel sippy cup, listening to every word.

"You're learning by leaps and bounds, dude," Fletcher says.

A car pulls up in the driveway.

"Jehovah's Witnesses?" Fletcher asks.

"Ugh. Why do I attract false puritanical belief systems?" I ask. "I'll go see what they want."

"Hello, I'm Chief Putridt. Are you Mary Howard, founder of Wilmington Island School?"

He's got a scowl and a forty-pound gut.

"Who wants to know?"

"DHEC food police."

They wave badges at me.

"Sergeant Putridt," one guy says.

"Sergeant Doob," the other one says.

"Are those Cracker Jack prizes?" I ask.

"Scarcely. We're here to inform you that you are facing closure for breaking Georgia Department of Health and Environmental Control codes of conduct," Putridt says.

"You are in violation of the DHEC Bureau of Food Facility Licensing," Doob says.

"You have one month to comply with Georgia Code Section 66-89-6(3), Regulation 61-10, Section DDT#6, that mandates sterilizing produce with bleach," Putridt says. "You are now subject to mandatory inspections, and we will shut down your school if you are not in immediate compliance."

"Bleach is poison. Shame on you for enforcing rules that prevent humanity from balancing Mother Earth."

"I'd recommend you read these brochures carefully to familiarize yourself with unannounced inspections," Doob says.

"I'll fight this stupidity to the Supreme Court."

"Ain't no swanky lawyer can keep you in business if you ain't in compliance with DHEC, little lady," Doob says.

He gives me a stack of pamphlets. Lizard brain spits.

I shake my fingers and summon Mami Wata. When I start making poking gestures at their gluttonous stomachs, they back off.

"Be gone with you. I won't comply with your fear-based rules. DHEC will crumble." I stomp my right foot, "*GBO*," I holler.

They run away like wet rats in a flood tide.

"Who were those dudes?" Fletcher asks.

"Government pigs preaching the 'Hundred Year Lie: Better Life through Chemicals.' How can they still claim bleach is safe?" I ask.

Fletcher thumbs through the *DHEC Rules and Regulation*s pamphlets.

"Dudes, they've mandated a bazillion rules that private schools are required to follow," Fletcher says.

"Government propaganda laced with professional sports stars, fast-food restaurants, addictive junk food, and of course, soda," Pearle says.

"Pictures of farmers on vintage tractors and dancing cows," I say.

"As if slaughterhouses are wholesome," Pearle says.

"The Secretary of Agriculture pushes milk, meat, corn, and wheat just like Big Pharma pushes poisonous pills," I say. "Government lawmakers get away with blatantly ignoring the World Health Organization."

"Still the same food pyramid with a sirloin steak, whole turkey, and an eight-ounce glass of milk that graced my elementary classroom in Atlanta," Fletcher says.

"We had this chart in our classroom on Daufuskie Island," Pearle says.

"And Wilmington Island," I say. "The Standard American Diet—SAD."

"I bet Mr. Nicopane called DHEC on us," Pearle says.

"What was I thinking when I contracted this incarnation next door to a puritanical roadblock?" I ask.

"When we are on the other side, we are love-based. It's when we get down here that fear creeps in," Pearle says.

"True that. DHEC is fear-based. Okay, let's collectively think DHEC *will* crumble."

"DHEC will crumble," we chant.

Millie surprises us when she screams "cwumble."

"Ah, the power of positive thought," I say.

"Faith will allow magic to happen," Pearle says.

"I think I'll stroll down the avenue and enjoy the yard work we did yesterday," I say.

I grab my hat and walk outside. Halfway down the avenue, I get a hit to give Cecil Lloyd a call. His secretary puts me through.

"Hello, Mary. Are you enjoying this spectacular day?"

"Yes, today is gorgeous."

"How can I help you?"

"I'm calling because DHEC Food Police came by here about thirty minutes ago. They want me to bleach my produce. And bleach is poison! Anyway, I'm calling because they were extremely intimidating."

I walk to the mailbox listening to Cecil explain policies and procedures within various departments of DHEC. I lose myself in his eloquent dialog. The Cumberland trip pops into my head. My root chakra heats up. Ain't it a shame Cecil Lloyd is a lawyer?

"DHEC is corrupt, outdated, and has out of proportion control over lawmakers," he says.

"I want to do everything in my power to make DHEC crumble."

"I'll look into the allegations. When they show up again tell them you are not officially open for public registration, give them my number, and let them know they need to talk directly to me."

Cecil is super professional when he asks me to refrain from telling DHEC that I intend to cause their demise. When I open the mailbox, it's stuffed with DHEC literature. I mark everything "Return to Sender" and put up the red flag.

When I get back to the house, I let everyone know that Cecil Lloyd is now on board. We devise a plan that substitutes bleach with straight white vinegar. Pearle and I perform the *Gho* Ritual for protection. We vow to give DHEC zero power.

Crew, Marshall, and Rosemarie come over around eleven. We

walk out to the dock and meet our guests as they arrive by dories.

When everyone docks, we walk to the lawn and form a power circle. The bare-breasted drummers begin the ritual, and Pearle, Doc, and Supreme Chief Isle start chanting in *Fon*, French, and Prayer talk.

"*Sê doo nú wê. Gbe Tome*. We welcome Millie into the Land of Life." Supreme Chief Isle says. "I invite *Lêgba* to dance my body and free Millie from jealousy, unpredictability, and daily tragedies that are beyond good and evil. *Agbe*, the *Vodun* who gives life, *Du*, the Supreme Being, bless Millie on her second birthday and keep her safe in the land of life, *Gbetomê*."

We tour the veggie garden, head inside, and get everybody seated at the dining room table.

Pearle and I have been a wreck tweaking the ancestral oyster stew recipe. We've replaced the bacon grease and heavy cream with smoke-infused olive oil and coconut milk.

Everyone raves about the entire meal. We sing "Happy Birthday," Millie blows out her two candles, and we slice Fletcher's mile-high coconut cream cake.

Supreme Chief Isle gives Millie a charm bracelet. He explains the meaning of the lion charm and the three-monkey "hear no evil, see no evil, speak no evil" charm. Millie is delighted.

After the tribe shoves off, we grab a Dogfish Double IPA from the dock fridge and jump into the river.

"Now that Wisdom Seeker is free from Animal Agriculture, GMOs, food chemicals, and Big Pharma, I invite you to climb another rung of the ladder," I say.

"I'm still acclimating. What are you suggesting?" Crew asks.

"Join Millie and me at sunrise for daily group meditation," I say.

"And Ouida," Millie says.

When Rosemarie suggests we practice Spiritual Yoga after we meditate, Fletcher gives us all sloppy kisses.

Is this really happening?

"Maybe you should wait until DHEC isn't breathing down your neck," Crew says.

"Crew, DHEC will crumble," I say.

"Cwumble," Millie shouts.

"My intuition says we start Monday morning," Pearle says.

"Are you in?" I plead with Crew.

"I suppose meditation and yoga could help balance the overtime I rack up at the station," Crew says with his elfin grin.

"Alright, alright, alright," Fletcher says.

"Tenke, tenke," Pearle laughs.

We walk Crew, Marshall, and Rosemarie to the car.

"Gratitude, Mr. Nicopane is still away," Crew says.

"Yes, thank you, Universe," I say.

That night, I sketch Supreme Chief Isle in a trance.

NINETEEN

Monday morning we meet on the dock at sunrise. I explain there are as many ways to transcend waking and sleeping states as there are stars in the sky. I ask everybody to get comfortable, close their eyes, imagine the mind is like a still river, and radiate love to humanity for as long as they feel comfortable.

We're amazed how much power we generate from our first session. My urge to magnify goodwill to humanity intensifies. We walk to the lawn and Rosemarie lays out colorful yoga mats. We start with a constructive rest pose that softens our bodies. We focus our pranayama on moving inward as spiritual warriors. Then we move through the Mountain Pose.

"Relax into the pose," Rosemarie says.

She is patient and encouraging. We learn Downward Facing Dog and Warrior I and II. We wobble through Tree Pose. My left side is completely off balance. Who knew? We somehow get ourselves into Pigeon Pose. Then we find Child's Pose and Happy Baby, my two faves.

"Only move into the pose as much as feels comfortable. Breathe in from your heart center and out through the channel of your arms," Rosemarie says.

Fletcher and Pearle are naturals, but Marshall and Crew are struggling as much as me. After a heaven-sent *Savasana*, Rosemarie reads to us in Sanskrit.

We're joyful to start practicing yoga.

We roll up our mats and head inside.

"After boycotting Chiquita and Dole bananas for the last two years, I offer you the first creamy substitute," Crew says.

"Way to go, dude," Fletcher says.

"Soaked organic Medjool dates and chia seeds," he says.

He pours us all a gloppy concoction that requires spoons.

"It's gelatinous," Rosemarie says.

"Strange mouthfeel but delicious," Marshall says.

"Love the raspberry and spinach zing," Pearle says.

"Millie wants more," Marshall laughs.

"It reminds me of tapioca; I'm hooked," Fletcher says.

Wisdom Seeker splits up after the morning routine, and at high tide we meet in the river to discuss books we are reading, universal laws we are practicing, and ways to make Unity real.

After 'family supper' we either do our own thing or meet in the library to work on the Wisdom Seeker Curriculum that teaches love, understanding, soul work, and finding our unique ways to be of service in the cosmos and beyond.

We celebrate our one-month sunrise group meditation and yoga anniversary during green smoothie klatch.

"I definitely feel more alert," Fletcher says.

"And balanced," Crew says.

"We all do," Rosemarie says.

Marshall gets our attention and takes Rosemarie's hand.

"I have a big announcement," Marshall says. "We're tying the knot."

"Fantastically romantic!" I say.

"Congratulations! When's the shindig?" Crew asks.

"April 20, 2013," Marshall says.

"We couldn't wait any longer for you to know," Rosemarie laughs.

"Does Professor Lowe know?" Crew asks.

"Not yet," Marshall admits.

"Are you still getting death threat texts?" Crew asks.

"Yes, but we're moving forward anyway," Marshall says. "I booked Benjamin One to perform the ceremony."

"Rosemarie, wait until you see Benjamin One. He is one hot Shaman. He looks exactly like the portrait of his father that graces your living room," I say.

"Benjamin One is a newlywed," Marshall says.

"Yuck. My soul told his soul to wait for me," I say.

The rest of the summer, I take midmorning hikes through the woods. I tell myself to be happy being single. I know Omar is who he is and that much won't change.

Universe, please send me a man who is fit, kind, intelligent, and spiritual.

By fall, I feel more in control of willing myself to stay present. For the most part, Wisdom Seeker is thriving.

A northeastern chill and strong winds come in late-November. We decorate the downstairs into a yoga studio and move group meditation and yoga inside.

Omar comes to Savannah at the end of December. We celebrate my twenty-sixth birthday out on the town, attend a private New Year's Eve bash on Skidaway Island, and soldier through two nights of Omar's Celeb Fund Raising Galas at the Brockington Hall Mansion.

After a hectic week with a million details, Omar charters an 85-foot Morgan sailboat for a Cumberland Island film shoot. Crew, Marshall, Rosemarie, Pearle, Millie, Fletcher, Omar, and I bundle up. A half dozen of Omar's young, glamorous staff are already on board. Even the captain looks GQ.

Omar's friends party hard. By the time we check-in to the Greyfield Inn, I have to sleep off my whiskey buzz before cocktail hour.

We party through cocktail hour, the seven-course dinner, and way past the lounge's official closing.

The next morning we're on location before sunrise. Omar shoots film nonstop for the next two days.

Our last morning we enjoy a leisurely Greyfield Inn Sunday Brunch before cruising back to Wilmington Island.

The next afternoon, my fake fiancé leaves for Egypt.

I bundle up, hop into *One That Got Away* and end up at Tubby's in Thunderbolt Village. After drinking a few too many with the locals, I motor home.

By the end of January, unexpected freezes hit hard. We buy row covers in hopes of protecting our cruciferous, strawberries, and lettuces.

Omar's mother drops her body so he cancels his trip to Savannah at the end of January. When his father sinks into depression, he cancels his mid-February trip, too.

I'm on edge. Our wedding date is fast approaching, and Omar is never here. What if Savannah figures out that I'm a fake or, worse, that Omar is bisexual? I attempt to balance myself.

March rolls around, we load up *Bottom Line* and *One That Got Away* and caravan to Daufuskie to celebrate Millie's third birthday.

We make our way to Daufuskie and upon our arrival, Supreme Chief Isle introduces us to wife number three, a young, fit, self-absorbed woman named Diane. Pearle gives her father the look.

He tells her he was lonely. Although it is immediately obvious that Diane is light years away from utilizing her goddess power to serve humanity, we attempt to be nonjudgmental.

The full moon rises. Drumming starts. Supreme Chief Isle summons the deities *Sakpata* and *Xevioso* to give Millie *da gu do* so she will not accept complicity with evil. Next, he summons *Dú*, who blesses Millie's entry into the land of life, *Gbetomê*.

The next morning, I hike to my secret cove and Spiritfly-meditate. I get a hit that the Universe wants me to upgrade to a Wisdom Seeker van.

I get back to camp in time for brunch. We feast on fried fish, duck eggs, and grits. It's early afternoon before we shove off.

On the way home, I interpret my vision. Should I get rid of my silver Honda and buy a passenger van? Why is something nagging me? Is it that Mama gave me the silver Honda as a gift on my fifteenth birthday? Is it that I need to wait for more free spirits to enroll in Wisdom Seeker before I buy a gas guzzler?

That night, I toss and turn trying to decide. By morning, I decide to follow my gut instinct. After the morning routine, Crew, Marshall, and I pile into the Honda and head to Auto World on the south side of town.

"Let's circle around the Oglethorpe Inn," Marshall says.

I hit the brakes and hang a left.

"Wow, look at all of the construction trucks," I say.

"It's been busy like this for a few weeks," Crew says.

I merge back onto Wilmington River Road.

"Look, Duane is out-front of Wise Hoe Woo Marina," Crew says.

"Let's stop," I say. I pull in.

Duane was part of our pack from kindergarten until, well, I was kicked out of the May Howard School for being a free spirit.

"Dudes, long time no see," Duane says.

"It's good to see you, man," Crew says.

"What's new?" Marshall asks.

"Well, due to THC in my pee I got laid off from the paper plant," Duane says.

"Bummer," I say.

"No worries, man; I'm better off not inhaling nasty chemicals forty hours a week anyways. I've decided to avoid repo man, and Wise Hoe Woo has generously given me permission to sell the van in his parking lot," Duane says.

"I'll take it!" I say.

"Do you need the Silver Honda?" Crew asks.

"Dudes, yes. Wheels and cash. I'm amped," Duane says.

"Gratitude, we saved haggling with car dealers *plus* we get to stay on the island," I say.

"Priceless," we all say at once.

Wise Hoe Woo downloads a bill of sale; I transfer funds to Duane's bank account, and we exchange car keys. Fifteen minutes later we pull up to the house, and I beep the horn.

"You just left," Pearle says.

"Genies pardoned us from traveling to the ugly side of Savannah," Marshall says.

"Nice ride," Fletcher looks under the hood. "Dude, she's in great condition. I can't wait to drive her."

"Just in time for Saint Patrick's Day," Rosemarie says.

"We won't have to take two cars this year," I say.

That night we dig out everything loud, green, and metallic.

The next morning, Fletcher confesses a love of driving oversized vehicles. I'm thrilled to relinquish the keys. We pick up Crew, Marshall, and Rosemarie and head downtown. Fletcher drives like he surfs and glides into a sweet spot a block away from Rousakis Plaza.

We set up base camp under the shade of a grand oak tree and wait for the parade to start. Soon bagpipes, tin whistles, Alee Temple Shriners, Keystone Cops in go-karts, marching bands, and the Oriental band wearing rainbow pantaloons and gold elf shoes stroll past us. Millie's favorite is the belly dancers who are playing tiny cymbals and flutes that are tuned in quartertones.

After the parade is over, we head to Kevin Barry's Pub. We belly up to the bar and order a pitcher of Southbound IPA and a round of Jameson. It's hard to ignore the heaping platters of corned beef and cabbage being served.

Whiskey buzzed, the waitress finally comes around to take our orders. After I order the Buffalo Shrimp Caesar Salad, everyone follows suit. Gratitude. One table in this bar is abstaining from the St. Patrick's Day tradition of killing, boiling, and eating cows.

The sun is crushingly bright when we leave. River Street is already shoulder to shoulder with celebratory drunks. We work our way out of the crowd and climb the steep cobblestone steps to Bay Street.

"Wait a minute, I left my pocketbook," I say. "I'm going back."

"Do you want me to walk with you?" Rosemarie asks.

"No, I'll just be a minute," I say.

When I get to the entrance of Kevin Barry's, I collide with the lady in black from Cecil Lloyd's office. She disappears in a hot minute. Why is she alone? I walk into the bar and slam into Cecil Lloyd.

"Mary, what a pleasant surprise. Are you just arriving?" Cecil asks.

"Hey, there. Nice to see you. Actually, I'm on my way out, but I forgot my pocketbook."

He follows me to the bar. "Here it is. Thank goodness."

"May I buy you a cocktail?"

My root chakra heats up.

"Um, no thanks. I better go." I blush.

"Aren't you staying for Irish music? The first band is starting at three."

"Um, my group is in the van waiting for me."

"I'd be happy to give you a lift home."

"Oh, no, thanks. I have to go home, and, um, paint. Yes, paint, lots of painting to do, always."

That's when Cecil Lloyd wishes me a happy St. Paddy's Day and kisses me square on the lips.

"Yeah, Happy St. Paddy's Day to you, too," I say.

Completely confused, I wave bye-bye like a toddler and back out. When I turn the corner, I run back to the van.

I hold up my pocketbook, and they cheer. We climb in the van, Fletcher eases out of a tight space, and glides through downtown traffic.

My heart is pounding. Who is the lady in black? Is she Cecil's lover? Does Cecil know that I'm engaged to Omar? Will I ever forget that kiss?

I doze off until Fletcher jumps out of the van to check the mail. I'm feeling sleep deprived and way too whiskey-buzzed.

"Here come the St. Patrick's Day protestors," I say.

They march around at the end of Mr. Nicopane's driveway carrying their 'God Hates the Unholy, Unworthy, and Unpatriotic' and 'Repent and Be Obedient' banners.

Fletcher pushes his way through the small band of haters. "Lighten up fire breathers," Fletcher says. "God loves us and angels watch over us."

Fletcher grabs the mail and jumps back in the van just before Mr. Nicopane appears.

"Whoa, Mr. Nicopane's stomach is the size of a Crenshaw melon," I say. "It's an omen."

"But what does it mean?" Pearle asks.

"I wish I knew," I say.

Fletcher hands me a bundle of DHEC threats, and we drive past the haters. When we get inside, Pearle performs *Gho*. Her powerful voice resonates healing energy.

At the end of the summer, Mr. Nicopane loads three big suitcases in his yellow Mercedes and drives away. The rest of the winter, Wisdom Seeker is free of him.

March brings earthworms and ladybugs to the garden and Millie's fourth birthday celebration on Daufuskie. Thankfully Diana is no longer in the picture.

When we get home, we begin to tackle the multitude of details for Marshall and Rosemarie's big day.

The morning of Marshall and Rosemarie's rehearsal dinner, we walk over to their house and start yard work. We break at noon. Fletcher and Rosemarie are organizing lunch when Marshall gets my attention and signals me to follow him to the library.

"I still haven't heard from Professor Lowe. Did you try dialing him from your number last night?" Marshall asks.

"Yes, he never picked up," I say.

"Professor Lowe haunts me. I'll give it one last shot," Marshall says.

We're shocked when Professor Lowe picks up.

"Hello, this is Marshall Portunus."

"I have caller I.D."

"Thank you for taking my call."

"Keep it brief, Mr. Portunus."

"Rosemarie and I would be honored to see you at our wedding tomorrow at six."

"You brainwashed my daughter. You have slandered the Lowe name."

"Professor Lowe, I am begging you to understand that we are madly in love with one another."

Professor Lowe spits obscenities and hangs up.

"I've only offered him kindness, patience, and love," Marshall says.

"I'm sorry."

We join the others in the kitchen.

"Well, your parents won't be attending the wedding," Marshall says.

"They thrive on shame and disappointment. A joyous occasion like their daughter's wedding day, not so much. My parents have been stuck in the negative illusions of network news since forever. I only hope that they will one day evolve past the spiritual equivalency of evil-spirited brats," Rosemarie says.

"Some parents teach us how not to be," Crew says.

"Okay, I'm letting go," Marshall says.

"Love and peace, Professor Lowe," I say.

"Amen to that," Pearle says.

"Hey, big news. A few weeks ago Savannah Bright interviewed me about our green wedding. Well, I just got a text, she's airing it tomorrow morning," Rosemarie laughs. "She's going to expose unethical wedding industry standards."

Fletcher finds the link, and we watch the video. It starts off with a segment taken from hidden cameras exposing wedding gown sweatshops: Chinese migrants, locked into walled factory compounds forced to work ninety-hour weeks. They receive no overtime, are routinely beaten and earn less than fifty cents per hour. Even more disheartening, is watching little kids working on the fast-moving assembly lines.

Rosemarie is next. She calmly talks about local seamstresses and a slew of green wedding alternatives.

Next, Savannah Bright shows a clip from *The Blooming Business*, a 2010 documentary about the dirty secrets of the global flower industry; military cartel in Columbia and Equador beating and murdering laborers and raping women and girls when they use the bathroom. One woman says roses for her means thorns, rape, blood, and chemical poisoning for her, her family, and her people.

"Wow, in two minutes, Savannah Bright nailed social injustice," Fletcher says.

"The primetime shift to compassion," Marshall says.

"Light is lighting darkness," Pearle says.

"Please, send free spirits to Wisdom Seeker," I say.

We head to the dock to fish the incoming tide. Luckily, we catch plenty of whiting and stripes for tonight's fish fry. We gut and fillet the fish, decorate the dock house and change into clean clothes.

Benjamin One arrives with his new wife, Sha Sha. She is enlightened, genuine, and married to the coolest, kindest, hottest man on the planet.

Benjamin One smudges the entire property, inside and out. Afterward, Tiffany, the wedding coordinator, arrives and walks us through the rehearsal. I'm completely distracted standing next to Benjamin One.

At sunset, we tap the keg of premium rum and officially start cocktail hour on the dock. The sky is ablaze with radiant bursts of pinks, reds, purples, and oranges. We reminisce about Mr. and Mrs. Portunus' research on Shaman plants, Hawaiian Forgiveness, Mali Indian Dances, and the Amazonian Shaman diet.

The rehearsal dinner is a blast. We get home around eight. I make a pot of mint tea, let it steep, and then enjoy the first aromatic sip.

Headlights come up the driveway. I flip on the outside floodlights. An old-fashioned station wagon pulls up in a cloud of black smoke. I go outside and see Louisiana license plates. A hefty woman in a polka-dotted muumuu gets out waving her enormous arms.

TWENTY

"Hey, I'm Mandy Dubois. Are you the one with the psychic school?" She asks.

I am nonjudgmental when I realize she can't afford dental care.

"Yes, I'm Mary Howard," I say.

She jerks away from my handshake.

"Do you take woo-woos?" She asks.

"We can schedule an interview."

"Look here, girly," she opens the back door. "I'm their mama."

I gasp. Two little girls and a Jack Russell terrier are in the backseat.

"Hello, I'm happy to meet you. My name is Mary Howard."

Their blue eyes penetrate me with hope, love, forgiveness, and happiness.

"Mary Howard, Marjorie, Greta, and their feisty dog Manfred," Mrs. Dubois says. "They can figure things out 'fore they ever happen."

"How old are you two?" I ask.

"Six-years-old," Mrs. Dubois says. "And they ain't much trouble, but my brothers and sisters at The Bright Light Fundamental

Baptist Church believe that they are Satan in person, the author of sin, and the cause of the Fall of Man."

"Please, come inside."

"Only if we can bring Manfred," one twin says.

"Manfred is welcome," I say.

Manfred rips the leash away, pees on Mr. Nicopane's garage, and comes right back. I shudder to think how bad it would be if Flambé and Juicy were home right now.

"Manfred is robust. I like his expressive eyes," I say.

"He's eager to please," one twin says.

I take in the twin's thick blond pigtails, Oshkosh B'gosh striped overalls, and pink tennis shoes.

After introductions, Fletcher takes Millie to the library, and Pearle comes to the office to help me with the interview.

"I got some health problems with my lungs," Mrs. Dubois says. "And I came here with donations raised by The Bright Light Fundamental Baptist Church because I ain't got no money."

I fire up the computer and print out the Wisdom Seeker Admittance Form.

"Greta and Marjorie, why do you think Wisdom Seeker would be a good fit for you?" I ask.

"Look, I was sent here because my preacher said that Greta and Marjorie are enemies of God who will lead us to eternal punishment in the Lake of Fire."

The twins sit perfectly quiet. I tune Mrs. Dubois out and hear their sweet voices telling me that they are philosophical, spiritual, kind, and sensitive beings of light. But strange, something is stopping me from reading their auras.

"So, what my brothers and sisters at The Bright Light Fundamental Baptist Church want to know is, how much would it cost if you jes took 'em?" Mrs. Dubois blurts out.

"Pearle, I'd like to follow my heart and offer Greta and Marjorie full scholarship," I say.

"I feel the same way," Pearle says.

The twins high five. Mrs. Dubois signs on the dotted line and hightails it back to her life as the Bright Light Fundamental Baptist Church fear-based rule follower.

"I am happy you selected us to be your guardians," Pearle says.

"You two are gifts from the Universe," I say.

Fletcher and Millie join us in the library.

"Welcome to Wisdom Seeker," Fletcher says.

Manfred stands on his hind legs at Fletcher's side.

"Dudes, animals sense that I am a critter protector," Fletcher says holding Manfred like a baby.

"Fletcher, Marjorie and I love critters, too," Greta says.

"Well, y'all will love island exploring Wisdom Seeker-style. Right, Millie?" Fletcher says.

"Let's go see Ouida!" Millie says.

"Ouida is off fishing," Fletcher says.

"Who's Ouida?" Marjorie asks.

"Our pewican," Millie says.

When laughter fills the room, my peripheral vision catches a glimpse of the twins' eight-foot-wide, kaleidoscopic, zig-zag, psychedelic, shimmering rainbow aura.

"We have incarnated with the full spectrum of light," Marjorie reads my mind.

"We are here to give humanity the light they need to assimilate serotonin in their bodies," Greta says.

My head is spinning from their wisdom.

"Humanity will soon realize that peacemakers are now inundating our planet," Greta says.

"When did you find out you were psychic?" Fletcher asks.

"We have had vivid memories of communicating mind-to-mind since we were babies," Greta holds Marjorie's hand. Adorable.

"At first, it was weird trusting our intuition because it was completely opposite from what we saw happening around us," Marjorie says.

"But by the time we turned five we started having the same lucid dreams," Greta says. "And they always came true."

"This is the first incarnation on earth for Rainbow Children," Greta says. "Our earth journey is karma-free."

"So you incarnated love-based?" I ask.

"Yes," Greta and Marjorie say at the same time.

"You have good timing," I say. "We're going to a wedding tomorrow. Would you two like to be flower girls?"

"Now, that sounds fun," Greta says.

"Millie would love for you two to join her," Pearle says.

"We don't have fancy clothes," Marjorie says.

"I'd be happy to sew you dresses tomorrow morning," Pearle says.

"I'll do it if you will," Greta says.

"Sure, let's go for it," Marjorie says.

"Dudes, I can't tell y'all apart," Fletcher says.

"Greta is graceful, loyal, cheerful, and persistent," Marjorie says.

"Marjorie is grounded, pessimistic, and merciful," Greta says.

The Twins shut their eyes and hold hands.

"Mary and Pearle are Indigo Adults who are here to quash caste systems, and Fletcher is a light-keeper who is here to help the animal kingdom," Greta says.

"You are old souls," Pearle says.

"Our biggest feat has been surviving fanatical devotees for the past six years," Marjorie says.

"Kindred souls," I say.

"We've always visualized starting our seventh year with those who understand premonitions, angels, other dimensions, and parallel realities," Greta says.

"Now we can begin to hone in on the gift of peace," Marjorie says.

Manfred falls asleep on Fletcher's lap.

"Have you read *Psychic Intelligence* by Linda and Terry Jamison?" Fletcher asks.

"PI rocks!" Greta says. "Linda and Terry Jamison are our idols," Marjorie says.

"When we told our librarian, Miss Bee, that her boyfriend was two-timing her, and it turned out true, she found esoteric kid's books for us," Greta says.

"She wanted us to know we had validity," Marjorie says.

"How did you find Wisdom Seeker?" Pearle asks.

"We both dreamed about a 'W' swimming in the river," Greta laughs.

"Night after night we saw 'W' swimming. Then we saw the word Wassaw, then Wilmington, and finally Wisdom Seeker," Marjorie giggles.

"Miss Bee searched online and found out Wisdom Seeker actually existed," Greta laughs.

"And you were located on the Wilmington River!" Marjorie cracks up.

Millie starts to fade, but Greta and Marjorie are wide awake.

"Are you hungry?" Pearle asks.

"No," Greta says.

"We pigged out at Krystal," Marjorie says.

"And Krispy Kreme," Greta says.

I evoke a silent cry to the House of Shamballa to stop corporations from poisoning humanity.

The digital clock flips over to 11:11 and Marjorie and Greta shout 'twin flames' together.

When I give gratitude for the Universal Law of Attraction, Greta reads my mind.

"We hear the inner thoughts and feelings of others," Greta says.

"We sense dishonesty like Manfred senses fear," Marjorie says.

"Do you have visions or impressions?" Pearle asks.

"Both, really," Marjorie says.

"Impressions when we're awake and visions in our dreams," Greta says.

"Whenever it happens, it happens to both of us at the same time," Marjorie interjects.

"Pretty much, we've learned how to stay in the moment and see pure truth," Greta says.

"It's pretty easy. We'd be happy to teach you." Marjorie says.

"The biggest challenge is steering clear of naysayers who feel threatened by truth and light," Marjorie says.

Greta and Marjorie crawl in my lap. My urge to serve humanity is amplified. A heavenly host of angels fills the office.

Millie starts dozing off so we head upstairs. Pearle puts Millie to bed, and Fletcher helps me put fresh sheets in the guest room. Greta and Marjorie make a bed for Manfred out of towels and throw pillows and unpack all of their belongings from one small suitcase.

When Pearle and Fletcher say goodnight, Greta and Marjorie are still wide awake.

What to do?

We climb up in my four post bed with mama's jewelry box. Manfred circles around and passes out at the foot of the bed.

"Our guides have taught us that our purpose on Earth is to teach patience, honesty, intuition, spirituality, and compassion," Marjorie says.

"But little kids who try to fix broken education and religious systems get themselves in a heap of trouble," Greta says.

"So, we focused on controlling our emotions in order to be more open channels to receive the light from other dimensions," Marjorie says.

"When did it dawn on you that there was good and evil in the world?" I ask.

"We figure out that God is good," Greta said.

"Yeah, God wouldn't send her children to eternally burn in hell for following soul desire," Greta laughs.

"Then we figured out that we were seers, not sinners," Marjorie says.

We sort out earrings, untangle bracelets and necklaces, and try on rings. Greta and Marjorie teach me how to hold the crystals and precious stones to calm myself.

"What should we call you?" Marjorie asks.

"Mary or Miss Mary. What do you prefer?"

"Mary. Proper etiquette needs a total do-over," Greta says.

"Mary, do you grocery shop?" Marjorie asks.

"Sure, what do you need?"

Marjorie digs into her pocket and pulls out a shopping list: dog food, smoky bacon Pringles, Blue Razz Blow Pops, Dr. Pepper, and Diet Mountain Dew. I cringe that their mother's vices have become par normal.

By midnight, they start yawning.

"I think these necklaces will be just right for the wedding tomorrow," I say. "How about we get some sleep?"

"I'm not sleepy," Greta says.

"She's scared of the dark," Marjorie says.

"You are, too," Greta says. "Honestly, neither one of us have acclimated to the new three A.M. energy waves we've been experiencing."

"They're way intense," Marjorie says.

"Yeah, especially with the full moon tomorrow night," Greta says.

"What do you do to calm yourself?" I ask.

"We go outside barefooted," Greta says.

"It grounds us," Marjorie says.

"Me too!" I say. "Gardening grounds me."

"Do you grow food?" Marjorie asks.

"Yes," I say. "We grow vegetables, herbs, and flowers."

"We've always wanted to garden," Greta says.

"Maybe we should take a barefoot tour?"

Manfred shakes off, and we head outside.

The almost full pink moon is rising. After Greta and Marjorie dig their toes into the Bermuda grass, they start feeling sleepy.

We go to the kitchen, drink a glass of water, and go upstairs. Manfred circles his bed, ruffles the towels into a nest, and collapses. Greta and Marjorie put on their pajamas, brush their teeth, and go to bed like little grownups.

"I'll leave this lamp on the night light setting. If you need anything, please wake me."

We kiss goodnight. Love, love, love.

We wake up early enough to catch a sublime yellow and pink sunrise on our walk to the dock. Halfway across the yard, Manfred rips the leash out of Fletcher's hand and races ahead to the floating dock. Thankfully, Ouida flies off toward Wassaw Sound.

When we catch up with Manfred, he is barking at the incoming tide.

"Okay, sit comfortably. Let's practice meditating."

Manfred barks and barks.

Millie gets the giggles and that gives Greta and Marjorie the giggles.

"Alright, let's get comfortable," I say. "Manfred, settle down. Ok, let's shut our eyes."

"Manfred, please," Pearle says.

Giggling, barking.

"Okay," I say. "Let's invite monkey brain to take a nap and invite our souls to rest in our hearts," I say.

They quiet down. About five minutes pass before I ask them to give gratitude and open their eyes.

Success. We are all smiling. We get a collective hit that we are vibrating at a higher frequency.

When we get back to the house, Fletcher goes out for organic dog food and the rest of us head to the sewing room. Greta and Marjorie find a bolt of fabric with bold sunflower print.

"I was your age when my Mama and I found that fabric in Barcelona, Spain," I say.

As soon as we scroll through the first Online sewing site, it is obvious that Greta and Marjorie thrive on creativity. They pick a pattern with a sassy yellow sash, a large side bow, and ruffles around the neck and scooped back. Pearle takes their measurements and prints out the pattern. She cuts the fabric and cranks up the vintage 1950 Singer sewing machine.

Millie shares her secret treasure chest with Greta and Marjorie. They love the Voodoo charms, Shaman rattle, eagle feather, magenta lithium quartz crystal, deep purple amethyst crystal, and malachite tree frog.

Pearle and I witness Millie's social world unfold as she has one ah-ha moment after the next. She becomes aware that she has the ability to express her spirited temperament.

When I go downstairs, Manfred picks up his lead and follows me. And before I can start breakfast, he herds me to the kitchen door. Communicative. As soon as I open the door, Manfred rips the leash out of my hand. Inch for inch Manfred is one mighty dog.

"Manfred, come!" I call him.

He pees on the corner of Mr. Nicopane's garage, scratches the earth, and then heels beside me.

"Manfred, no," I command. "Flambé and Juicy are big trouble."

DHEC propaganda is spilling out of the mailbox. I allow disgust to pass by me and invite truth to guide me. I vex the envelopes, mark everything 'return to sender,' and put up the red flag.

Fletcher returns an hour later. He had to drive all the way to Habersham to find organic dog food. Manfred woofs down his kibbles, licks his chops, and falls asleep in front of the kitchen door.

Fletcher and I make veggie omelets and Ezekiel toast with coconut butter, maple syrup, cinnamon, pecans, and raisins. We call everybody to breakfast. We sit down for our first meal together.

The twins are good eaters and they haven't mentioned needing junk food today. What a relief.

After breakfast, Pearle takes the kids back to the sewing room, and Fletcher and I head to the library and research Rainbow Children.

"Rainbow Children are spiritual, multi-dimensional beings who resonate with the morphogenetic field," Fletcher says.

"They are capable of allowing trappings to pass through them, hold onto nothing, and are constantly in the ultimate state of detachment," I say. "The biggest challenge for Indigo, Crystal, and Rainbow Children, we're warned, is staying grounded."

"Dude, Wisdom Seeker was custom-made for Greta and Marjorie," Fletcher says.

"Gardening is going to be good therapy for the twins," I say.

At noon, we turn off the computer and head to the kitchen to prepare lunch. We make wraps stuffed with radish sprouts, sprouted basmati rice, green lentils, cos, and raw goat cheese.

"Wisdom Seeker serves beautiful food," Greta says.

"Dollar menu fast food and peanut butter and jelly sandwiches pale in comparison," Marjorie says.

By early afternoon, the sashes, bows, and ruffles are complete. Pearle's sewing is stunning. The dresses are darling.

We take Manfred for a walk. The twins move Manfred's bed downstairs and place it next to the kitchen door. They give him kisses and tell him to guard the house.

I lock up the house, and we walk to Marshall and Rosemarie's house. By the time we arrive, I figure out that Greta crosses her arms when she speaks, and Marjorie talks with her hands on her hips.

Gratitude, just in time for introductions.

TWENTY-ONE

"Surprise! Wisdom Seeker is materializing," I say. "Marjorie and Greta Dubois. They are animists, just like the rest of us!"

We talk over each other. Millie is even chatty. Greta and Marjorie surprise us with their outgoing personalities. It blows my mind that this is their first earth journey.

Soon everything is a whirlwind. Equipment trucks, caterers, florist, and photographers are swarming. Up goes the forty by fifty clear-roof tent. In comes the porta potties with canned music, air conditioning, and chandeliers. Tiki bars are set up on opposite sides of the lawn.

Tiffany, the wedding coordinator, is like several people in one. One minute she reminds us to walk down the aisle slowly and keep our eyes on Benjamin One; the next minute she's twenty feet up on top of a tent hanging lanterns.

I'm intrigued when Marshall and Rosemarie ask us to meet in the library.

"We've been in premarital bliss for almost two years," Marshall says.

Rosemarie blushes, "And we have a big surprise."

Dead silence. Pregnant?

"Wisdom Seeker is invited to join us on our honeymoon," Marshall says.

"Tomorrow morning?" I ask. "We go with you two?"

They nod.

"I've already told them there is no way I can get away from the station this week," Crew says.

"In addition to our honeymoon suite, we booked a family suite. There's plenty of room for all of you," Marshall says.

"Get out," I say.

"While Rosemarie and I stow away, Wisdom Seeker can explore Key West," Marshall says.

Millie is sitting in Marshall's lap. Marshall explains that it will be fun, but we'll need to stop in Miami to shop for bikinis, flip-flops, sunglasses, and straw hats.

"I've always wanted to snorkel in the Keys, dudes," Fletcher says.

"If you don't think we will interfere with your privacy, sign me up," Pearle laughs.

"What about Manfred?" Marjorie asks.

"Dogs are pack animals. They don't understand the passage of time like people do," Greta says.

"I'd be honored to babysit Manfred," Crew says.

The twins close their eyes, hold hands, and determine that Crew is trustworthy.

"Road trip!" Fletcher says.

Tiffany finds us. She puts flowers in our hair and escorts Pearle, Marshall, Rosemarie, Greta, Marjorie, and Millie to Crew's house.

Crew's favorite local band, Sol Torso, sets up and starts sound check. Caterers finish setting up the outside kitchen. The entire property smells like fried shrimp and crab cakes.

Benjamin One and Sha Sha arrive right on time. I escort them to the guest room, light incense, and leave them to meditate.

TVPD officers are directing traffic, Crew and Fletcher start to usher guests down to the river, and the ceremony musicians start the prelude music.

A red Range Rover barrels past the parking area and slams on brakes just shy of the front porch. Officer Lardus shows up in a minute.

"I'm Professor Lowe, father of the bride. Stop this wedding. Stop this wedding!"

Benjamin One appears and sweeps Professor Lowe inside faster than the eye can see. Shaman magic? Shear strength? I follow them inside. Professor Lowe is swinging wildly, but Benjamin One gets him upstairs like a trickster. We pile into Mr. and Mrs. Portunus' empty bedroom.

Benjamin One places his massive right hand on Professor Lowe's right shoulder.

"Be present, release your negative energy, and be one with Marshall and Rosemarie's love," Benjamin chants.

"Get out of my way you half-dressed woo-woo," Professor Lowe shouts vulgarities.

"Rosemarie and Marshall are consenting adults. Their love is invincible," Benjamin One says.

"That muddled pothead isn't marrying my daughter!"

Professor Lowe's bumpy nose is running.

"Mary, please ask Tiffany to start the cocktail hour at six and postpone the ceremony until seven."

Professor Lowe takes an unexpected swing. Benjamin One leaps back. I find Tiffany, and she makes the switch quickly. The ceremony musicians fade out of Bach's "Arioso" and crank up "Love Me Do."

"Why the change-up?" Crew asks.

"Professor Lowe is in the house. He reeks of booze. Benjamin One is trying to calm him down. We're switching the ceremony and cocktail hour," I say.

We find a place at a tiki bar and sip primo rum punch.

"Let's toast," I say. "May the Shaman Way and majestic oaks heal Professor Lowe."

"Here, here," Fletcher says. "May the sun, moon, stars, heavens, nests, whirlwind, trees, rainbows, and raindrops heal Professor Lowe."

"May Professor Lowe find his sacred circle and connect to all things," Crew says.

We clink punch glasses, enjoy another round, and indulge in crab cakes, shrimp kabobs, and smoked Florida mullet. When the breeze dies down, the air gets thick, the humidity gets sticky, and the no-see-ums descend upon us.

"Seven until seven," Crew says.

"I'll go check," I say.

When I get upstairs, it's quiet. I open the bedroom door, and Professor Lowe shoots me a peace sign and says 'love-based.'

"What gives?" I ask.

"A common Shamanic practice called soul retrieval," Benjamin One says. "Professor Lowe traveled to other realms to locate and bring back wounded pieces of his soul so we could reintegrate the soul fragments into his physical body and help him understand the truth."

"How did you get him to do that?"

"I prayed to Great Spirit and spiked his bourbon straight up with peyote so he would be willing to vacuum up his demons and transport them to the center of the earth where they have been returned as pure love."

Professor Lowe giggles.

"Professor Lowe, the Wheel of Time is ready for your daughter to find true happiness. Remember, this is a sacred ceremony, and you are very high, so no giggling. Come on, fella."

Tiffany lines us up and cues the musicians to start "Gabriel's Oboe."

Benjamin One, Crew, Fletcher, and Professor Lowe begin the processional. Professor Lowe plops down in the first row. "A Thousand Years" is our cue to walk. I go first, and Pearle goes next. I keep my eyes on Benjamin One. Stop monkey brain. He's married.

The girls passionately toss wildflowers before Marshall and Rosemarie, hold hands, and walks down the aisle to "I Will."

"Rosemarie Lowe and Marshall Portunus, I honor your decision to be joined in holy matrimony, to be conscious of the shifting seasons, and to walk in a sacred way that is full of marvel and wonder, for all the days of your lives.

"Perform rituals of continuous dance, and remember to thank spirit guardians, animals, plants, and stone spirits.

"Stand firmly in the center of your life. The wheel is around you and within you. Center yourself, heal your past, and climb the rainbow to seventh heaven.

"Intimacy is what makes a marriage. Love-making opens your chakras and energizes the *Ka* body. Learn the Kama Sutra and enjoy each other's naked bodies. Make love regularly for vitality, fire, and passion for life. Raw sexual power is grounding, brings peace of mind, and creates healing power for Mother Earth. Remember to belly laugh, pray, and fast.

"Grandmother Earth and Grandfather Sky make spiritual energy available when we quest for power over ourselves under nighttime rituals using San Pedro psychotropic plants.

"I smudge you with sage, rosemary, cedar, lavender, cannabis, and sweet grass smoke. Fill your senses and allow words of love to come from your mouth like flowers in spring.

"Turn to the north, I know, white, the body. Turn to the east, I see, yellow, the mind. Turn to the south, I feel, black, the soul, and turn to the west, I sense, red, the spirit.

"Rosemarie Lowe and Marshall Portunus, I now pronounce you husband and wife. Please kiss one another to seal your promise," Benjamin One says.

They grind. Wow. We recess to "Marry Me" by Train.

Since cocktail hour already happened, we head to the big tent for dinner. Professor Lowe is euphoric.

Servers pass Grilled Spotted Sea Trout with creamy dill sauce, cracked blue crab claws in a drawn butter and Tabasco dipping sauce, delicately fried creek shrimp, scallop au gratin, and veggie shish kabobs.

The shift to local, organic, and in-season wedding food is happening now. Yippee.

Marshall and Rosemarie cut their three-tier organic carrot cake with brandy-soaked Georgia peach aphrodisiacal icing. We dance the rest of the night. The tide is high, and the full Pink Moon is casting silver rays across the rippling river.

The next morning, we wake up before sunrise and Spiritfly-meditate. After we take Manfred for a long walk, we head inside and make oatmeal and fruit salad. We race around, pack the van, and take off to Crew's house.

Saying goodbye to Manfred is teary. My guides tell me to keep moving. As soon as Marshall and Rosemarie load up, we leave. The streets of Savannah are deserted on Sunday morning. We catch every green light on Victory Drive and Martin Luther King

Boulevard. Crew sends a dozen pics of Manfred right when we merge onto southbound I-95. Manfred loves Lardus the most. They made him a little bed in the lounge. The cops are all gaga.

The van is soon full of laughter.

We stop in St. Augustine. We visit the Fountain of Youth and drink from the historic spring. After picnicking on leftover wedding food, we're back on the road.

Despite endless bathroom breaks, we make good time on the Florida Turnpike. Everyone comes alive when we start seeing signs for Miami. Fletcher takes the downtown exit, and we follow the signs to the MiMo neighborhood.

Rosemarie made reservations at the Blue Collar. We order their famed veggie plates. Our servers bring out platters of Napa cabbage, curried cauliflower, roasted artichoke hearts, garlicky wilted spinach, caramelized Brussel sprouts, and cheese grits family style. The food, casual vibe, and super friendly servers are five-star.

After lunch, we hit a trendy kids shop in Coconut Grove and buy bikinis, flip-flops, shades, hats, shorts, and t-shirts for all. We find the car, and merge back onto the Southbound Florida Turnpike.

"We've received vivid psychic impulses since our third year," Marjorie says. "But we never saw ourselves in Miami, Florida, buying bikinis."

"We're thrilled," Greta laughs.

"How did you teach yourself to interpret psychic impulses?" Pearle asks.

"By reading esoteric books and practicing mental exercises," Marjorie says.

"One thing we've learned is that we will all be communicating telepathically in the New Age," Greta says. "It will be fast, direct, and honest."

"Unlike the way humans communicate now," Marjorie interjects.

"What type of mental exercises will help humanity learn telepathy?" Rosemarie asks.

"We have to get people to participle in full moon, rain, and sun dance ceremonies," Marjorie says.

"And value meditation. Meditating is a vibration-changer, even after a measly two days," Greta says. "Especially for us Rainbow Children who are born with the urge to hone in on their intuitive sensibilities."

"We are here to strengthen the ability to send and receive love telepathically," Marjorie giggles.

When we cross the Overseas Highway, we long to dive into the turquoise water. We pass Islamorada, Marathon, Big Pine Key, and finally arrive at bustling Key West.

Fletcher follows Flagler Street to Zero Duval Street and checks us into the Ocean Key Resort and Spa.

Marshall and Rosemarie slip away to their honeymoon suite, and the rest of us settle into our luxurious new space.

We change into our new suits, take the glass elevator down to the ground floor, and order signature rum-infused cocktails at Liquid, Ultimate Poolside Bar. The sunset is glittery.

We shower, change, and head to the Hot Tin Roof for our dinner reservations. We order caramelized grouper, spinach risotto, and grilled asparagus family style. Fantastic.

After supper, we take a walk down Duval Street. Fletcher takes off solo, and the rest of us head back to the Ocean Key Resort.

Pearle puts the girls to bed. I soak in the Jacuzzi tub. How is it that love eludes me? I stop myself. Now is the time to be happy for Marshall and Rosemarie. I imagine them tangled in tantric bliss, surrendering to co-mingling magnetism, achieving the Egyptian alchemy of Horus, and sex magic of Isis, as taught to Yeshua by Mary the Magdalene.

We make the first snorkeling tour of the day. By midmorning, we are taking the lighthouse tour. During lunch Greta and Marjorie teach us the basics of gazing at objects, buildings, colors, faces, animals, and plants as they are, without interpretations, to search for hidden meanings and deeper truths.

"Stopping monkey brain from imagination-painting when my eyes are open will be a big challenge," I laugh.

"We'll help you," Greta says.

"Yeah, we have to learn to control our thoughts before we are ready to communicate telepathically," Marjorie says.

"Thoughts will soon be public information," Greta says.

We go ocean kayaking every morning and explore a different beach every afternoon. When we get back to Ocean Key, we head to Liquid for the ultimate cocktail hour, sipping the signature Limonada Azul in their glamorous pool. When we start to get wrinkled, we get out in time to walk to Mallory Square to catch the Sunset Celebration.

On the third night, Marshall and Rosemarie emerge from their honeymoon suite. Love, love, love.

After the Sunset Celebration, we follow our noses to the sweet aroma coming from a tiny family-owned kitchen off the beaten path. We're seated on the outside patio, dine on mystical grilled seafood and veggies, and enjoy the ultimate view of the waning alabaster moon.

By the end of the week, we know our way around the gingerbread trim and pastel shades of Old Towne, the Key West Butterfly Nature Conservatory, and every nook and cranny of the Key West Tropical Gardens.

Our last day we head out to celebrate the Blessing of the Shrimp Boat Festival. Duval Street is a parking lot. We push our way into the big crowds, past TV vans, satellite antennas, and camera crews.

Highway patrol cars, swat teams on bikes, and white Ford Crown Victoria canine units inch their way through the pedestrian traffic.

Decorated winged outriggers pack the Gulf. Thirty or forty activists are dressed-up like shrimpers, wearing white rubber boots and yellow slickers. They chant 'Stop Net-Killing Turtles' and 'Make Safety O-Hooks and Turtle Excluders Mandatory.' Fletcher tracks down the organizers, who are a husband and wife team. We thank them for their activism and make a donation to help their plight.

The next morning, we load up the van and head north to the mainland.

"Did you read that sign?" I ask.

"Yes. There's another one, dude," Fletcher says.

"They're hand-painted. Look, there's another one," I say. "'Wild Organic Fruit.' Let's see if we can kick green smoothie klatch up a notch."

Fletcher glides over two lanes and exits the Turnpike. We travel west for fifteen miles, hang a left at the next sign, and head down a dirt road with deep potholes and a long stretch of dilapidated trailers.

"Environmental refugees," Fletcher says.

"This looks like our hood in Wacko," Greta says.

"Poverty and famine in our backyard," I say.

"Marshall and I recently watched the *Harvest of Shame*," Rosemarie says. "It's a 1960 CBS documentary that exposed horrendous work conditions for South Florida migrant workers."

"Loopholes between corporations and Federal Labor Laws continue to make it legal to profit from slave labor," Marshall says.

"The tide is turning," Greta says.

"Goodwill and sharing will soon be popular," Marjorie says.

They shut their eyes and hold hands.

"Film will make the shift happen," Greta says.

"Dudes, that's what I've always believed," Fletcher says.

Millie attempts to explain Omar to Greta and Marjorie. She says that Omar is pretty, funny, and makes good movies. When Greta and Marjorie learn that Wisdom Seeker is partners with a Film Institute, they high five.

The road forks and we enter a tropical paradise. Fletcher parks under the lush greenery of an enormous tree that is laden with creamy white flowers. We follow a walkway oozing with good *feng shui* and arrive at a jerry-rigged table made from pallets and cinder blocks.

I take in the hand-painted menu on the busted longboard, rusted cashbox, stainless steel cleaver, and fancy red blender plugged into a 1950s' generator. Two kids run out and greet us. Vroom, look at that girl's voluptuous titties. She could attract men of great power to risk their careers, families, dignity, and self-respect. Why did I ask for small breasts this incarnation?

These two must be siblings. They have the same tall, muscular build and jet black wavy hair.

TWENTY-TWO

"Welcome to Homestead. I'm Bridget, and this is my brother, Bo."

Bridget squats down to talk to the twins at eye level. I take in her long legs, cut-offs, and worn cowboy boots.

Fletcher is in a trance. Pearle snaps her finger.

"Fletcher, will you hold Millie?" Pearle asks. "She's dead weight when she's asleep."

Greta and Marjorie introduce themselves. They explain they are clairvoyants and that they will be turning seven on September sixteenth.

Millie wakes up in a good mood, hops down, and introduces herself.

"How old are you and Bo?" Rosemarie asks.

"I'm eighteen, and Bo is sixteen," Bridget says.

"Are you graduating from high school this year?" Marshall asks.

"No, we both earned our GEDs."

"Me too!" I laugh.

We high five. Rule-breakers, I love them already.

We study the menu, but the ingredients are the unknown.

"Merciful heaven, do you need help deciding?" Bridget asks.

"Canistel, Mammy Sapotes; we don't know what this is," Marshall says.

"The Grocery Manufacturer Association brainwashes us," Bo says. "They want us to believe fruit has to be uniform in size, shape, and color.

"What the GMA doesn't tell us is that blemish-free, overly hybridized fruit is void of nutrients," Bridget says. "May I suggest the Tropical Bliss Tutti Frutti Smoothie?"

"Yes," Marshall says. "Tutti Frutti for all."

Bo and Bridget slice, dice, and juggle fruit like magicians. They dole out short, fat, black-skinned ice cream bananas, and we're hooked. Next, we sample vine ripened mangos, chocolate-pudding-tasting sapotes, and sapodillas with an Asian pear and coconut combo sensation. Ambrosia. Unsurpassed.

Bridget stuffs fruit in the red blender. Nothing is refrigerated, and they don't use ice. Bo cranks up a blender that sounds like a jet plane taking off. A minute later they serve us extra thick fruit shakes.

"Out of this world," Pearle says.

"This is the best thing I've ever tasted," I say.

"Dudes, rad," Fletcher says.

We order another round.

"It tastes like heavy whipping cream," Marshall says.

"Bridget and I are vegans, brother man," Bo says. "We don't consume animals."

"Interesting. What do you eat?" Marshall asks.

"Organic fruit, vegetables, seeds, and nuts," Bridget says.

"Why does this taste so creamy?" Pearle asks.

"Wild bananas have viable seeds, seeds have fat, and fat is creamy," Bo says.

"I totally get that," I say.

"Why, are you, vegans?" Rosemarie asks.

"The question is 'why do people eat animals,' not why we don't," Bo says.

I get a hit that pescetarians are very different from vegans.

"Humanity won't learn compassion until they stop killing sentient beings," Bridget says.

I feel like a hypocrite killing fish and teaching peace.

"Gorillas don't eat other animals, right?" Greta asks.

"Right! Gorillas are vegan just like Bo and me," Bridget laughs and flexes her hot feminine muscular biceps.

Fletcher is gone. I elbow him.

"How long have you been vegans?" Marshall asks.

"Seven years," Bo says.

"This smoothie could make a vegan out of me," I say.

"Well, drink up. Today is our last day on this farm," Bo says.

"Is it the end of the growing season?" I ask.

"Hardly. The owner of this land was sued for infringement rights after Monsanto's armed thugs planted a patented GMO soy in the mango grove," Bridget says.

"That's criminal," Marshall says.

"Monsanto and Congress have teamed up with a clear message to small farmers: be big or get out," Bo says.

"Five generations of sweat and toil building this fruit farm, only to be bulldozed in one single day.

"By Black Friday this fruit farm will be a factory outlet mall," Bridget says. "And in Homestead, where poverty and famine are an epidemic."

"Criminal," Marshall says.

"Such a shame," Pearle says.

"Do your parents work here with you?" Rosemarie asks.

"Our mother died when we were young, and our father still lives in Puerto Rico," Bridget says.

"Will you go back to Puerto Rico?" I ask.

"No, we'll never go back," Bridget says.

"We're sensing fear," Greta says.

"Why are you scared?" Marjorie asks.

Marjorie and Greta's magnetic personalities radiate unconditional love.

"Our father is an abusive drunk," Bo says and squeezes Bridget's shoulder. "I don't know why I'm telling you this. I guess there is something about you that I trust."

"One thing we learned from our father is that we have unlimited power to make a new start in life."

"How did you get to Homestead?" Pearle asks.

They tell us how they took the *ferrie del Caribe* from Puerto Rico to the Dominican Republic. In Dominica, they sharecropped by day and built a little raft named *Fate* at night. They beat the odds and made it to the Caicos Islands where they found work on a low budget cruise ship headed to the mainland.

"We worked on a chemically laden tomato farm in Immokalee our first two summers," Bo says. "The conditions were horrendous."

"The library was the only thing that kept our spirits from breaking," Bridget says. "And the library is where we met Guy, the owner of this farm."

"The past five years of organic fruit farming has been a dream come true," Bo says.

"What now?" Marshall asks.

"We're looking for work," Bridget says.

"Any luck?" Fletcher asks.

"Well, organic operations in South Florida are rare. Most of the farms we've interviewed with are still using DDT that they hoarded in the 1950s. I don't know about the rest of the states, but conventional farmers in Florida get away with murder," Bo says.

"We've started Wisdom Seeker on Wilmington Island, Savannah, Georgia, and are currently accepting free spirits with a desire to use the imagination to co-create solutions that will heal Mother Nature," I say.

"Sounds New Age," Bo says.

"Let her finish," Bridget says.

"We are using the Law of Attraction to create a parallel system that is love-based," I say.

"Wisdom Seeker is cool, dudes. We're unaffiliated and degree free," Fletcher says.

Greta, Marjorie, and Millie make a hard sell for Wisdom Seeker.

"That sounds nice, but we don't have money for, um, is it a school?" Bo asks.

"Not a school, a hub," Pearle says. "We meditate, explore nature, and take the time to ponder solutions to balance Mother Earth."

"I'd be happy to offer both of you full scholarships," I say.

"Bo, I feel like the Universe is providing," Bridget says.

"I trust Bridget's intuition," Bo laughs.

"What would our responsibilities be?" Bridget asks.

"Cultivate an Edible Education program for Wisdom Seeker, Savannah School District, and beyond," I say. "We offer room, board, and a stipend."

"The Universe is abundant," Bridget says.

"Help and be helped," Pearle says.

"Welcome to Wisdom Seeker!" We sing.

Bridget and Bo give thanks to one hundred saints and pack everything they own, including the red blender, in one duffle bag.

We go deep into the food forest and learn to climb trees and pick fruit. We overload the van with fruit and head home.

"Why did you start Wisdom Seeker?" Bridget asks.

"I need help shifting humanity to love-based by 2020."

"Are there more people enrolled at Wisdom Seeker?" Bo asks.

"Crew Potalis, Marshall's next door neighbor and our lifelong friend," I say.

"He is a peace activist and police chief," Marshall says.

Bo and Bridget get quiet.

"Crew is a hip popo, dudes," Fletcher says.

"Ouida, our pelican, is a Wisdom Seeker," Millie says.

"Manfred, our terrier, is a Wisdom Seeker," Marjorie says.

"We're growing," Rosemarie says.

"Mary, you share your name with the Holy Mother Mary of Christ, who is the Virgin Most Prudent, Queen of Angels, Queen of Martyrs, Queen of All Saints, Queen of Peace, the Mirror of Justice," Bridget says.

"Bridget shares the name with Saint Bridget of Ireland, who was the original lifeforce governing all organic processes," Bo says.

We all say 'no coincidences' at the same time.

"I'm a healer," Pearle says. "And I can't help but notice how healthy the two of you look."

"We eat an alkaline diet, exercise, and get plenty of fresh air," Bridget says.

"If we do get sick, we practice the secret alchemy of herbal healing that Saint Hildegard of Assisi taught in 1200," Bo says.

It's late when we drop Marshall and Rosemarie off, and since Crew's lights are out, we have to wait until tomorrow to get Manfred.

We put the girls to bed as soon as we get home and then fix the two rooms at the end of the hall for Bo and Bridget.

Next we carry a hundred pounds of fruit inside and sort it by ripeness. When every surface in the kitchen and dining room are covered with exotic tropical fruit, we go to bed.

I hear people stirring early. Pearle and Millie are in the twins' room. I flip my pillow over the cool side and doze off for a few more minutes.

When I get dressed and open my door, Bridget is walking down the hall. She stops and gives me a sweet hug and tells me that she had the most peaceful night sleep of her life last night.

I sneak a peek at her tight purple tank top. 'Would You Suck the Tit of a Sick Cow?' Ha, and I thought I was an activist.

Marshall and Rosemarie pull up in the green Packard followed by Crew in his cop car. Manfred rolls over on his back and gets lavished with belly rubs.

"Hi, I'm Bridget, and this is my brother, Bo."

Crew shakes their hands.

"Welcome to Wisdom Seeker," Crew says.

We head inside.

"I've never seen so much fruit in one place," Crew says.

"It's sorted by variety and ripeness," Pearle says.

I catch Crew's expression when he reads Bridget's top.

"Hey, let's head to the dock so we can catch the sunrise," I say.

The kids are disappointed that Ouida is still away. We close our eyes and ask monkey brain to be still. When we open our eyes, Greta and Marjorie tell us how much they enjoy spending less time in the third and fourth dimensions and more time in higher dimensions.

"Meditating seems like a good idea," Bo says.

We walk to the lawn for Spiritual Yoga. Bridget and Bo are naturals. After yoga, we head to the kitchen for green smoothie klatch.

"This is how to eat a ripe mango," Bridget laughs. "Suck it so the juice doesn't drip down your chin."

Marshall winks at Rosemarie.

We unpack the Vitamix and whip up Tutti Fruitti Smoothies.

Who knew South Florida grew organic tropical fruit? Manfred laps up his smoothie and stands on his hind legs begging for more. I walk Crew outside when he is leaving for work.

"Bridget is going to cause Fletcher pain with her Carmen Miranda looks," Crew says.

"I know, I know," I say. "But no need to be fear-based. Two consenting adults, right?"

Crew leaves for work and I join the others in the garden.

"We can definitely increase food production," Bo says.

"Worm poop is good for the soil," Marjorie says.

"Vermiculture," Greta says.

"You two are smart," Bridget says.

I'm confused. I thought organic gardeners were supposed to squish worms. I keep quiet. I've got a lot to learn.

We flag the sunny spots and start shoveling. By noon, we are beyond dirty and sweaty.

"Double digging is the bomb," Bo says.

"Sustainability will end world hunger," Bridget says.

"Planting peace," I say.

I get Pearle's attention, and she follows me inside.

"I need help making lunch. I'm clueless," I say. "Pearle, I use butter, goat cheese, eggs, and seafood in everything."

"I was raised to believe I would die if I didn't eat meat," Pearle says. "I've never even heard of vegans before now."

"Fruit salad and Ezekiel toast with coconut butter, maple syrup, cinnamon, raisins, and pecans are vegan, right?" I ask.

"Right, but what else?" Pearle looks through the fridge.

We come up with fruit salad, grits with olive oil instead of butter, and kale, onion, and mushroom stir-fry. At the last minute, I make goat cheese omelets for the omnis.

We sit down for our first meal together.

I say the blessing and we pass the fruit salad. When we bring out the main course, Bridget and Bo eat more fruit salad and pass on everything else.

"The grits, stir-fry, and toast are vegan," Pearle says.

"Everything is organic and GMO-free," Rosemarie says.

"Thank you, but Bo and I are raw vegans," Bridget says.

My narrow mind explodes.

After Greta and Marjorie ask questions, they push their omelets to the side. Millie imitates them.

I think about Roy Day showing me eggs covered in poop and blood before he washed them for the market. I get an off-taste in the back of my throat and, just like that, I'm over eggs.

"Dudes, when I became a Wisdom Seeker, I gave up deli meat and the apex sacrifice: bacon," Fletcher says.

"We heal Mother Earth in unique ways," Bridget says.

"How do you feel about boiled peanuts?" Marshall asks.

"Peanuts are unhealthy because worldwide peanut seeds have been infected with Aflatoxin mold," Bo says.

"I knew peanut butter was making us sick," Marjorie says.

"And I knew you were right," Greta says.

"I'm going to take conscious eating to the next level," I say. "Veganism makes sense to me."

"George Bernard Shaw said, 'While we ourselves are living graves of murdered beasts, how can we expect any ideal conditions on this planet?'" Bridget says.

"Animals have souls just like us," Greta says.

"Bridget and I will blow your mind with living food. Raw Pad Thai, pizza, chili, curries, and desserts," Bo says.

"Mary, I know you would love the *World Peace Diet* by Will Tuttle," Bridget says.

"Let's run downtown after lunch," I say. "We can hit the library and go shopping for vegan food at the health food store."

"If I want to experiment with a vegan diet, can I still eat sprouted rice and peas?" Pearle asks.

"Yes, you don't have to be raw to be a vegan," Bridget says.

"I'm game," Fletcher says. "If I can eat toast and grits."

At this point, Fletcher would eat anything Bridget asked him to eat.

"It sounds fun," Greta says.

"Let's go for it," Marjorie says.

We're psyched. When Marshall and Rosemarie take off to a Mad Mother's Against Monsanto meeting, the rest of us pile into the van and head downtown.

We give Bridget and Bo the lowdown about Mr. Nicopane.

"He goes away for months at a time," Pearle says.

"But when he is home, we avoid him," Fletcher says.

"We visualize a 'For Sale' sign in front of his property," Greta says.

"We give him zero power," Marjorie says.

We circle around the Oglethorpe Inn and explain that this will be the future home of Wisdom Seeker and the Omar Victor International Film Institute. When we pass Wise Hoe Woo Marina, we point out where we get our magic compost.

"I've fought animal sacrifices forever so I get 'as long as we are the living graves of murdered beasts...', but what about raw goat milk or raising backyard chickens?" Pearle asks.

"Mama goat secretes baby goat growth hormone intended for a baby goat's consumption," Bridget says. "And eggs are almost the same as a hen's period. Gross, right?"

"Animal Agriculture is immoral and unnecessary. Animals don't deserve to be imprisoned in backyards, organic farms, or factory farms," Bo says.

"When will it be considered unjust to rip a calf or a goat away from his mother and steal her milk?" Bridget asks.

"How is it legal for the dairy industry to forcibly inseminate cows using an apparatus referred to as a 'rape rack'?" Bo asks.

"Did you know that 21,000,000 male calves, every year globally, immediately travel to a slaughterhouse to be used for cheap ground meat or much worse?" Bridget asks. "They are slated for the horrifically evil veal industry."

"First, we kill the animal, and then the animal kills us," Bo says.

"Dudes, it's hard to believe I could graduate first in my class from Atlanta Country Day School, study Biology at Emory for three semesters, and still be suckered into believing dairy industry propaganda," Fletcher says.

"Unfathomable," Marjorie says.

"Barbaric," Greta says.

"Millie refuses to drink goat milk," Pearle says. "She always has."

"Because it smells like butt," Millie says.

"Females, no matter what species, do not exist to produce food for other species," Bo says. "I mean, imagine a freaking businessman sucking an udder."

"Humanity needs to grow up and self-wean," Bridget says.

We find parking and walk to the library.

We are in our element. We research permaculture, raw vegan recipes, quantum physics, the power of love, and metagifted children. Everyone gets their own library card, and we check out. We pile back into the van with a mountain of books.

On a whim, we take a walking tour through the City Market and River Street. The dogwood trees and azaleas are in full bloom.

We pile back in the van and drive to Brighter Day Health Food Store. We grab a cart and pile into the small produce department.

Right off, Bo finds the produce manager.

"Is this section "Local" or "Organic"? Bo asks.

"Local," The produce manager says. "We proudly support the Buy Local Campaign."

"Brother Man, I have to tell you that dark leafy greens and beans have been added to the dirty dozen list. Believe me, "local" non-organic beans are sprayed with sixty different carcinogens and neurotoxins," Bo says while charismatically smiling.

The produce guy apologizes. He had no idea. Bo says, 'One Love' and gives him a hug.

"Hey, please wear gloves when you handle this stuff," Bo says. "Skin is a big drinker."

Bridget gets my attention. I follow her to the deli.

"I know talking about money is taboo," she says, "But, we only have sixty bucks."

She hands me a wad of ones. I hand the money back to her and give her a hug.

"Bridget, Wisdom Seeker is prosperous. Now is the time when we come together to be receptive to ways we can balance Mother Earth."

"I've worried about where our next meal was coming from our whole life. I don't know what to say."

"Help us change the world to love-based," I say.

"Thank you," she says.

We head back to the produce department. Fletcher calculates how much produce we will need for eleven people to eat vegan for one week.

We fill the cart with a case of romaine lettuce, ten bunches of herbs, a case of Napa cabbage, six pounds of snow peas, twenty-five pounds of carrots, a case of spinach, and all of the winter squash, Florida avocados, and US organic fruit they have in stock.

The second cart gets loaded with Medjool dates, Turkish figs, cashews, walnuts, pecans, sundried tomatoes, buckwheat groats, oat groats, cocoa nibs, maca powder, hemp seeds, chia seeds, boatloads of kelp and nori wraps, wild rice, and seeds for sprouting wheatgrass, broccoli, radishes, and alfalfa.

We give the fridge a total makeover, pack a cooler, load *One That Got Away*, and head to Little Tybee. The sun is bright, and the river is as smooth as glass.

We anchor off the south side of Little Tybee. I'm the first one in the river. Wow, Bridget in a bikini. She could easily get a modeling gig.

When the outgoing current gets too swift, we picnic on mangos, ice cream bananas, and chocolate sopotes, and then explore the maritime forest until sunset.

We get home right before Crew, Marshall, and Rosemarie arrive for family supper.

After they take pictures of the fridge, we get busy soaking, slicing, dicing, chopping, food processing, and Vitamixing our first raw family supper.

We start off with gazpacho. Amazing. The main course is romaine lettuce taco shells stuffed with walnut taco meat, radish sprouts, and collard ribbons, and topped with cashew sour cream and guacamole. Unreal. The Spanish rice, made with raw cauliflower, sundried tomatoes, onion, garlic, celery, and herbs, blows us away. Bo's raw fudge bliss bites leave us completely satiated. Joy. Laughter.

That night we go online and order three Excalibur nine-tray dehydrators, a professional-grade Cuisinart food processor, a second Vitamix blender, and two mega masticating juicers.

Within a week, we have learned how to massage kale, Vitamix soup, and sauces, spiralize vegetable noodles, food process dressings, sauces, and dips, and juice wheatgrass. We help flip trays of dehydrated veggie burgers, pizza crawlers, compost cookies, and the raw vegan dog bones of Manfred's dreams.

We eat more produce in one day than a Savannah restaurant would serve in a week. Healing crises hit hard, but within a month our gut floras adjust, and we stabilize in healthy alkalinity.

At the end of June, we build a hoop house and start seed trays. In August, we install drip irrigation and sturdy trellises.

Wisdom Seeker develops a comfortable routine of meditating, practicing yoga, swimming, island exploring, helping marine critters, gardening, reading esoteric books, and co-creating New Age curriculum.

On September sixteenth, we load up *Bottom Line*, *Driftwood*, and *One That Got Away* and head to Cumberland to celebrate Greta and Marjorie's seventh birthday.

By October, we plant out hundreds of cruciferous seedlings and direct sow tiny radish, carrot, and lettuce seeds. At this point, Wisdom Seeker believes veganism, meditation, and organic food forests will end world famine by 2020.

On the full Frost Moon, the twenty-fourth of November, I take my three prodigies, Greta, Marjorie, and Millie, to the forest for their secret initiation into Fairy Magic. Afterward, we go in search of the portal and find Mossy Snellbaad. He is sober and kid-friendly, gives fairies validity for a hot minute, and poof, he's gone.

Omar visits Savannah at the end of December. We celebrate my twenty-ninth birthday and attend a New Year's Eve Party at a private home on Skidway Island.

I sink into a deep funk when Omar leaves. Fletcher picks up on my low vibe and talks me into going surfing with him.

The next morning, we head to High Tide Surf Shop on Tybee. I buy a Kechele 'Grinder,' a black Quicksilver Zipperless Wetsuit, gloves, boots, and a hood. I also get a red Roxy bikini, because I will date again.

We hit the beach. My first session I catch a wave for ten seconds, and I'm hooked. By February, I can hang ten.

TWENTY-THREE

THE FIRST DAY OF SPRING WE MOVE MEDITATION AND YOGA OUTside. The azaleas are in bloom and the bluebirds are chirping.

The garden takes off when the days get longer. We harvest a bounty of lettuce, herbs, Asian greens, cabbage, kale, sweet peas, and strawberries.

By the end of March, the citrus trees are in full intoxicating bloom.

I wake up before dawn, open my window, jump back in bed, and flip the pillow over to the cool side. I love this time of year.

Millie checks to see if I'm awake.

"Good morning, Millie. Happy Birthday!"

"Thank you. Mama said I'm starting my sixth year."

"But you're turning five today."

"Yeah, but I was born a year before I turned one."

"Oh, I see what you mean."

I follow her to her room and patiently wait while she dresses. Hurrying or helping are not options when she is putting together one of her eccentric outfits.

We meet everyone on the floating dock and greet Ouida. We get comfortable and close our eyes. By now, everyone has discovered a unique way to calm the mind.

We gather on the lawn for Spiritual Yoga. Rosemarie helps us get the hang of the Spring Equinox Sun Salutation. She reads a Sanskrit prayer about spring cleaning thoughts that no longer serve us so we can create space for ideas beyond our imaginations.

The intense flavors wafting from the dehydrators have Manfred salivating. We flip trays of candied almonds, mushroom-walnut burgers, sprouted buckwheat-sesame buns, crispy pizza crawkers, and spicy kale chips. And because it's raw food, the samples are always ready. Manfred stands on his hind legs begging for raw vegan dog biscuits.

The way that Bridget and Bo make Millie's birthday cake is something I could never have imagined. They food process sprouted oat groats, sprouted sunflower seeds, soaked pecans, cocoa powder, and soaked dates for the batter. For the icing, Bo cracks open young Thai coconuts, and Bridget adds the seeds from vanilla beans. Next, they create a three-layer quarter sheet cake masterpiece.

We pass around the bowls for a sample.

"Savannah is going to love Bo and Bridget's organic raw vegan desserts," Rosemarie says.

"The shift," I say. "Sheet cake sans flour, sugar, and eggs."

"Scrumptious," Pearle says.

"Not too sweet and not too heavy," Marshall says.

"Chocolatey, coconutty, creamy bliss," Fletcher says.

We pop the cake in the fridge and head to the dock to greet the tribe. Supreme Chief Isle and Doc arrive in the first dory. They are in full regalia. The minute Supreme Chief Isle steps on the floating dock, Millie jumps into his arms.

Drummers signal the start of the *Gho* ritual. Supreme Chief

Isle spits palm wine and gin on Millie's third eye, pours some on the ground to honor the Deities, and passes it around for us to share with the spirits. After the ceremony, Supreme Chief Isle gifts Millie with an owl charm, the Wisdom Seeker mascot. Millie is delighted.

After we introduce Greta, Marjorie, Bo, and Bridget to the tribe, we take a garden tour.

"Cold-hardy grapefruit, satsuma, and lemon trees," Bridget says. "Smell the blossoms."

"Ah, so tender and sensual," Supreme Chief Isle says.

He's obviously checking Bridget out from her head to, well, her breasts. Pearle gives her father the evil eye.

"Blackberry, strawberry, raspberry, loquats, and pecan trees," I say.

"Bridget you are very powerful. The Deities have invited you to be initiated to perform *Gho*," Supreme Chief Isle says.

"I'm game," Bridget says.

Fletcher's soul is itching to get out.

Supreme Chief Isle places his enormous hand on Bridget's head and spits palm wine and gin down her tank top. Unreal. It's easy to see why Diana divorced him last winter.

"Let's go inside," Pearle says.

"The aroma stimulates all of my appetites," Supreme Chief Isle's laughter bellows through the downstairs.

When we get seated, Supreme Chief Isle switches his name tag with Bo's and plops down next to Bridget. Pearle is livid. Fletcher is a basket case. We bring out platters of sliced fruit for the first course.

"Bridget, I've never seen a girl so thin eat so much fruit in one sitting," Supreme Chief Isle says.

She pops a strawberry and shrugs.

"These pizza crawkers are divine," Supreme Chief Isle says. "Who made them?"

"I did," Bridget says.

"Then I will have you for my wife."

Supreme Chief Isle kisses Bridget on the mouth.

Fletcher chokes on a kale chip. Bridget says she's happy being single, but Supreme Chief Isle doesn't let up. Everybody takes seconds of the walnut mushroom slammers. After we serve the birthday cake, Supreme Chief Isle starts bragging that the raw food has given him a giant erection.

The tribe is in high spirits when they leave for Daufuskie.

"Other than Daddy hitting on Bridget, I think that went well," Pearle says.

"And we were worried about raw food," Marshall says.

We grab Dogfish Double IPAs and head to the dock. The tide is high, the sun is hot, and we swim until the outgoing tide gets too swift.

That afternoon I head to the art room. I've been working on the same still life for weeks. Whenever I iron out one detail, a hundred more scream for my attention. I put on my smock, prepare my palette, and chant my mantra that time is an illusion.

Hours pass. Monkey brain chats about Supreme Chief Isle chasing Bridget. He's sixty-years-old. Why in the world would he act that way? Bridget's breasts?

I clean my brushes at three A.M., walk out to the verandah, and fall asleep in my Yucatan hammock.

The next morning, I wake up to an electric orange and pink sunrise. I give gratitude, say love, love, love, and get up as the others are coming outside. We walk to the dock, greet Ouida, and meditate.

After green smoothie klatch, everyone heads out to help with a garden install. For the first time since I can remember, I'm going to devote the entire day to painting.

I put the kettle on and make a pot of tea. When it is steeping, a red Mercedes SUV pulls up to the house. What in the world?

I go outside. A fit blonde wearing a pencil skirt and a starched white sleeveless linen shirt gets out and shakes my hand.

"I'm Mrs. Lark," she says. "Stage mother of child cello prodigy, Ella Lark."

I sense major adrenal stress under her extremely tidy appearance.

"Mary Howard, nice to meet you."

"Ella found you online. She wants to study here."

"Ella is a cellist?"

She holds up her hand and stops me.

"I am prepared to pay your tuition."

"Look, um, Mrs. Lark, we are not a music conservatory."

She opens her designer purse and takes out a sterling silver case engraved with 'L, L, & L' in curly cursive and hits her electronic cigarette.

"Yes, darling, I understand that you are not a conservatory," she sighs. "But Ella skypes cello lessons so that will not be a problem. What I need from you, is to make it happen ASAP."

She gives me her card and pulls out in a hot minute.

'Lark, Lark, & Lark; SAND – GLASS; Cleveland, Ohio.'

The rest of the day, I cast Mrs. Lark out to sea, and she crawls right back. When we finish family supper, I tell the others about Ella Lark.

Greta and Marjorie shut their eyes and hold hands.

"Ella isn't pushy like her mother," Marjorie says.

"She's been with our group before," Greta says.

"And we all love the cello," Marshall says.

"Law of Attraction, it's how we roll," Fletcher says.

That night, I take a long soak. I think about the building chemistry between Fletcher and Bridget. I face the fact that my relationship with Omar is disillusioned. When will I figure out dating?

'Don't ask how' pops into my head. I shift.

'If it is in accordance with the Universe, I will attract a kind, fit, spiritual, vegan, altruistic, *available* man soon.'

I crawl into bed with *Woman River Saints*.

The phone rings.

"Hello?" I say.

"We've been waiting for your call," Mrs. Lark says.

"Really? I said I would call you in the morning."

"But have you scheduled Ella's interview?"

Mrs. Lark's rude persona floods my mind.

"Yes. We'd like to interview Ella tomorrow afternoon at one."

"Eight A.M. works best."

"Fine. Eight it is, Mrs. Lark. Goodnight."

Has she ever used the words please or thank you? I toss and turn all night. I have to be forthright and tell her we are unaffiliated and degree free. I talk myself out of mentioning anything about DHEC lawsuits.

The next morning monkey brain chatters nonstop during Spiritfly-meditation, and I'm completely unbalanced during yoga practice.

"The Universe only needs one percent of us to look inward for one-quarter minute every day, to shift humanity to love-based," Rosemarie says at the end of Spiritual Yoga.

During green smoothie klatch, I try to get my head around how Wisdom Seeker could be the right fit for a child cellist prodigy?

Mrs. Lark pulls up twenty minutes early. Rosemarie, Pearle, and I go outside to greet them. Ella jumps out. She has a charismatic purple aura.

"Could she be any cuter?" Pearle asks.

When Mrs. Lark gets out, Ella shuts down.

"Welcome, I'm Mary, this is Pearle, and this is Rosemarie. Please, come inside."

We get seated in the library.

"Let's spare the formalities. I'm driving back to Cleveland today and flying to Italy tomorrow night. I'm anxious to start my new life," Mrs. Lark sighs.

"Very well," I say. "First of all, we are not a school, we are a Wisdom Seeker hub."

"Spare me the syntax," she interrupts.

"Secondly, we are unaffiliated and degree free."

"Ella has talent and drive," says Mrs. Lark. "Ella doesn't need a degree."

Mrs. Lark takes out her silver case and hits her electronic cigarette. Pearle and Rosemarie collectively gasp.

"Ella and I don't see eye to eye on anything," Mrs. Lark says.

"Yeah, like your toxic fumes you make me breathe," Ella is soft-spoken.

"You are the reason I smoke!" Mrs. Lark throws her head into her hands.

"Ella, why do you think Wisdom Seeker is a good fit for you?" I ask.

Ella's smile melts my heart. I take in her slight frame, see-through blue eyes, cropped jet black hair, and long slender neck.

"Wisdom Seeker is a good fit for me because I want to concertize less and practice and compose more. Also, your degree in Fairy Magic intrigues me because of my love of the mythological *Rusalka*. And finally, I want to study with Marshal Portunus because of his books, *My Thoughts, My Things* and *My Soul, My Intuition* helped me cope on and off stage."

"How so, Ella?" Pearle asks.

"My high school is segregated. Kids that study Math and Science twenty-four/seven are treated to well-funded Gifted and Talented programs. The rest of us are labeled slow learners and sentenced to remedial drudgery."

Mrs. Lark sighs like a female Woody Allen.

"Ella, will you thrive in our remote location?" I ask.

"My intuition says yes," Ella says.

"My intuition says yes, too," Pearle says.

"I agree," Rosemarie says.

After Mrs. Lark scrutinizes every word of the ten-page Wisdom Seeker Admittance Form, she signs.

"Ella, welcome to Wisdom Seeker," I say.

Mrs. Lark says 'Hallelujah' and 'Hail Mary' and we follow her outside. Ella looks younger than fifteen in her black skinny jeans, small white V-neck t-shirt, and red Converse shoes.

"Ella has a private bank account. I'm making a donation to the school for a quarter mil, and I'm asking you to have the good business sense to invest in a security system."

She gives me the insurance appraisal for Ella's Italian cello and priceless French bow. We unload Ella's backpack, purple cello case, a crate of music, black padded fold-up chair, and cherry wood music stand.

"The help in Cleveland will send Ella's attire and library," Mrs. Lark says.

She blows Ella a kiss and waves goodbye.

"Let's leave everything in the kitchen so we can meet the others," Pearle says.

Ella admires every painting and sculpture she passes. When we get outside, she hugs the grand oak tree. We check out the garden and the fast-running fiddler crabs scurrying to their burrows as we approach.

We introduce Ella to Marjorie, Greta, Bo, Bridget, Millie, Fletcher, and Marshall. We tell Ella about the tides, the critters we protect, and the rich estuary system of the Georgia Barrier Islands. Ella tells us that she's looking forward to devoting more energy to composing after the last four years of hectic touring.

"Ouida is away fishing," Millie says.

"Who's Ouida?" Ella asks.

"Our pet pelican," Millie says.

Ella balances my charkas with her belly laugh.

"We break at high tide to take a dip," Fletcher says.

"We're more productive after swimming," Pearle says.

"High tide is at three today. We hope you will join us," Bridget says.

I take Ella back to the house and help her get settled into her new digs.

"This is way cool," Ella says. "I love the view of the garden and the river."

"Look, Ouida just got home," I say.

Ella's laugh is contagious.

"Do you want to see my cello?"

"Yes, I'd love to."

She unlatches the case.

"Where are *your* parents?" She asks.

"They're deceased."

She strokes a cake of amber rosin across the horsehair of her Pernambuco bow.

"Do you miss them?"

I'm surprised when she doesn't say she's sorry like everyone else. I decide to keep my gloomy can of worms closed.

"Well, we have to honor the exit plans we make on the other side. I'm comforted to know that they are just three feet above us, basking in the love of the spirit world and that their love is always in my heart."

Ella takes out her Italian cello circa 1750. It has a maple neck, silver strings, complex varnish, curved bouts, slender neck, carved scroll, inlaid purfling, and a curly maple back. I imagination-paint Ella adjusting the end-pin, holding the cello between her knees and balancing her sit bones.

She takes a deep breath, plays long tones, adjusts the pegs, complements the room sound, and then plays the opening of the Elgar Cello Concerto.

I shut my eyes. I'm transformed. The cello releases tangled-up negativity. At the end of the first movement, Ella stops playing.

"Ella, you play so expressively. Your tone is bravado."

"Thanks! I've been working on the Elgar since I was like twelve. I've vowed to memorize the other movements this summer."

I soak up her youthful exuberance.

"How long are your practice sessions?" I ask.

"I strive for three-hour sessions twice a day," she says.

"Me, too," I say.

"Ella, please let me know if you need anything."

"Um, Miss Mary, I don't eat meat, but no worries," Ella says.

"Ella, we're all vegans! Everyone will be so happy that you self-weaned!"

"The Law of Attraction in action," she laughs.

"So, true. I'll let you practice."

I head to the art room, slip on my smock and prepare my palette. I listen to Ella glide up to a high pitch, hold it with a wobbly vibrato, and then glide back to the original pitch.

That summer, Ella joins us for group meditation, yoga, high tide swims, and family suppers. Otherwise, she is in her room listening to YouTube videos, web-conferencing, skyping cello lessons, and ironing out details of the symphony she is composing.

We strive to move freely in time and space. We remain conscious of our plight to be rule free. We dive deeper into our imaginations to create a curriculum that teaches peace, compassion, meditation, yoga, and organic edible plant-based education.

We start online blogs, and every Friday night we meet to discuss our trials and tribulations.

"Thanks for participating in my new online blog, *Perfect is the Enemy of Good*," Pearle says.

I think about Pearle's mother committing suicide. Pearle is noble.

"We're discussing skepticism versus cynicism, the high stakes that perfectionists feel for risk-taking, thinking outside the box, love-wisdom versus know-it-alls, and emphasizing process over perfection," Pearle says. "Fletcher, you're next."

"Pearle, the comments have been boss. My 'rents teach math at Emory, and they freaked me out about being perfect. Teaching process over perfection is rad, dudes. Great blog. Thanks, Pearle. So, dudes, the ocean remains flat. I know, right? No surf sessions again this week," Fletcher says.

"Let's take a moment to think waves," Marshall says.

We shut our eyes. I see myself hang ten.

"This is a big week for Island Explorers with the full Blue Moon and flood tides. We'll be leaving the dock around ten P.M. all week. Let's remember to cat nap so we have the energy to evoke a solid cry to the House of Shamballa. Bridget and Bo are up."

"The past three Grow Kids' Veggie Patches' installs are rocking," Bridget says. "Thanks for volunteering."

"Tomorrow, we invite you to join us for the Mella Elementary

School install. Remember, nothing feels better than helping kids get their hands in the dirt."

"Teaching kids how to grow their own food is the ticket," Bridget says.

Millie, Greta, and Marjorie take turns.

"We have been throwing seed bombs," Millie says seriously. "Cosmos, collards, and kale are sprouting all over Savannah. I think this is a good way to spread the love."

Greta and Marjorie have more hits on their blog than the rest of us combined.

"Okay, this just in," Greta laughs. "We've started a new post called Staying Grounded," Marjorie says.

"We're talking about asking Gaia to help keep us grounded. We're teaching how to exhale negative energy to the center of the earth and inhale positive life-giving earth energy back," Marjorie says.

"We help people learn to fully shield themselves in 'the bubble of white light,'" Greta says.

"We're excited to connect with thousands of Rainbows, Crystals, and Indigos," Greta says.

Next, they invite Rosemarie to speak.

"Mad Mother's Against Monsanto loved Bo and Bridget's raw vegan class. Not only did they rave about the cuisine, but they also say they're serving their families more living enzymes. And I have twelve more moms signed up for next month's class," Rosemarie says. "Mary is up next. I love the comments on your new blog."

"Thanks, I call it *Emotional Intelligence 101*. The comments have been stellar. We're discussing ways to stay upbeat, ideas to improve our listening skills and express our feelings, and positive ways to release negative emotions."

"I liked the comment that a real smile makes the orbicular oculi muscles dip down," Marshall says.

The kids lose composure when we practice genuine smiling.

"Let's listen to Crew. He has big news," I say.

"The feds slapped Doolittle Development with a whopper fine and revoked his permits. Right now, Pigeon Island will remain pristine."

We cheer.

"Like my Grand used to say, 'Ya gots dado it mo dan ten thousand times to gits the magic!'" Pearle says.

When everybody erupts in celebratory side conversations, I slip away to the art room. I've been working on this still life for weeks. I deep breathe. Time is an illusion.

Fletcher knocks on the studio door.

"Hey, Mary, can I talk to you?" he asks.

"Yes, of course, Fletcher."

"I know I have a rose-colored version of reality. I'm generally chill, but I can easily get my feelings hurt."

"Fletcher, is this about Bridget?"

"Maybe what I'm doing isn't working. Maybe I should try something else."

"Keep your power, Fletcher. Keep your loggerhead-alligator spirit. Be true to who you are."

"Day and night, night and day, I can't get her out of my mind, and she doesn't see. She just doesn't see."

"You are being asked to learn patience."

"I'm like an inept young sloth grabbing my own arms and legs instead of the tree limb and falling out of the tree."

"Talk to yourself in the same spontaneous, forgiving, loving, laughing voice of the man we all admire."

"Thanks, Mary. You build me up, but, dude, the ocean is flat.

There hasn't been a wave in weeks. When I'm with my most precious possession, my longboard, clandestine inside the barrel, all is good. But working with Bridget in the garden and taking her on full moon cruises is sick."

He spills his guts. I radiate love and understanding.

TWENTY-FOUR

After the morning routine, I take Manfred for a walk down the avenue of oaks. The record heat persists. We're visualizing that the nor'easter that is predicted to hit this weekend will bring cooler temps and big waves.

I open the mailbox. DHEC propaganda, a letter from Grandmama Sharon, and a note from Omar. I open Grandmama Sharon's letter first.

Dearest Mary,

I hope this letter finds you well, love. Everything is good in Dingle. My two Irish Folklore classes are off to a good start and, as usual, my students bring me joy.

The faculty at Diseart Institute sends their love. We are excited that Wisdom Seeker is materializing. Isn't the Law of Attraction a wonderful thing?

Mary, love, I awoke last night at three A.M.. Isis was present, and she asked me to throw the stones for you.

Love, brace yourself. Although Savannah won't be hit

directly, a hurricane will cause massive destruction from the tropics to the Carolinas.

Mr. Nicopane is moving back to his home on Wilmington Island, and he is intent on destroying Wisdom Seeker. Mary, love, it gives me the shivers how the hurricane energy will fuel Mr. Nicopane's vindictiveness.

Again, love, it is the size of his stomach that will determine when the time is right for you to act as a Change-Agent. Isis is confident that you will know, love, if only you will listen and be receptive to her soft voice, she will always be there to guide you.

On a bright note, my heart is with you and Omar as your wedding day approaches. My blessing is that you will be surrounded by happiness, joy, and peace forever.

Mary, stand tall in that church and radiate pure love where feminine truth is so desperately needed.

Love,
Grandmama Sharon

I reread the letter. Why does Mr. Nicopane always crawl back? Why?

I open Omar's letter. More delays make it impossible for him to leave Egypt. Yuck, I have to call the church lady and cancel our counseling session again. Omar is exasperating.

I paint until the tide comes in, join the others on the dock, and dive into the river. Manfred is chill floating on his little raft. Finally, Ouida and Manfred can tolerate one another.

Pearle debuts Ella's awe-inspiring Peace Mantra called "Sounders," inspired by the didgeridoo, planetary gongs, chimes, and Tibetan singing bowls. Pearle's soprano voice is unworldly.

Greta, Marjorie, and Millie pretend to be wish-givers. They grant

Mother Earth, humanity, and the animal kingdom a fun life with plenty of clean air, pure food, good soil, and connectedness to our unique place in the cosmos.

Our group is diverse yet one. We share our wisdom, wit, and some pretty good jokes. After a few hours, we pull ourselves out of the river and layout on the floating dock to sun-dry.

"This heat sure doesn't feel like fall," I say.

"I did feel a chill in my bones this morning," Pearle says.

"The chill is from what's to come," Marjorie says.

"We might as well tell you now," Greta says. "We both dreamed a hurricane is heading this way."

"The hurricane's name starts with 'N.' We saw grand oaks down and pine trees being snapped like toothpicks," Marjorie says.

"I received a letter from Grandmama Sharon today. She also predicts a big storm," I say.

"Not a big storm, a hurricane," Greta says.

"Grandmama Sharon is right on," Marjorie says.

Bridget and Bo tense up. Hurricanes have hit Puerto Rico and Homestead hard. Pearle is noble. Daufuskie has been devastated, too.

"We will be prepared and hope for the best," Rosemarie says.

"Grandmama Sharon also predicts Mr. Nicopane is coming home." I wait for the disappointment to settle.

"Let's attempt to be optimistic and visualize peace," Marshall says.

"Hey, it's been twelve hours; I bet the pizzas are ready," Bo says.

"Dudes, I've been dreaming about those pies all day," Fletcher says.

When we get back to the house, it smells like an Italian restaurant. The spiralized zucchini, hemp seeds, rosemary, and thyme crust is sublimely chewy, and the sundried tomatoes, Medjool date sauce is intense. The cheeze is a creamy blend of soaked macadamia nuts, sea salt, apple cider vinegar, lemon, basil, and oregano. Too good. Live Enzymes. One hundred percent nutrient dense. Who knew raw vegan pineapple, shitake, black olive, and spinach pizza would be this off the charts delicious?

"Living food rocks my world," Ella says.

"Ditto," Millie says.

"What's not to like?" I say.

That afternoon, my Fairy Magic Class graduates to fieldwork. Greta, Marjorie, Millie, and I walk to Wise Woo Marina and buy two quarts of Roy Day raw organic goat cream. We cut across the May Howard playground, slip into the maritime forest, and enter the portal. Mossy Snellbaad is nursing a brown jug of poteen. He's clad in Dickey cargo pants and a 'Crumble Corporate America' t-shirt. He's kicking up his heels, dancing a fast gig, and holding onto his pot of glistening gold. His unkempt green hairy feet are matted with twigs and leaves.

"*Dia Duit*, Kali goddesses."

He bows deeply and loses his balance.

The girls get the giggles. It's all over.

They offer Mossy Snellbaad the cream.

"Well knock me over and steal muh' teeth. It don't take much: meditation, muses, and cccreammm."

He gulps the entire pint down in one long swallow.

"Oh jah, oh jah. Come with me. Let's take a look-see."

Underneath a dense patch of palmettos and scrub oak, Mossy's possum, Scarlatti, is nursing seventeen baby possums. When we fill the wooden bowl with cream, Scarlatti lifts her hind leg and pushes her babies off her cracked nipples.

Scarlatti's mate, O, Scarlatti, and Deer Helen, Mossy's sweet miniature deer, lap up the second pint of cream. Adorable. Mossy takes out a tin whistle from his hidden pocket on the side of his top hat and plays a strange adagio. Then the tempo kicks up and we Irish Step Dance until we get dizzy.

"Ok, yous best get going now. Lil chilen in da woods after dark is scccery, sccery."

Owls hoot when we're crossing the golf course. We jog down the avenue of oaks and get back to the house just as Crew, Rosemarie, and Marshall arrive for family supper.

Tonight is sunburger night. We pull warm flax buns out of the dehydrator. Bridget Vitamixes a cream of sweet potato and butternut squash soup. I make rainbow slaw with red and green cabbage, purple carrots, celery, dill, ginger, turmeric, orange and yellow sweet peppers, parsley, kale, and dill. Bo makes a lemon juice, date, cashew cream dressing.

We fix beautiful plates, bless the food, and take a moment to visualize humanity desiring and having access to clean food. We savor our aromatic gourmet raw food creations.

"Omar wrote. Phase one of the Oglethorpe Inn is finally complete. The property is officially asbestos, lead, and mold free."

We toast.

"Divine timing," Bo says. "We're ready to start the kitchen garden Monday morning."

"Crew, we don't know how to thank you enough. That Kubota is fast," Bo says.

"My pleasure," Crew says. "That's what trust fund babies are for."

"We finished planting the citrus, blueberries, blackberries, and raspberries in one week," Bridget says.

"Tomorrow we're digging into the butterfly and cut flower gardens," Bo says.

"Bridget rocks the red Kubota," Fletcher says.

"You're not bad yourself," Bridget says.

"Mary," Crew changes topic, "Will Omar be arriving this weekend?" Crew asks.

"No. He's still stuck in Egypt."

Ella ignores Crew's long sigh and changes the topic.

"I watched the trailer to Omar's new film. The soundtrack, composed by Rik Seixas, blew me away."

"Good news," Bo says. "May Howard School approved our Grow Kids Veggie Patch install proposal."

"I applaud you for your persistence and charisma," I say.

"The shift," Ella says.

Resisting my urge to hang out, I slip away to the art room. Tonight's the night I will finish my still life. I put on my smock and prepare my palette.

Monkey brain is relentless. Omar keeps canceling. The press is crazed. The church lady seemed suspicious when I blundered on why I was canceling our third counseling session. What if Savannah finds out this wedding is fake, or worse, that Omar is bisexual? How cruel will *the Tongue* be then?

I finish my painting at three A.M.. Yippee, *fine*. Sleep deprived, I thank my muses, walk out to the verandah, and collapse in my Yucatan hammock. I watch the half-moon reflection shimmering across the choppy river until I fall asleep.

The next day, Mr. Nicopane, Flambé, and Juicy return home. Within twenty-four hours, his evil spirit has seeped into every nook and cranny of our psyches. We make positive affirmations, perform *Gho*, and ask our spirits to allow negativity to pass by us like the wind. Flambé, Juicy, and Manfred constantly fence fight. Time moves like we're walking through pluff mud.

Omar arrives in Savannah a week before the wedding. The calendar is packed with nonstop meet and greets. He doesn't miss a beat. Omar prides himself on memorizing names and faces. He's quick-witted and has the uncanny ability to make stuck up people chuckle. I stay focused on keeping my facial expressions neutral in a sea of pretentiousness.

The morning of our counseling session, I feel despair. The limo takes us to Christ Episcopal Church.

"The Mother Church of Georgia founded in 1733." Omar reads the commemoration.

"In the New Age, Mother Church and the rest of humanity will shift and finally worship Mother Earth, who provides their homes," I say.

We climb the marble stairwell, open the enormous red double doors, and enter the nave.

"It's cold as a morgue in here," I say. "What a waste of coal."

A lanky man materializes from nowhere and scares us both.

"Hello. I'm Father Nose."

"Pleased to meet you. I'm Omar Victor, and this is my fiancée, Mary Howard. Your sanctuary is exquisite," Omar says.

"Yes, and we have the rarest Paul Revere and Sons Bell in the country."

Father Nose speaks with a Geechie-Brit accent that immediately gets under my skin. Right off the bat, we're quilted into joining Christ Episcopal Church. I cover my solar plexus, put up psychic vampire mirrors, and refrain from telling him I am proudly unbaptized.

We follow Father Nose to his office. When we're seated, he looks over his reading glasses and goes into another long-winded rant to tithe to Christ Episcopal Church or else.

When Father Nose exhausts all hope of getting us to pledge membership, he lunges into fees for the parish, off-street parking fees, custodian fees, celebrant service fees, altar server fees, and pre-marital counseling fees.

Omar writes a dozen checks and then Father Nose starts the counseling session.

"Why have you chosen to submit to Omar Victor?" Father Nose asks.

"Submit?" I cringe. "Well, at first, I fell for his exotic skin tone, then his hot ripped body, but ultimately, between you and me, the deal-maker was his enormous," I pause for drama, "bankroll."

Surprisingly, Father Nose is okay with my answer.

"Although my wife is a woman of the Bible and Christ, our Savior, she's gotten very fat in the hips and butt," Father Nose says. "Isn't that a shame?"

Dead silence. Is this a sacramental confession or what?

"Now she is involved in a class-action lawsuit against Thunderbolt Village. Have you heard about this?"

"No, what's up?" I ask.

"Thunderbolt housewives claim thieves are raiding their larders."

The Leprechauns that Mossy Snellbaad warned me about pop into my head.

"Peace be with you," Omar says.

"And peace with you," Father Nose says. "Listen, what I struggle with is if thieves are stealing all of the ice cream, butter, and hard cheeses, then why has her badonkadonk grown trunk sized?"

"Consumption and expenditure of calories control weight," I say.

"I just don't know who to believe," Father Nose buries his head in his hands.

"May God make you succeed," Omar says. "Will that be all, Father Nose?"

"Yes, I give you my consent to marry in this holy place of worship. And do be warned that we take overtime very seriously at Christ Episcopal Church."

"I'll keep that in mind," Omar says. "Good day."

"Hey, good luck with your wife," I say.

We head to Johnny Harris Restaurant and hide out in a dark booth. When the cocktail waitress finally appears, we order double Bushmills 1608 and study the same menu that has featured brown food since 1924.

Omar orders fried oysters and onion rings. I order a salad and steamed broccoli. After forever, our food arrives. Yuck, could vegetables be any more lifeless?

After the second round of Bushmills, we head outside.

"Unreal, the heat hasn't let up," Omar says.

We hit heavy traffic on the way back to Wilmington. By the time we get home, we have under one hour to get cleaned up and leave again. I shower, tie my wild red hair on top of my head, and slip on my new glam gown.

I push and twist the locking closures to all four Cleopatra white gold necklaces laced with pearls, chrysoprase rock, crystals, and carnelian. Ha, this is who I am to the elite.

Traffic doesn't let up. Omar constantly checks his watch. High society takes cocktail hour seriously.

We roll into the private country estate on Hutchinson Island right on time. I visualize busting up the fabulously manicured lawn and installing raised beds, cover crops, and fruit and nut trees. I am a change-agent. I will shift Savannah to love-based.

Cocktail hour is a glamorous buzz. Champagne is nonstop.

Servers pass an occasional tray of grilled veggies, but I can never get away from well-wishers.

Mayor Archibald Doolittle III, squeezed into a tux, waddles over to congratulate us. Trickster is testing me. What would Isis do right now? She would shut up about the poor, the homeless, animal agriculture, GMOs, and farmer suffering until she lured her opposition to her side. I take a deep breath. Patience. Everyone achieves Unity in an average of seven-hundred-and-seventy-seven lifetimes, even Mayor Archibald Doolittle III.

I shake hands with the Mayor, penetrate him with vexes, and move as far away as possible from his sleazy spirit.

By the end of cocktail hour, I'm drunk. Slow down.

The elegant wait staff escorts us to the grand dining room. The décor is lavish, but the art is cheap. Why?

When Omar's friends cheer us on, we drink a shot of Bushmills and smooch. Finally, servers start bringing out dinner. My vegan meal is the last to arrive. What in the world? Everything is dripping with cheddar cheese, butter, sour cream, and bacon crumbles. I send it back and wait for eternity. The next attempt is a small bowl of broccoli covered in cheese sauce. Pass. Are southern chefs trying to kill us with cholesterol?

Wine is raw vegan. Relax.

Mayor Archibald Doolittle III leaves when we're heading to the dance floor. Thank you, Universe.

Drunk is drunk, and things get wild on the dance floor. When guests cheer us on, Omar kisses me, and I kiss back. We go on and on like this until three A.M..

I wake up on the big day with a killer hangover. I'm dragging during the morning routine. Makeup and hair artists arrive at two in the afternoon. An hour later, I have a sneezing fit from the chemicals they are using. Shortly after, I get the first nosebleed of my life.

"Sit down and lean forward," Pearle says. "It reduces blood pressure in your nose veins."

"That feels better," I say. "Gratitude for Voodoo healers."

The limo arrives, and we drive downtown.

The church is freezing. The wedding coordinator, Anne-Linda, introduces herself. How is she not wearing a coat in here? I bend down to tie my shoe and get another nosebleed. Anne-Linda pinches my nose, tells me breathe through my mouth, and rushes me upstairs. I'm freaked.

I think through Pearle's relaxation techniques and begin to imagine five sounds, smells, and tastes. By the time I'm on the third or fourth sight, the nosebleed stops.

Right before ceremony time, wardrobe arrives and helps me into my forty-thousand-dollar silk tulle beaded pearl bias-cut gown and matching beaded pearl slippers.

Anne-Linda helps me downstairs. Crew and I wait for the sixteen bar cello quartet fanfare, and then walk hand and hand down the aisle. I'm trembling.

We walk to the altar and Crew lifts my veil. He kisses me and gives me to Omar. I recognize the two dozen professional models, our bridesmaids and groomsmen, from the rehearsal dinner last night.

"Dearly beloved, we are gathered together here in the sign of God and in the face of this company to join together this man and this woman in holy matrimony, which is not to be entered into unadvisedly, but reverently and solemnly," Father Nose says. "If any person can show just cause why they may not be joined together, let them speak now or forever hold their peace."

Good, let's move on Father Nose, I communicate with him telepathically.

I invite my soul to rest on my heart and focus on radiating feminine love and pure truth into the church.

Father Nose starts out preaching about submissiveness, pain, suffering, and poverty before going on a twenty-minute rant about death, lost hope, despair, bitterness, pity, and oppression.

His Geechie-Brit accent stings like biting flies.

After we recite the vows, Father Nose pronounces us husband

and wife, and Omar performs the sweeping *Gone with the Wind* kiss.

We turn to the congregation. Father Nose presents us as Mr. and Mrs. Omar Victor, and we recess to Ella's original for two violins, four cellos, oboe, two French horns, and piccolo trumpet.

"I want to kiss this concrete," I say.

"The ceremony was suitable for the dead," Omar says.

"No need to ask why the divorce rate is sky high," I say.

"Cocktail hour will alleviate our pain."

"Not until we greet three hundred guests."

"I'm melting," Omar says. "Record heat this late in the fall is one detail I overlooked."

"Look, paparazzi," I say.

"And here comes the guests. Smile," Omar says.

I only allow myself to think about Unity Consciousness and our love-based take-over scheme.

We arrive at Brockington Hall, pound French champagne, and then switch to Mint Juleps. I'm past hunger when the hors-d'oeuvres are served and fall off the vegan wagon with deviled quail eggs, oysters rockefeller, and Beluga caviar on cucumber slices.

When we get to the dining room, we switch to Bushmills. Bridget and Bo are nonjudgmental when I chow down on lavender pheasant and Bluefin tuna. Ten percent debauchery, right?

After we cut the triple-layer caramel cake, we switch to premium Jamaican Rum and dance nonstop until it's time to make our grand exit through pelting rice.

"Big relief," I say.

"You perform well," Omar says.

"I do my best under pressure."

"I've got your back, Mary Howard."

Uneventfully, we head to the airport and Omar leaves for Egypt.

Everybody is asleep when I get home. I escape from the wedding dress, scrub the makeup off my face, and crawl into bed. Naked and alone isn't cliché anymore. Yuck, my poor digestive system. I trashed my temple. I drift off to sleep.

When the phone rings the next morning, I jolt out of my recurring barracuda nightmare. Ouch, hangover. Daddy, I accept your exit plan. Please free me from seeing your bloody demise again and again. Love, love, love.

"Good morning."

"Hey, Mary, Crew here. Wow, that was some shindig last night. I'd like to see Omar's real wedding."

"You're funny. Thanks for walking me down the aisle. What's up?"

"I've been waiting for a break in your social life. I need to talk. Can I come over?"

"Yes, of course."

"Thanks, I'm on the river. I should be there within the hour."

"Great, see you soon."

Oh, my poor gut flora. And the poor birds and fish I ate. What a screw-up. I stop myself. I am a warrior. As of this moment, I am back on the vegan path.

When Ella breaks from practicing, I knock on her door.

"Good morning," Ella says. "Come on in."

"Hey there," I say. "The music you composed for the ceremony was stunning."

"Thanks much," Ella says. "I bet you feel relieved."

"Major relief. How's the third movement coming along?"

"Way cool. I do believe that every single transition is finally committed to my long-term memory," Ella says.

"Wonderful. Where is everybody?"

"They just left for the library and Brighter Day," Ella says.

"What time is your lesson today?"

"Noon," Ella laughs. "I can hardly wait I love my new teacher so much!"

"The principal cellist of the Atlanta Symphony?" I ask.

"Yes. I love the way he plays and teaches," Ella says. "Are you stretching canvases today?"

"Maybe later, but right now I'm heading to the dock to meet Crew."

"Miss Mary, sorry, but DHEC was here today, and Wisdom Seeker kitchen is officially shut down," she says.

She puts her cello down and gives me a hug.

"We are warriors. No regrets," I say. "Hey, happy practicing. See you at high tide."

I walk to the dock and Spiritfly-meditate. Monkey brain is crazed thinking about no kitchen. How can they do that? I stop myself. Warriors don't ask how. I have the unbending intent to quash DHEC. I am in alignment with good and have Universal support.

Crumble DHEC.

Crew pulls up in *Bottom Line*, ties off, and gives me a bear hug.

TWENTY-FIVE

"What I'm about to do is against police code." Crew takes a mini digital recorder from his backpack.

"You have my word," I say.

"This is regarding a situation on Pigeon Island."

"Isn't Pigeon Island uninhabited?"

"It is, except for one lady who is Deep South-eccentric."

"You pique my interest."

Crew hits play.

"Please state your full name."

Beep, beep, beep.

"Address?"

"One, Pigeon Island," The voice says.

"Occupation?"

"Mermaid, um, seductress," she snorts.

"Have you had cream stolen from your property?"

"Does this look like a body that consumes cream?"

"Do you have a description of the thieves?"

"Three feet tall, green coats, red breeches buckled at the knee, woolen stockings, wide-brimmed top hats worn slightly askew with secret pockets, move quicker than the human eye can see, constantly smoking foul-smelling pipes, surly and sour dispositions, argumentative, drunken, moody, and not noted for personal hygiene."

"Do you take any types of mind-altering drugs?"

"Eewee, baby, yes, recreational Colorado K.B. in my Aladdin bong, every two hours."

"Please answer the questions 'yes' or 'no.'"

"You're silly," she giggles.

"Ma'am, no police procedures, no complaint filed, and no investigation."

"You wear your police uniform tight. I like a man who is looking for a woman full of surprises. Baby, let me…"

"Please, focus on the cream crimes."

"Eewee, I got hot when you said cream crime," she snorts. "How about you unleash my hundred-year mermaid itch, Chief?"

"Do you feel that you are of sound mind?"

"I'm not the most enlightened avatar in the deck, but I've evolved past the karma phase. Chief, my hard body is loads o'fun. Feel my arse."

"Ma'am, follow the rules."

She snorts and laughs.

"Do you, or anyone you know, have information about the cream crimes?"

"Hard to get or good and hard?"

"Stop that. Please."

"Boys will be boys and so will men."

"Is there a specific time the cream is stolen?"

"Full moons."

"Describe the sounds you hear."

"They speak in ultra-high-pitched Gaelic with a Glocca Morra lilt. Jeez, don't you know anything?"

"Continue."

"Leprechauns raid fat people's larders to lark with their karma. If you help me wrangle the leprechauns, you will win the race for Mayor."

Silence.

"Ma'am, I am not running for Mayor."

"Smartypants. Straight A student. Gold sticker winner. Know-it-all. Brat."

I raise one eyebrow. Crew blushes.

"Please, can we get back to the cream crimes?" Crew persists.

"Mr. Big Ego," she keeps roasting him. Five sensor."

"Ma'am, why should I listen to you?"

"Because lil' old me, a run of the mill, straight-talker multi-dimensional has been assigned by the Masters to urge you into New Age Politics because of your understanding of trust and sharing. And I have permission to whack you on your arse if need be."

"Ma'am, do you have any further information about the cream crimes?"

"Meet me at the next full moon and I'll show you the proverbial cream flying."

"Do you consider this to be a potentially dangerous situation?"

"It is more mysterious than dangerous."

"Is there anything else?"

"Yeah, when you come back, bring me some Jack H. Skunk Weed. Eewee, baby, I'll sure show you a good time."

Crew hits the stop button.

"Have you been back?"

"Yes; it is terrifying paranormal stuff."

"It could be a hoax."

"That's what I suspected. But dozens of victims have come forward with the same three feet, striped breeches, and green top hats, and all of the crimes occur during full moons."

"Did you sleep with her?"

"I can't believe I fell for the whole pent-up mermaid story."

"What now?"

"She's got million dollar legs; she's hot."

"I mean with the cream crimes."

"Sorry, I'm distracted. We caught the Leprechauns on thermal camera, but the whole 'ethereal' mess is a roadblock. You're the fairy expert. What should we do?"

"Leprechauns are tricky. Do you think your friend will allow Mossy Snellbaad and me to help?"

"Yes, she has already agreed," Crew says. "Mary, if this leaks, I'll be the laughingstock of Thunderbolt Village."

"No worries. Mossy and I will make this happen under the radar," I say. "Crew, what's up with her Mayor prediction?"

"I wanted you to be the first to know," he says. "I've joined the race."

"Alright! You've built an impressive constituency."

"I'm going to roll up my sleeves and get to work."

"Mayor Crew, the voice of New Age government."

"I'm happy marriage didn't change you," he gives me a bear hug.

"You're funny."

"Marshall and Rosemarie invited us to brunch," Crew says.

"That sounds fun. I'll motor over in a few."

Crew takes off, and I jump in *One That Got Away*. I shove off just as Mr. Nicopane, Flambé, and Juicy walk out on their dock. The dogs race to the floating dock barking wildly. I whistle for Ouida; she nestles against me, and I open throttle.

Marshall greets me. I change it up today and burn one, like every morning before high school, in the olden days. Oh, jah baby.

When we get back to the house, Crew and Rosemarie are putting out an amazing raw vegan spread. We sit down at the kitchen table, and Marshall blesses the food.

"Everything is enzymatically delicious," I say.

We talk about eye candy last night and thankfully move on.

"Hey, what's up with the bizarre string of thefts in Thunderbolt Village?" Rosemarie asks.

"A group of pranksters is stealing ultra-pasteurized dairy products," Crew says.

"Strange, the victims have all been fat," Marshall says.

"Did you ever think they might be good guys removing temptation and fighting obesity?" Rosemarie asks.

"I never thought of it that way before," Crew admits. "These guys do go for the hard cheeses, butter, and ultra-pasteurized heavy cream."

"Maybe animal rights activists are involved," Marshall says.

"From notmilk.com to milkthemostmucusyfoodontheplanet.com, every activist organization is clean," Crew says.

"You always crack the case," I say.

"Hey, I don't know if you've heard yet, but family supper will be here tonight," Rosemarie says.

"Ella told me we failed inspection this morning," I say. "Were you there?"

"Yes, when we finished green smoothie klatch, the DHEC food police busted in like the Gestapo. They tore the kitchen apart searching for bleach. When they came up empty-handed, they said we weren't allowed to boil hotdogs or even make toast.

"Bridget was livid. She chased them out with tongs, screaming, 'Get your filthy colons and dark yellow pissy-selves out of my sacred kitchen,'" Rosemarie says.

We laugh.

"It was a good thing I slept through the ordeal," I say.

"DHEC's tangled web of stupidity," Crew says.

"They will crumble in a sea of lies," I say.

"Meanwhile, we give them zero power," Marshall says.

"Absolutely," I say. "Hey, Crew has an announcement."

"I've entered the race for Mayor," Crew says.

We group hug.

"My platform is sustainability and peace," Crew says. "If the Thunderbolt Police Department can shift to be of service then Savannah will shift, too."

"The 'Savannah Shift' campaign!" Marshall says.

"Hey, that's catchy," I say.

"Let's make it stick," Crew says. "I'll announce my candidacy at the Cucurbit Pepo Pageant next week."

"Parallel Reality times infinity," Rosemarie says.

The vision I had during the last Full Blue Moon Evocation when Guide said change is coming soon, pops into my head.

"Hopefully, storms will hold off another week," Crew says.

"Grandmama Sharon and the twins' predictions are looming," I say.

"I'd suggest that we get started on some overdue chainsaw work," Marshall says.

"Sounds like a good plan," Crew says.

"Good, we need fresh oak limbs to inoculate more shiitake spores," Rosemarie says.

"I'll round up the troops and come back with the van," I say.

I walk back to the dock, whistle for Ouida, and we motor home. A wave of sadness floods my emotions. I dig down to the root of the matter. Oh, it's Omar. I kindly coax my inner-child to let go.

When I get home, we load the van with coolers, chainsaws, and ladders and bust out yard work on all of our properties until dark.

We head back to Marshall and Rosemarie's house for a fun first family supper change-up. Before we leave, Crew fills us in on the tropical depression that is stalled over the Atlantic.

The next morning, the system is upgraded and named Hurricane Nadia. During meditation, we radiate love to the island people and animals in the path of Hurricane Nadia.

Wednesday and Thursday, Hurricane Nadia stalls over the Atlantic. Thursday night we make a call to go ahead with the Cucurbit Pepo Pageant this weekend.

Saturday morning we load up the van and head to the May Howard School playground. Record heat persists.

By five P.M., I make the final rounds. The vendors have doubled this year. We're set. I take Manfred for a quick walk before the twins start their first psychic reading.

Freak out. What is Mr. Nicopane doing here? Yuck, his stomach is personal watermelon-sized. What does it mean? Manfred rips the leash out of my hand and pins Mr. Nicopane against the red brick corner of the primary wing.

"Manfred, come!"

He ignores me, growls, and bares teeth.

"Manfred, come!"

Manfred lifts his short leg and pees on Mr. Nicopane, backs away, and heels by my side. Mr. Nicopane's evil spirit penetrates me. I shiver.

"I'd be happy to buy you new pants."

"Judgment Day has cometh for heathens, heretics, witches, sodomites, and Satan worshipers. You and yours will be tortured for eternity for your transgressions."

I look straight into his yellow-grey eyes and tell him I don't believe his ill omens. He leaves.

I oxygenate. Tonight is for Unity.

I take Manfred back to the twins' booth, run to the stage, and cue Marshall to start.

"Welcome, friends. I'm Grand Marshal Marshall, here to kick off the annual Cucurbit Pepo Pageant Unity Consciousness celebration. Thank you all for being here!" Marshall says. "Without further ado, let's give it up for Mayor Archibald Doolittle III, the one, and only permit-giver."

Seven vultures land on the stage. Mayor Archibald III waddles to the mic and drops his two-page speech. When he bends over to pick it up, he exposes his curvaceous woman's behind. The crowd chuckles.

"Ladies and gentlemen, distinguished guests, and esteemed colleagues," he says, whistling S's and creating mic feedback.

"Another twenty-minute speech based on myth, his private set of beliefs, and a secret agenda," Rosemarie says.

"Vote for me! Land development is the vaccination shot Savannah needs! Magna Carta, Magna Carta, Magna Carta. Thank you, goodnight."

Crew takes the mic. The crowd cheers.

"Mayor Doolittle, Magna Carta was a power tradeoff between the king and the land-owning barons. Magna Carta represents a gang of hairy, unwashed pilgrims, showing up on the Indigenous People's beloved shores and stealing the corn they had preserved to survive winter. Magna Carta does not support group responsibility, make provisions for free speech, or freedom of assembly."

Crew points to the Mayor leaving the parking lot in his green Range Rover Holland and Holland. The crowd boos.

"Magna Carta is not the birthplace of civil rights, and Savannah demands more than power tradeoffs!" He waits for wild cheers. "I stand before you tonight, to officially announce my candidacy for Mayor of Savannah."

The crowd is deafening.

"We will end oligarchy."

Group energy skyrockets.

"Unity, equality, and justice."

Crew waits for applause and cheers after every sentence.

"The time is now to be visionary, focus on truth, and honor Mother Nature. The time is now to teach peace and compassion to every walk of life. The time is now for the Savannah Shift."

We chant, 'Savannah Shift.' Strangers embrace. The AME Gospel Songbirds C-3 organ player hits a crazy chord that lifts our spirits to seventh heaven for a rock solid hour of spirituals.

Afterward, the Savannah Rhythm Section takes the stage. They kick it off with a funky bass groove that gets the crowd dancing.

Wise Hoe Woo's silent firework show caps off the perfect night. We're supercharged.

That night, Mr. Nicopane visits me in my dream. Fear consumes me; he slays my Goddess Power and destroys Wisdom Seeker.

The next morning, Hurricane Nadia turns. The National Weather Service predicts Georgia will be spared, but the Carolinas will be hit by midnight.

"Psychic predictions are more reliable than Doppler Radars," Greta says.

"We're in for high winds and heavy flooding," Marjorie says.

I wait until we finish green smoothie klatch before I spill my guts about Mr. Nicopane.

"I couldn't stop shaking," I say.

"I know the feeling. Mr. Nicopane has been looking at me through the fence," Bridget admits.

"Mr. Nicopane has been visiting me in my dreams, again," Pearle says. "Last night he got past me and took Millie away."

I hold Millie tight.

"Our light is lighting Mr. Nicopane's darkness," Greta says.

We tighten up the buddy system and update the hurricane plan. Crew takes off for work, Marshall and Rosemarie head home, and the rest of us load up the van and head to the projects.

"How'd you find Mella Elementary School?" I ask.

"We look for schools with the lowest standardized test scores," Bridget says.

"That's where Edible Education will most likely strike a chord with the principal," Bo says.

Guards unlock the gates. The new raised beds and citrus grove totally transform the vibe of this campus. Miss Tangib, the principal, comes outside to greet us. She has wild gray hair and is wearing a tie-dye hippie outfit.

"Miss Howard, we appreciate your generosity," Miss Tangib is soft-spoken. "Bridget and Bo are givers of hope."

"We appreciate your support of Organic Plant-based Edible Education," I say.

"Let's tour the raised beds, shall we?" Miss Tangib exudes compassion. "I've been in public education for forty years, and I've never seen students more excited about any other project."

"Everything is growing," Bridget says.

"The children treat these seedlings with tender loving care."

Bo and Fletcher grab the coolers, and we follow Miss Tangib to the auditorium. Chatty garden volunteers from the fourth and fifth grades file in, pull out the bleachers, and sit down.

Miss Tangib claps her hands three times, and the kids quiet down. She invites Bridget and Bo to take the podium. Bridget is wearing black skinny jeans, a white V-neck tee shirt, and purple rubber boots. Bo has on cargo shorts, a black t-shirt, and flip-flops. The students are rapt.

"We were born in Puerto Rico," Bo says. "Farmed wild fruit in

South Florida, and then moved to Wilmington Island, Savannah, Georgia, to join Wisdom Seeker."

"In addition to teaching people how to grow organic fruit and vegetables," Bridget says, "we teach people to eat healthier."

"Bridget and I are raw vegans. We advocate spiritual and physical purity, enrichment of the soul, protection of the planet, and compassion for all living creatures," Bo says.

"The Essenes, a peaceful desert tribe that lived 3000 years ago, were also raw vegans," Bridget says.

"Jesus is the most famous raw vegan Essene," Bo says.

After questions and answers, Millie, Greta, and Marjorie pick six volunteers.

"Okay, this is the fun part," Bo says.

Bridget and Bo start food processing sprouted oat groats, flax seeds, Medjool dates, Brazil nuts, young Thai coconut, coconut manna, and cocoa powder. When it is a fudge consistency, the volunteers roll out 'Raw Vegan Dough-not Holes' and sprinkle them with coconut flakes and finely chopped pecans. Big hit.

The bell sends the kids racing back to class. A shy girl with long flaxen hair stays behind. She wants to eat what Bridget eats. Principal Tangib writes her a late pass.

That afternoon, Hurricane Nadia stalls over the Atlantic east of St. Croix, St. John, and St. Thomas. That night, she races north before stalling again, two hundred miles east of Miami.

The next morning at group meditation we radiate love to island people. Although the twins predict the hurricane is fast approaching, it seems unlikely because the river is as smooth as glass, the sun is blazing through the thick haze, and the unreal, record heat persists.

TWENTY-SIX

Before Crew leaves for Thunderbolt Village, we make plans to spend the night at Marshall and Rosemarie's house so we'll all be together in case we need to evacuate.

After lunch, Marshall and Rosemarie take Fletcher, Greta, Marjorie, and Manfred back to their house to help organize meals and sleeping arrangements.

Ella volunteers to babysit Millie during her afternoon nap so Bo and Bridget can juice and dehydrate. Pearle and I make a run to the health food store.

Traffic is backed up getting off the island. By the time we hit Johnny Mercer Boulevard, the sky turns black, the wind picks up, and it starts to rain.

Victory Drive turns into a parking lot. The rain is hammering.

"It's ominous," Pearle says. "I think we should turn back."

"Good idea," I say.

After waiting an hour to get around a fender bender, we turn around. The rain is blinding. Limbs and debris are everywhere.

When we get back to Wilmington, the grand oak at the entrance to the Oglethorpe Inn is swaying.

"We'll get everybody in the van, load the coolers, and head straight to Marshall's house," I say.

We hear an explosion.

"Look out!" Pearle cries.

I slam on brakes. A massive oak crashes in front of us.

"I have a bad feeling," Pearle cries. "Run!"

We run down the avenue of oaks in the pelting rain. The house is pitch dark. I open the door. Ella is sobbing. I light the sconces. Bridget, Bo, and Ella are sitting at the kitchen table. All of us are soaked.

"We were in the library. Millie wanted to play hide-and-seek," Ella says. "I checked all of her usual spots."

"What happened?" Pearle asks.

"I was upstairs when I saw her on the floating dock. I ran out to get her. I was almost there when I saw her go airborne," Ella drops her head in her hands and weeps. "And then she vanished."

"When?" Pearle asks.

"Just now," Bo says. "We phoned Crew, and he's calling the Coast Guard."

Pearle breaks down.

"It's my fault; I'm sorry," Ella says.

"Ella, you didn't do anything wrong," I say.

Pearle and I embrace Ella.

"We're warriors," I say. We will find her."

Pearle and I suit up in slickers and hoist *One That Got Away* into the churning river.

Boston Whalers don't sink, right?

Marshall and Fletcher phone. They are heading toward Savannah, so Pearle and I take off toward the Isle of Hope.

A few hours later the wind dies down, and the rain lightens up. When the rain finally stops, I know our Guides are leading us to Millie. The phone rings. It's Crew. The Coast Guard must have found Millie.

"Hey, the Coast Guard needs you to tell them what happened, again."

"Get out!" I scream. "They've heard the same story three times. Tell them to get off their bureaucratic arses and start searching. It's a new moon. We need searchlights already."

We rendezvous at Wise Hoe Woo Marina for gas and supplies. Everyone is there. I break down, but Pearle is noble.

"There are no accidents," Pearle says. "Nothing and no event have a life of its own. *Loa Agwe* is the divine presence of the hurricane, and *Loa Agwe* will keep Millie safe until we find her."

We get back on the river. After a long night, the brilliant dawn sky gives us renewed hope. Pearle has a lucid vision of Millie sleeping in a bed of soft grass, surrounded by earth angels.

Crew phones and tells us that the Coast Guard has officially started the search. Meanwhile, Rosemarie, Bridget, and Bo have organized dozens of volunteer search teams.

Thoughts are things. I visualize seeing Millie at every bend in the river. We rendezvous back at Wise Hoe Woo Marina at noon, swap coolers, gas up, and assign new territory to cover.

Right before we shove off, Crew's phone rings.

"It's Diek Bric with the US Coast Guard Search and Rescue," Crew says. "I've got you on speaker phone. Did you find Millie?"

There's a deafening pause.

"No sir, we have not found the child. I'm calling to inform you that we are calling off the search due to Clause 666," Diek Bric says.

"Look," Crew says. "We're not talking about some devil clause; a child's life is at stake here."

"Airborne victims are subject to a maximum twenty-four-hour search. Why? Because the wind is unpredictable," Diek Brick says.

"Look, Diek, this is your opportunity to be a hero," Crew says. "What could be more important to the US Coast Guard than saving the life of a child?"

"The War on Drugs."

Marshall busts a gut. Crew hangs up.

"We're on our own," I say.

"Intuition will lead us to Millie," Pearle says.

"The twins predict Millie is safe and that we will find her soon," Rosemarie breaks down.

"Visualize Millie rescued," Marshall says.

We head out. The river is calm. We nose around river banks calling Millie's name. Thoughts are things. The sun sets. The night sky fills with stars. The waxing moon rises and lights our way. We hug the shore calling Millie's name and listening to owls hoot back. Dawn revives our hope, again.

The phone rings. Greta and Marjorie are on the line. They have a lucid vision of Millie holding a messenger bird.

"Pigeon Island!" I scream. "We're headed there now."

"I'll phone Fletcher and Marshall," Rosemarie says.

I open throttle.

We approach Pigeon Island. I slow down at the sharp bend at the mouth of the Moon River.

"We came back here on date night to smoke pot and make out," I say.

Pearle smiles indigo, and I get a positive mojo hit.

Marshall and Fletcher come around the bend. They tie off *Driftwood* and search by foot while Pearle and I motor around the circumference of the island.

"There's Millie!" Pearle screams.

Millie is sitting in the pluff mud, surrounded in a bloody battlefield of dolphins aggressively strand feeding.

"Millie, I'm coming."

"Pearle, wait!" I scream. "Oyster beds make it impossible to get there."

A woman runs out of the maritime forest. She whistles a deafening shrill and the dolphins glide back to deep water. She grabs Millie and carries her back to shore.

We follow her to a patch of beach, throw the anchor, and wade to shore. Millie. Bliss. Love, love, love.

Wait a minute. I recognize her murky green aura and million dollar legs. Is she the lady in black from Cecil Lloyd's office? What?

"I'm Pearle Isle, and this is my daughter Millie. How can I thank you enough?"

"*El gusto es mio*. The name is Moon, Moon River," she says.

Moon River, Moon River, my mind swirls.

"How did you know Millie needed help?" Pearle asks.

"I'm an Intuit. I picked up a signal from the Dubois twins. Those two pack a powerful telepathic punch," Moon River laughs and snorts.

I immediately recognize the snort from Crew's taped police interview. Could Crew and Cecil have the same lover?

"What can we ever do to repay you?" Pearle asks.

"Seeing this wee' lil' one safe is o' plenty," Moon River says.

I text Rosemarie and Marshall.

"Millie is safe. We can't stop kissing her sweet face."

Rosemarie texts back. "Woot, woot. Love you, Millie! Just got a text from Marshall. They are lost, and Marshall's phone is dead."

We board *One That Got Away*, and Moon River leads us back to *Driftwood*. Millie tells us wondrous nonstop stories. What an adventure for a five-year-old.

Fletcher and Marshall stumble to the beach. They are covered in insect bites and shaken from an encounter with a five-foot gator and they walked into a bed of baby copperheads.

Next Crew and three TVPD cops barrel out of the forest.

Moon River purrs and rubs her breasts against Crew.

"Officers, thank you for your help," Crew throws his voice. "Please take the patrol car back to the station. I'll catch a lift home by boat."

"I thought I felt your vibe deep down in my Lowcountry," she says.

"You two know each other?" Marshall asks.

"Police work," Crew says.

"Liar, liar, pants on fire," she snorts.

Now I see how Moon River got Crew to run for Mayor.

The day before the full moon, I accept my invitation from Isis to be initiated to the fourth ring of power. That afternoon, I cruise to Daufuskie and hike to my secret cove. That night I receive awe-inspiring instruction on new ways to interpret symbols that will improve my receptivity to unlock my soul's desire.

The next morning I shove off at daybreak and motor home.

That afternoon, Crew texts to say Moon River is launching the Leprechaun raid at midnight tonight. I sneak out at eleven P.M.. The rising moon lights my way to the portal.

"Namaste, Carthead!"

"Namaste, Mossy Snellbaad," I say. "Let's do this thing."

"Mossy Snellbaad at your woodsy service."

We run to May Howard School, cross the playground, and jump in the back of Crew's cop car.

"Leprechaun raid," I say.

"Where's Mr. Snellbaad?"

"Ethereal," I say.

Moon River is at the Leprechaun Camp when we get there. She cracks Mossy Snellbaad up telling Grogoch jokes.

"Okay, girls, let's do this," she snorts and whacks Crew on the behind.

Mossy Snellbaad flies to the treetop. The rest of us hide in the bush. Soon, a dozen little green guys file back to camp. How hard could this be? They pig-out on ultra-pasteurized cream, butter, ghee, cottage cheese, and brie. Gross. The cholesterol starts to clog their tiny arteries.

Mossy Snellbaad sings a soft high pitch Druid tune and lulls them into euphoria before he materializes, flies down, and scares them silly.

We make quick work wrangling the little green guys.

"Who knew a mortal chick, a popo, and a Grogoch would help me complete my earth mission?" Moon River asks.

The leprechauns, happy for a lift home, board their life raft.

Moon River strips naked. Mama.

"You were fun to play with rock candy," Moon River rubs Crew. "I bid you *adieu.*"

Moon River dives into the Moon River, changes shape, soaks us with her whale tale, and departs for the Emerald Isle.

I get home and fall into a deep sleep for a few hours before heading to the dock for sunrise meditation.

My soul is on fire with the will to do good, and I feel like anything is possible.

I spend the whole day painting, only breaking for a high tide swim and family supper. Around ten P.M., my eyes start playing tricks, and I head to bed.

I must have just dozed off when the phone rings. It's Mr. Pope.

"Mr. Pope, hello. How are you?"

"Fine, dear, it's lovely to hear your voice. How are you?"

I sense something is very wrong.

"Fine thank you. How is Grandmama Sharon?"

"She's ill, dear, and, of course, she refuses to see a physician."

"All the women in my family are that way."

"Regretfully," Mr. Pope says, "I feel her time may be soon."

"I'm sorry. I know you two are close."

"Yes, dear, we are lifelong friends," his voice cracks.

"Mr. Pope, Grandmama Sharon has always been against contaminating Mother Earth with diseased physical vehicles," I say.

"Yes, dear," Mr. Pope says. "She's made the necessary arrangements for her cremation."

It hits me that this is real.

"I'll leave Savannah tomorrow morning," I start crying. "Please let Grandmama Sharon know I'm on my way."

"That's comforting, dear. Thank you," Mr. Pope says.

When we say goodnight, I sob. I walk down the hall and knock on Pearle's door.

"What is it, honey?" Pearle asks.

"Grandmama Sharon is preparing to transition."

I break down. Pearle massages the base of my skull.

"Pearle, you and Millie come to Dingle with me. I need help."

"Sure, honey. That sounds great."

The next morning, thunderstorms make getting to the Savannah Airport stressful. We get to Atlanta on time, but our flight to New York is delayed. Millie calmly reads her books and people-watches. Two hours later, we board the flight to New York.

When we get to LaGuardia, the flight to Dublin is showing a two-hour delay. Monkey brain spirals to worst case scenarios.

We head to the food court. Millie wiggles loose, runs over to the Great American Cookies' sample tray, grabs a sugar cookie with an inch of vanilla icing and sprinkles, and stuffs it in her mouth.

"I want more!" She screams.

I'm horrified. Millie hasn't finished what's in her mouth.

"More!" She stomps her right foot.

"No way," Pearle says. "We only eat healthy cookies."

"More Mommy, I want more!"

Millie's lips quiver, she wails and throws herself down. In horror, we witness her first temper tantrum. Pearle peels her off the floor and holds her tight.

"Wow, just one bite of FDA approved preservative and flavor chemicals and Millie's peaceful warrior spirit vanishes," Pearle says.

"Shame on the FDA for profiting off of addictive chemical poisoning," I say.

When Millie calms down, we order steamed vegetable plates. Millie is defiant. When we offer her broccoli, her favorite, she holds her hands over her mouth and shakes her head, no.

When we board the flight to Dublin, Millie falls asleep.

Nerve-racking thunderstorms and headwinds make for a rough flight across the Atlantic. We land in Dublin and have no time to spare. The rains are torrential. We hail a cab and barely make the Iarnród Éirann to Limerick.

TWENTY-SEVEN

At dawn, the rain stops and the bright Irish sunshine illuminates the lush countryside. We have an hour layover in Limerick, so we take a brisk walk to a new place called Zomato, Raw and Real Juicery. We order much-needed wheatgrass shots and kale, avocado, fennel, pineapple, and coconut smoothies. Five stars. We grab vegetable wraps from the takeaway case and head back to the train station. The vegan shift is happening worldwide.

We arrive in Tralee, rush to the bus depot, and depart at noon. We arrive in Dingle on time, collect our luggage, and walk to Grandmama Sharon's cottage.

Mr. Pope answers the door. We hug.

"She's so thin," I say.

"She radiant," Pearle says.

"She remains a bright lamp for humanity until the bitter end," Mr. Pope says.

Mr. Pope leaves for some much-needed rest. Pearle, Millie, and I sit by Grandmama Sharon's side another hour before she opens her eyes.

"My beautiful earth angels, I'm happy you are here. And this must be Millie. What a wee cutie pie and with such a pure spirit."

I kiss Grandmama Sharon on the cheek and start crying. Millie nuzzles on my lap.

"Mary, love-based, joy," Millie says.

Grandmama Sharon blankets me in love.

"We've shared a beautiful earth journey together," Grandmama Sharon says. "Now, God has invited me to rest in his loving light, and I must respect my exit plan. I have removed precious stones and metals and am prepared to journey to the other side."

"A host of angels is filling the room," I say.

Grandmama Sharon squeezes my hand and then dozes off. I watch her chest rise and fall as she labors to breathe. When she wakes up, she takes my hand again.

"Mary, this is the original touch. I pass the mantle of Ancient Wisdom to you," she says.

Grandmama Sharon gasps her last breath, drops her physical body, and we witness her natural death.

"I disengage Grandmama Sharon's chakras and loosen her luminous body," I say with tears streaming. "She is prepared for Spirit Flight. The veil between worlds is thin. Grandmama Sharon is transitioning easily."

"*Sê* is back to her original state," Pearle says. "Grandmama Sharon is home now, in the metaphysical world of *Yêsùnyimê*."

"She's watching all the good she did on her earth journey," I say. My tears are unstoppable.

We call Mr. Pope. When he comes over, he covers Grandmama Sharon in soft Irish linen.

Dingle holds a three-day wake to celebrate One Hundred Years of Grandmama Sharon's truth, kindness, beauty, compassion, and love.

The day after the wake, Pearle, Millie, the kids at the orphanage,

Mr. Pope, and I set out to hike the Spiritual Way Pilgrimage.

We arrive at the base of Mt. Brandon by early afternoon. After a profoundly peaceful meditation, Pearle performs the *Yêsùny-imê* Ritual.

"Until we meet again, may God hold you in the palm of his hand," I say as I scatter Grandmama Sharon's ashes.

The kids recite WB Yeats, *A Child Dancing in the Wind* in unison. *Dance there upon the shore; What need have you to care for wind or water's roar?* I drift away to Grandmama Sharon's loving arms.

Halfway back to Dingle, racing black clouds and a sudden wind chill send us racing to the nearest town. We find an opening at the Imeall na Mara B&B and enjoy a grand view overlooking the Smerwick Harbour.

After a good night's sleep, we hike back to Dingle. For the next two days, we clean out Grandmama Sharon's cottage and donate many of her belongings to the local charity.

When Cecil Lloyd texts to let me know Grandmama Sharon's estate is organized, I book our flights back to the states.

The night before we leave, we celebrate at Dick Mack's Pub. After dinner, I make an announcement.

"Grandmama Sharon has a surprise for you," I say. "She's donated her entire estate to the Dingle Orphanage. Blueprints are in order and contractors will start gutting out the cottage Monday morning. Grandmama Sharon has designed the space to house modern showers, a modern kitchen, and girls' sleeping quarters."

We embrace. Love, love, love.

"Altruism," Pearle says.

We walk home by the light of the half moon. Hugging good night is bittersweet.

"Mary, you know you are always welcome in Dingle," Mr. Pope says.

"Thank you," I hold back tears. "I trust that each one of you knows to phone me if you need help."

"Grandmama Sharon always told us that the Universe provides for those who nurture Mother Earth with love," Mr. Pope says.

"She healed many of us," Pearle says.

Millie is surprised when I start crying, again.

The next morning, we finish packing and stop by the orphanage for breakfast.

"Good morning, come in," Mr. Pope says.

We sit down and bless the food.

Mr. Pope hands me a picture of a boy who looks exactly like Mick Jagger at age fifteen.

"Grandmama Sharon has a surprise for you."

"What in the world?" I ask.

"Meet Beck Atwood. He will be interviewing with Wisdom Seeker this fall."

"That explains why the seventh bedroom has been vacant this long," Pearle says.

"What's he like?" I ask.

"He's a sixteen-year-old sculptor making quite a stir in Belfast," Mr. Pope says.

"What medium?" I ask.

"Marble," he says.

"My garage *will* have good *feng shui*," I say belly laughing. "Hallelujah!"

"Grandmama Sharon was a remarkable woman," Pearle says.

"Yes, and her predictions were always spot on accurate," Mr. Pope says.

We walk outside.

"Thank you for always being here for Grandmama Sharon," I say. "I love you. Goodbye."

Here come more tears.

"I bid you farewell," Mr. Pope says.

We embrace, and he kisses me on the cheek.

We walk to the Dingle Depot. I wonder if I will ever be here again. We arrive in Dublin eight hours later, hail a taxi, and check into the Shelbourne Dublin.

I take a long soak in the claw foot tub and slip into a dark, lonely funk. Sad hurts. I crawl out of the tub and slip into sweats. I wish I hadn't confided in Omar yesterday. What I need is a red hot lover, not Omar. Why did he have to be in Dublin this week?

Pearle and Millie come in to check on me.

"I have puffy eyes and jet lag," I collapse on my bed.

"Mary, you said you wanted to tell Omar you are tired of the façade," Pearle says.

"Cocktails with Omar tonight feels counterintuitive," I say.

"Honey, my intuition says go and speak your peace," she says.

"Intuition is always right. I can do this," I say.

"We are warriors," Millie says.

I get dressed, go out in the pouring rain, and hail a taxi to Keogh's on South Anne Street.

When I arrive, Omar is sitting at the bar. We order pints of Guinness and shots of Teelings Small Batch Whiskey.

"To Grandmama Sharon," Omar says. "May strife be removed from the populace, and the Two Shores toil after the transition."

"Sláinte," I throw back my whiskey and order another round of Teelings.

Omar talks about how grueling post-production was on his last project. I finish my Guinness and order another pint. He goes on to fill me in on a myriad of details about his new film, *Egyptian Spiritual Pilgrimages*. How much more can I endure?

"Mary, my life partners and I have come to the realization that keeping our bisexuality a secret is a disservice to ourselves and our bisexual brothers and sisters."

"What in the world?"

"As you say, warriors have no regrets and accept the consequences of their actions," Omar says.

"Good for you, Omar," I order another Teelings.

"Mary, I've got your back."

"Way to kill my love-based take-over plan, dude."

Omar takes my hand, and I snatch it back.

"Look," I finish my shot of whiskey. "Stage a scandalous divorce and contact my attorney."

Omar is speechless.

I finish my pint and slam the glass down on the bar.

"I'm not some crone void of feeling."

I race out in the pouring rain. Chilled, I hail a taxi and slosh into the backseat. Humility and a full bladder make me feel like I'll burst.

The next morning I wake up from the Barracuda dream in a cold sweat. It is still pouring rain. Traffic is brutal getting to the Dublin Airport, but somehow we make our flight.

An hour later, we've passed through the storms. When the turbulence stops, I attempt to rest, but the thought of telling everybody Omar, The Oglethorpe Inn, food forest, and Good Karma Cafe are dead in the water keeps me wide-awake.

I balance myself. Guide says to be receptive. I shift my attention to sending Ella love and peace.

We land in Atlanta and taxi to the Omni. We have just enough time to slip into our gowns. Millie is styling in her black party dress. We walk to Symphony Hall. The whole gang is right outside of the lobby.

I get kind hugs and kisses. Their condolences raise my vibration.

I hear Pearle's voice telling me not to worry about anything at all when we are finding our seats.

The house lights dim. The concertmistress enters, cues the oboe, and the orchestra tunes. Ella enters the stage wearing a tuxedo. She takes the baton and cues the timpani, piccolos, French horns, trombones, and tuba.

The opening theme to *Wilmington Tides* is transcendent. Although I've heard these unearthly themes for the past three years, when the sea of strings enters tremolo, it's euphoric.

Ella is in her mind, body, and spirit zone and the orchestra responds. After ten thousand hours of dedicated work, she produced a musical composition capable of raising group vibration.

The concertmistress holds a high harmonic and then fades. The audience hangs on to the last bit of silence and then erupts into thunderous applause, shouting '*brava, brava*.' My heart is pounding.

Ella bows deeply to the audience, who is giving her a standing ovation.

After intermission, Ella returns to the stage with her cello. She's wearing a purple flowing crinoline and taffeta gown. She sits down, adjusts her endpin, tunes, and cues the Maestro.

The opening of the Elgar concerto is cohesive. Ella is agile. She flies. The energy is pure truth and beauty. We collectively travel through the emotional extremes of the slow movement and precision and grace of the third movement.

After the concert, we race backstage. The twins and Millie present Ella with flowers, and we line up to congratulate her.

We clear out for Ella's fans to meet her. When the crowd thins, we taxi to the after party.

Bigwigs surround Ella and tell her that she is vital, intellectual, expressive, and mesmerizing. Ella is completely down to earth. The hosts thoughtfully made the entire spread vegan in Ella's honor. Yippee.

"Hello, Lawrence Sciles, principal cellist of the Atlanta Symphony and Ella's private cello teacher."

The night takes a sudden twist when Lawrence and Pearle lock eyes. Holy Isis. Love at first sight just won.

"Hello, Pearle Isle and this is my daughter, Millie."

"Isle is the name of ancient nobility where my people come from."

"Would that be Benin, West Africa?"

"Why, yes," Lawrence laughs.

"I'll take the kids to check out the buffet," I say.

Around midnight, we head back to the Omni. Pearle is glowing. I fall asleep making affirmations that I won't give the Savannah Tongue any power. It is none of my business what other people think.

The next morning I make some lame excuse to skip breakfast. When everyone leaves, I soak in the Jacuzzi tub. My nerves are a tsunami of hurt and humiliation. Why was I so naïve?

I drag myself out and dry off. Yuck. The fluorescent lights are brutal. What type of man would marry a woman with a house full of kids? I get dressed and finish packing. Monkey brain spirals to worst case scenarios.

"Mary, can I come in?" Pearle asks.

"Yeah, sure," I say. "Tell me about Lawrence."

She tells me that love feels like recognizing the energy you've been intimate with for lifetimes.

"Hey, are you okay?" She asks.

"Pearle, Omar asked for a divorce."

I fall on the bed and start crying.

She squeezes the base of my skull, rubs between my shoulder

blades, and massages down my spinal cord to the base of my spine.

"Last night I had a dream," Pearle says. "You were on the beach riding the gray horse, which means that you will soon be happily married."

She leans her knuckles into my lower back, and I moan.

"I'm clueless on how to start dating," I say.

Pearle adjusts my lower back. The cracks are a relief.

"Divine time," Pearle says. "Speaking of which the others are waiting in the lobby."

"Let's bask in Ella's success," I say.

"There's no rush, honey."

Fletcher eases through downtown traffic and merges on 1-75 South. We talk about the latest psychic predictions, uncook class ideas, and garden install progress. Then Ella tells us about common personality traits like loaded basses, high strung violinists, and brash trumpeters.

Good conversation makes the four-hour trip seem like a minute. When I get home, I realize that I'm sleep deprived.

After family supper, I head to my room, shower, and joyously finish reading *The Age of Enlightenment: When Quantum Physics was Reborn*.

I get a hit. If I want to make the Deep South love-based, I have to start with Mr. Nicopane. And as weird as it seems, the size of his stomach says the time is now.

TWENTY-EIGHT

During Spiritfly-meditation I receive a lucid vision on how to proceed with our love-based take-over plan. After the morning routine, I meet privately with Pearle and Bridget and we gather the courage to act on gut instinct.

That night, we sneak out of the house at midnight. The low waning moon cast long nightmarish shadows down the avenue of oaks.

Bridget throws Flambé and Juicy raw vegan dog bones. They sniff, collapse their haunches, and we are allowed entrance into Mr. Nicopane's backyard.

We make it to Mr. Nicopane's back porch. Bridget cuts the wires and disarms the alarm system. We sneak upstairs. My heart is pounding. We tiptoe down the hallway toward the flickering TV. When Bridget signals us, we storm the bedroom.

Mr. Nicopane and Superintendent Dr. Cross are in bed, naked, and reading Gideon's Bible. Bridget jumps on the bed and ties them together. Pearle is hand clapping, foot stomping, and chanting in *Fon* and French. I throw the top sheet over their heads.

Bridget gets them tied off to the headboard.

Pearle coaxes them into a trance.

We swig palm wine, allow the alcohol to disrupt our astral bodies, and chant; 'Mam-i Wa-ta Dam-bal-lah, Af-do-wei-do, Dam-bal-lay, Mam-i Wa-ta Dam-bal-lah, Af-do-wei-do, Dam-bal-lay.' We clap and stomp and go into a trance: "Mam-i Wa-ta Dam-bal-lah, Af-do-wei-do, Dam-bal-lay, Mam-i Wa-ta Dam-bal-lah, Af-do-wei-do, Dam-bal-lay.

"Go in peace n sin no mo," Pearle says. "I affect magic and put you in a voodoo spell to release all of yo demons. No longer are you bigots who speak in the name of divinity."

Mami Wata dances our bodies until we free ourselves of inhibitions. We strike the ancient prayer bowl and summon peace.

"*Ayi Vodun*, the *Vodun* of the earth, whose power is feared and terrifying," Pearle's voice resonates, "*Lêgba*, the *Vodun* of unpredictable good and evil, *Da gu do*, we do not accept complicity with evil, Dú le we jo we, bo nu le ve we, he who has been exposed to anger must be purified."

Pearle chants the *Wuslasi* purification rite used for opening closed minds and then gives Mr. Nicopane and Dr. Cross root medicine through a dropper.

"We will walk the walk until the day all people are treated fairly," Pearle says.

"Every thought and action done by human beings impact all other living things on earth," Bridget says.

"Your destiny is the way you think and live," I say.

"Forgiveness and gratitude are virtues of the brave," Bridget says.

"When kindness is the modus operandi we change the world," I say.

Pearle places her hands on Mr. Nicopane's stomach and uses her Voodoo Chieftaincy Power to remove the invading spirit that is disrupting Mr. Nicopane's energy.

Mr. Nicopane starts heaving.

"Grossout," Bridget says.

"Is he faking?" I ask.

"He's not faking!" Pearle says.

Bridget executes the Heimlich maneuver.

Darkness flies out of Mr. Nicopane's mouth. God, protect us.

"Mr. Nicopane looks dead," Bridget says.

"He's got a pulse," Pearle says.

"A Changeling Fairy just lunged at me!" I scream.

Pearle and Bridget see nothing.

The Changeling lunges at me again. When it nicks my neck, my legs turn to rubber.

"I've been poisoned," I collapse, curl up in the fetal position, and get zipped up inside of an ice cube. I'll freeze to death. Why do the Howards die such gruesome deaths?

I vanish in a shelf cloud.

Wait. This is my dream. I summon the Hierarchy, Masters, Isis, Sophia, Osiris, Horace, Mother Mary, Mary Magdalene, Buddha, Shiva, Shakti, Krishna, Kali, Deities, Avatars, Saints, Archangels, Spirits, and Indigenousness Guides.

"Pearle, Mr. Nicopane, and Dr. Cross are fear-based. Church and state have shunned them, too. We're in this together," I say telepathically.

When Pearle nods yes, I realize I am in control of my dream. Time and space do not exist; deal with it. I regain some strength and stand up.

Pearle, Bridget, and I perform *Gho* until we surround ourselves by the white light of protection. A football-sized Changeling materializes in the shape of a stinkbug.

We gag from the stench.

Bridget coaxes the beast to take a raw vegan dog bone, and we capture it in an oversized towel.

We perform *Gho* nonstop. Getting the Changeling to the stairwell is physically exhausting. When we're dragging the entity downstairs, the rotten-meat-smell sickens us. We finally get outside. We balance our chakras, connect with the gold cord, and summon unworldly power.

With our combined strength, we hurl the beast to the core of the earth when instantaneously a swallowtail butterfly flutters out of the exact spot.

We hurry upstairs, radiate unconditional love to Mr. Nicopane's and Dr. Cross's hearts, and unfasten them. When Pearle snaps her fingers, we have three minutes before they regain consciousness.

We race home. The long night is over. I collapse into a deep sleep.

The next morning, I say, love, love, love and head to the dock for Spiritfly-meditation.

After the morning routine, I take Manfred for a walk down the avenue of oaks. All is quiet at Mr. Nicopane's house. My energy is completely peaceful. I feel like anything is possible. Yippee.

I check the mail. A cerulean note card from Cecil Lloyd piques my interest, and I open it right away. Congratulations? DHEC is shut down? What? I read the note two more times.

Guide says, "Wisdom Seeker won, and now others will win."

I read the note again. DHEC is dead. Yippee.

Crew moves from thirty-five percent to eighty-five percent popularity in online polls. The *Rolling Stone* coins Chief Crew the Rock Star of New Age Politics. The twins' landslide prediction is coming true.

Volunteers for the Crew Potalis for Mayor Campaign continue to double. We organize nonstop peace rallies, canvassing, phone-banking, interviews, and social events. Savannah is onboard to quash oligarchy.

Hours before the final Peace Rally, Crew supporters pack Forsyth

Park by the thousands. The energy is off the charts high vibe.

Crew starts his speech.

"Thank you for your support."

The crowd roars, 'Savannah Shift.'

"Our campaign will win this race. Citizens have united to take back the power of justice and democracy. We have started to build better relations with our brothers and sisters through kindness, gentleness, goodness, and happiness. Fear and hate are histories. The Savannah Shift is the move toward compassion, trust, sharing, balancing Mother Nature, and creating World Peace."

The crowd chants, 'Savannah Shift.'

"Read, every day, something no one else is reading. Think, every day, something no one else is thinking. Do, every day, something no one else would be silly enough to do. Creative is the place where no one else has ever been. Be the miracle that unifies our potential to make peace thrive. Pure justice and equality for all."

We cheer. Crew introduces the All AME Gospel Songbirds and jumps off the front of the stage.

A lanky young man with a French beret nimbly glides his fingers mournfully over the keys of the C3 Hammond Organ. The choir is one strong voice. They're well-rehearsed and having fun.

We chant 'Savannah Shift' with thousands of soaring spirits. The evening is magical. We drive back to the island in awe of the positive power of the love-based plan.

I'm tempted to curl up in bed with a good book, but head to the art room instead. A few hours later, when I break to let the paint dry, Fletcher knocks on the door.

"Come on in," I say taking off my smock.

He studies the still life I've been working on for months.

"I love how the sunlight hits that wave," he says.

"Thanks for knowing my art better than anyone else," I say.

My Guides demand that I be forthright.

"Fletcher, have you had the talk with Bridget yet?"

He takes a step back. "I've been attempting to tell Bridget I love her sassy, temperamental personality, her soft, loose curls and that she allures me to total distraction telepathically."

"Fletcher, bank in the bank and not in your head. Organize your feelings, call Bridget aside, and express yourself either in writing or with words."

"Dude, I don't want to blow it, and I'm hooked; bait, line, and sinker."

"Fletcher, you have to tell her that you are hooked," I say.

"She's a master at changing topics. If only there were waves."

"Don't mope. Bridget can spot a phony quicker than a kid."

"You're right. She abhors negativity."

"Hey, let's grab an ice cold Dogfish Double IPA and watch *Hear No Evil, See No Evil*," I say.

We do just that and belly laugh from the beginning to end.

"Thanks, dude," Fletcher says. "I feel better. I'll see you at morning meditation."

"Leonard Cohen said, 'Act the way you'd like to be, and soon you'll be the way you act,'" I say.

The next day we head back to City Hall. Unbelievably, Doolittle has land movers back on Pigeon Island.

When we arrive, the courtroom is already packed with Georgia Barrier Island Coalition Activists.

"All rise for the honorable Mayor Archibald Doolittle III," the regular bailiff says.

Vultures coo outside the window when the mayor waddles up to the podium. He's sausaged into a pink and tan pinstriped seersucker suit. Oodles of belly are tucked into his eel skin belt. His white straw hat screams Dixiecrat.

"He's an exemplary legacy of dirty money," Greta says.

"Land takeovers for name-recognition," Marjorie says.

"I'd like to see him transcend the physical desire for food consumption," Bridget says.

Crew shushes us.

Bridget speaks first. She gets the room's attention in her skinny jeans and purple 'Would you suck the tit of a sick cow?' tank.

"A recent government publication on marketing cabbage contains 26,941 words. The Gettysburg address contains 279 words. The sixty-seven words within the Lord's Prayer powerfully cause the chakras to vibrate at a higher frequency."

Bridget pauses to give Doolittle direct eye contact.

"Your intentions to proceed with Pigeon Island Paradise Park needs only one word," Bridget takes a deep breath for dramatic effect. "Rape. In the name of the Father, Son, and Holy Ghost, stop raping Mother Earth!"

The line of protesters is out the door. After Bridget's speech, everyone accuses the Mayor of raping Mother Earth.

"This is mumbo jumbo! I have built my reputation out of things that I said I was going to do. This project isn't based on myth, and we won't stand for private agendas," the Mayor storms out and doesn't return.

"He's criminal," Ella says.

"As soon as he thinks nobody's looking, he'll try again," Bo says.

When we get home, we take wheatgrass shots to detox from the negativity of the current judicial system.

"Here's to happy colons," Bridget says.

That night at family supper, Marshall tells us his writing muses have returned, and he's sketched out his third book, *Kind Kid, Kind World*. And Fletcher says a storm will bring big waves by the weekend. Yippee.

After supper, I don't have the guts to tell the others about Omar, so I head to the art room.

I stretch canvas and apply primer. While it's drying, I work on finishing a commissioned work. Almost there.

I stop to let the paint dry, sand the new canvas, and add the second coat of primer.

At eight P.M., after several months, I finish my seascape. Yippee. I thank my muses and head upstairs to soak in the tub.

When I'm drying off, my cell phone rings. It's Cecil Lloyd.

"Hey Cecil, how are you?"

"I'm fine, thank you. Is this a good time?"

"Sure, what's up?"

"I wanted to phone and offer you my personal condolences on the passing of Grandmama Sharon."

"Wow, thanks, Cecil. I'm touched," I say.

"Is there anything I can do to offer my support?"

"You're kind. I'll need time. I understand involution, evolution, and devolution in spiritual terms, but emotionally it's tough."

"I'm here if you need anything."

"Ah, you're a sweetheart. Hey, Crew's campaign is on fire. Thanks for your endless legal support."

"My pleasure. The momentum is phenomenal," Cecil has a rare static pause. "Mary, I received your divorce papers today. I'm sorry this happened at such a sad time."

"Irreconcilable differences."

"Are you available to sign documents tomorrow morning at ten A.M.?"

"Sure, I'm free; ha, literally."

The next morning, after green smoothie klatch, I head upstairs and figure out what to wear. I get a hit to change up my style. I squeeze into my brand new Citizens of Humanity Super Slim

Boyfriend Jeans and a flouncy top. Alright. Goddess roar.

I jump into the van and crank up the tunes. Goodbye Oglethorpe Inn, Food Forest, Good Karma Café, and the Omar Victor International Film Institute. Be gone with you, Omar Victor.

I know money is an exchange of power, but what good does it do to for Omar to throw it away and waste my time. In the New Age, scammers won't lark with other people's karma.

I find a sweet spot right in front of Cecil's building and dash up the marble stairs.

Cecil opens the door and kisses me on both cheeks. Has he always been this hot?

"Fantastic to see you," he says.

I adjust my top and follow him inside. Odd that he's wearing jeans and a t-shirt on Monday morning instead of the regular three-piece suit. And where is the secretary today?

"Please, have a seat," he says.

I flashback to my court case in high school. Horrific. I struggle to maintain my Divine Goddess Power.

"Mary, I read the divorce docs. I've never seen anything more generous. Omar gifted you with the entire Oglethorpe Inn, excluding the PGA golf course, of course. Omar has gone as far as covering maintenance, taxes, personnel, and much more."

"Yeah, yeah, yeah. What's the catch?"

"Omar requested to house the Omar Victor International Film Institute at the Oglethorpe Inn with full right of refusal," I listen to Cecil highlight the settlement.

Guide says, 'Omar *is* good.'

"It's a win, win," Cecil says.

"What a difference a day makes," I say.

"Congratulations, Mary."

"Thanks, Cecil. I'm just glad it's over."

"Mary, may I speak to you about something completely different?"

"Sure, Cecil."

He smiles. I half-smile back.

"There is an Irish limerick that says, 'if you must steal, steal my heart, and if you must lie, lie with me in bed, and if you must cheat, cheat death.'"

I'm silent. Where could this be going?

"Mary, you walked in here ten years ago," Cecil says. "And I've loved you ever since. I feel that we've been together for lifetimes."

"Cecil, I just got divorced."

"Mary, I worked with Omar when he was acquiring the Oglethorpe Inn. When I recently learned about his life partners in Egypt, I deduced that your marriage was a part of your love-based take-over."

Cecil stands up and walks over to my chair. Our eyes lock. He takes my hands and asks me to stand up.

"Mary Howard, I love you, and I want to spend my life with you."

The brush of his hand across my cheek triggers passion. I bask in the pleasure of his hard lips against mine.

"Cecil," I'm untraditional."

"I love that about you."

"I live with a bunch of kids."

"Mary, I'm an orphan. I love that about you."

He holds me in his arms and tenderly kisses my neck and lips. When I open my eyes, we're both grinning like Cheshire cats.

He balances with one bent knee.

"Mary Howard, will you marry me?"

He pulls a ring out of his pocket.

My heart chakra opens. Everything makes sense.

"Yippee!" I squeal.

"Yippee, yes?" he asks.

"Yippee, yes!" I say.

He pulls me in by the small of my waist and explores my mouth with his tongue. I follow his lead. We fit together perfectly. Time stands still. Gold and red serpents reach my crown chakra, release droplets, and energize my *Ka* body.

"I want to marry you right away and tell you I love you before you fall asleep and when you wake up."

When his hands explore my hips and the small of my back, physiology kicks into high gear. After the best make-out in my life, I feel as light as a feather.

We hold hands and walk outside.

"I'll see you around seven," I say.

"I love you. I am going to make you as happy as you make me."

I drive back to the island. My heart is pulsing with love chemistry. Love, the energy umbrella.

When I get out of the van, I hear Ella practicing Kodaly Capriccio for solo cello from her open window. Ah, reincarnation.

The minute I get into the kitchen I hear Fletcher and Bridget talking in the dining room.

I freeze.

TWENTY-NINE

"IF YOU ASK A TOAD WHAT BEAUTY IS HE WILL ANSWER THAT IT is a female toad, with two great round eyes coming out of her head, a large mouth, a yellow belly, and a brown back. If you ask me, it is you. Bridget, I love you, with all of my heart, but you forsake me."

"Fletcher, who has forsaken whom? You've never told me how you feel."

"Come on. You know that you've owned me from day one."

"I'm no mind reader," she snaps.

"Okay, dude, I'm focusing on the power of now. Bridget, will you be my girl?"

"Well, I do think that you're hot, smart, sweet, and kind of irresistible."

"Then let's hook up, dude."

"I'm not sure if you understand feminine mysticism," Bridget says.

"I do," Fletcher says. "And I will prove it."

"Would you quit drinking coffee?"

"Dude, my cup of Fairtrade, shade grown, locally roasted Joe gets me jacked up for my surf sessions. But no worries Bridget, being raw vegan gives me all the stamina…"

"Yeah, raw vegan gives you stamina, but I'm not having sex with a supporter of the multi-billion dollar conglomerate of the second largest commodity in the world that profits on drugging humanity with caffeine-riddled anxiety."

"Okay, Bridget, not a problem. Say yes, and I'll quit coffee cold turkey."

They grind and moan.

"Bridget, will you Common Law marry me?"

"Well, only if you boycott Hershey."

"I only buy the dark chocolate," Fletcher says between kisses.

"Hershey kills Mother Earth, steals our water rights, and profits from child labor."

"Fine, I'll never look at another candy bar. I promise."

When Fletcher asks Bridget to common law marry him, again, she says she has to talk to Bo.

The kids run inside. I slam the kitchen door like I just got home. Ella and Pearle hear the commotion and come downstairs.

"Hey, I've got big news. Omar and I are officially divorced. I just signed the papers."

Everybody is sad. Omar was really fun. We all loved when Omar was in Savannah.

"Hey, fifty percent of fake marriages end in fake divorce, right? And it's a win-win; Wisdom Seeker will still be housed in the Oglethorpe Inn, and Omar will be here for the Grand Opening."

They cheer up.

"There's more. After I signed the papers, Cecil proposed."

"Cecil Lloyd, the lawyer?" Marjorie asks.

"Yes," I nod.

"He proposed marriage?" Bridget asks.

"Yes. Who knew Cecil and I have both had a secret crush on each other for the past ten years?"

"What did you say?" Pearle asks.

"I said yes!"

We group hug.

"I've got some more good news," Pearle says. "Lawrence is coming to Savannah right after the Asia tour!"

"Love is in the air," Fletcher winks at Bridget.

"Let's celebrate at Tybee Beach," I say.

Manfred goes crazy when he knows we're packing for the beach. We swing by and pick up Marshall and Rosemarie.

Omar, Cecil, and Lawrence. What a difference a day makes when patience and Divine Time are at the helm.

The ocean is calm, the sun is bright, and the water is brisk. After a quick dip, we take a long walk. Love, love, love.

We get home, shower, change, and start making culinary alchemy from homegrown organic produce and love.

Cecil impresses us when he shows up with a bunch of fat organic purple carrots that he grew in his downtown square foot garden. We pour French Cabernet Sauvignon and tour paintings, sculptures, and the garden.

We refill our glasses and walk out to the dock to catch the sunset. I am loved. I am a Goddess Warrior.

We're seated at the dining room table.

"A Native American blessing for our first meal together," I say. "Give us the wisdom to teach our children to love, to respect, and to be kind to one another that we may grow with peace in mind."

The first course is green papaya coconut salad and lemony zucchini bisque. The main course is Kale Caesar Salad, Living Lasagna, and Shiitake Fettuccine with Cashew Alfredo Sauce.

Every bite balances salt, sweet, sour, bitter, and umami, creamy, and crispy. By the end of the meal, Cecil commits to going vegan. Yippee. Compassion will win.

When everyone leaves, Cecil and I walk out to the dock. The tide is high, the moon is almost full, and every kiss energizes my *Ka* body.

"I have to be in court first thing tomorrow morning," Cecil says.

"Will you come back tomorrow night?"

He holds me tight. "Yes, I'll get here early and help prepare family supper."

It's three A.M. when we walk back to his car and kiss goodnight.

"In addition to your beauty, personal charm, grace, perception, and intellect, you wake up my potential," Cecil says.

"You wake up my healthy instincts," I say.

I watch his taillights dim. Love, love, love.

Two pleasurable weeks later, Cecil arrives on *Fish to Fry* to join us for the We Saw Wassaw Camp Out. By six A.M., the house is packed with Peace and Preservation kids. We serve breakfast, give the safety talk, and take our biggest group to date out to the dock.

We suit up in PFDs, load *Fish to Fry*, *Driftwood*, *Bottom Line*, and *One That Got Away*, and drift away from the dock. Dolphins play off the bow the entire way to Little Wassaw Island. When we get to camp, we go swimming before unloading the boats and setting up the kitchen. We set up the privy, pitch our tents, and collect firewood before lunch.

The rest of the day, we explore the maritime forest.

That night we serve our first raw vegan camp-out meal, romaine leaf tacos with all of the fixings. They love it. Raising vibration with living food. Wow.

We gather around the Think Tank Bonfire.

"Let's start by outlining some of the positive trends we've successfully implemented," Crew says.

"My school is airing, 'This Day in Peace and Justice' on the morning intercom announcements," Chineka says.

"Most teachers are featuring Peace Activists on classroom bulletin boards," Meyer says.

"We've had two dozen schools take the Peace Pledge," Marshall says.

"My school started an after-school yoga club," Jimar says.

"Dannisha, Fayth, and I have started two more organic edible education after-school clubs," Keeara says.

"Bridget and I have talked three principals into letting us teach mindfulness," Bo says.

"Ten years ago, even with blind faith and creative visualization, I would have never predicted this would be happening this soon," I say.

"The tide is turning," Greta says.

"Soon the majority of humanity will be love-based," Marjorie says.

"In my neighborhood, we are teaching each other to resolve conflicts with silence, love, and understanding," Jimar says.

"The gap is closing. Sports, DARE, and ROTC will be replaced with the arts and edible education in public schools," Ella says.

"I'm leading a *pro bono* team that has crippled the Textbook Industry," Cecil says. "We have lawsuits ranging from illegal affiliate links, corrupt commissions, outdated and false information, and author and publisher kickbacks."

I fall in love with Cecil all over again.

We discuss ways to start policing the police programs, free farmer markets in food deserts, mass transit, and building tiny home communities for the homeless.

At midnight, we have a group meditation. When I think of the personal sacrifices we will have to make for Humanity to achieve Unity Consciousness, it seems light years away. Guide says, "Be happy, teach happy, and keep moving."

The third night Think Tank Bonfire is the best. We feel empowered to organize a campaign to speak with city planners and ask them to allow us to use vacant lots to build tiny home villages.

We turn in around midnight, but I'm wide awake. At three A.M., unable to wait any longer, I slip into Cecil's tent.

We wade out to *Fish to Fry*, surrender to raw premarital sexual bliss, and sneak back to camp right before dawn.

Love chemistry surges all morning. Love, love, love. After a lazy morning, we head back to Wilmington Island.

When the kids head back to Forsyth Park, we pour Dogfish Double IPAs in frosty mugs and walk out on the dock.

"We Saw Wassaw keeps getting better," Crew says.

"Cucurbit Pepo Pageant next week," Rosemarie says.

"Lawrence will be here soon," Pearle grins.

Cecil squeezes my hand.

The morning of the Cucurbit Pepo Pageant an unpredicted cold front lifts our spirits. When we get to the May Howard School playground, Savannah Bright's *Be Here Now Show* is already set with stage, camera, and lights.

Savannah Bright pulls up in a white Lexus sedan. I'm taken with her charisma and ageless beauty.

"I'm amped. I've supported this campaign since day one," Savannah Bright says before she's whisked away by make-up artists. "Roll sound!" the director says.

"Sound speed," the sound guy hollers back.

"Roll camera," the director says.

The slate slaps.

"Camera set."

"Sound set."

"Action," the director yells.

"Hello, I'm Savannah Bright. Welcome to the *Be Here Now Show*. We're live, on Wilmington Island, home of the Cucurbit Pepo Pageant with Chief Crew Potalis just days before Savannah votes for their next mayor. Chief, how is your team holding up?

"We're stronger than ever approaching the finish line," Crew says.

"At this point, is there anything you want undecided voters to know about your platform?"

"If I am elected Mayor of Savannah, expect better organization among citizens, communities, businesses, and city agencies. Expect the minimum wage to increase to fifteen dollars an hour. Know that we will implement prekindergarten programs in every Title One school and implement Housing First for the homeless. We will build a vast network of urban gardens, aggressively plant fruit and nut trees on every abandoned lot, and demonstrate to other cities that sustainability, trust, and sharing will win."

"Esquire coined you as the 'Rock Star of New Age Politics.' How do you feel about that?" Savannah asks.

"A powerful shift towards love-based is happening now. The Deep South is joining worldwide visionaries to create a meme that honors mutual need, support, understanding, tolerance, helpfulness, goodwill, and sharing the multitude of resources so generously provided by Mother Earth."

"New Age Now," Savannah Bright smiles for the camera.

They cut to a commercial break. The sky is azure. The wind is crisp. The sun is shining.

When Cecil arrives, everything he does makes me feel sexy. We make the rounds an hour before the gates open. My friends from

Moon River Brewery tap the kegs and give us samples of their seasonal organic double IPA. Nice and hoppy. Yippee, beer fairies.

The food court has tripled in size. Everything is one hundred percent plant-based and organic including outrageous Cuban sandwiches made with seitan and delicious flaky un-fish fillets made with jackfruit.

Bridget and Bo's booth is set-up in front of their latest Kids Grow Veggie Patch install. Pearle, Millie, and Lawrence join us. We take a group picture in front of the 'Organic Raw Vegan Treats' sign propped against the purple blooms of trellised sweet peas in what used to be the teacher's parking lot and sample heavenly, melt-in-your-mouth, cashew-corn crawkers with a variety of seed cheezes.

Rosemarie and Savannah Bright's booth is right around the corner.

"Awesome. I like the name change from *Mad Mothers against Monsanto* to *Happy Moms for Healthy Eaters*," I say.

"Now that Monsanto is guilty of worldwide pesticide poisoning, biospiracy, and patenting death, we give them zero power," Rosemarie says.

Greta and Marjorie are manning the Dubois Psychic Advisor booth. We work our way through their fans and snap a photo of their handpainted sign:

> Greta and Marjorie Dubois Readings $100.00.
> All proceeds benefit the Heirloom Seeds to Schools Program.
> What you can expect from your reading:
> We attempt to communicate with your guides in the spirit world.
> We provide you with ways to follow your soul's desire.
> We help you find your unique way to serve humanity.

We do not read about health, career, love, and ambition, and we do not read for skeptics or Puritans.

Be prepared to be wowed! Thank You!

Mr. Nicopane and Dr. Cross are love-based and out of the closet. We visit them at the new LGBTQ booth.

"Hey, Mary," Mr. Nicopane hugs me.

"What do you think of our sign?" Dr. Cross asks.

"'Love is the only path.'" I say. "I like that it's evocative, well-organized, and pioneering."

"Big news. We're retiring this spring, and a dynamic husband and wife team are taking over," Dr. Cross says.

"Where are they from?"

"London, England. They're completely organic, like you," Dr. Cross says.

"Wow, that's fantastic."

We head over to open the gates.

"Professor Lowe, I hardly recognized you with your turban, beard, and ponytail," I say.

Professor Lowe holds Rosemarie tight.

"How was metaphysical training in Bombay, Daddy?" She asks.

"I fell in love with India," he says.

"Who are these little cuties?" Pearle asks.

"This is Abhi, five, Zoya, seven, and Ayesha, nine. They were up for adoption. I had an aha-moment to start Wisdom Seeker, Isle of Hope, and within two weeks, it was official. I appreciate your inspiration, Mary."

"Awesome. Hey, let's get this Unity party started," I say.

Marshall and I work our way to the stage.

"Welcome to the Cucurbit Pepo Pageant," Marshall says.

"Celebrating Unity since forever," I say.

"And give it up for the man that signs the permits, none other than Mayor Archibald Doolittle III," Marshall says.

The mayor takes the mic. Vultures land on the stage.

"I quote Ross Perot, 'If you see a snake, just kill it: don't appoint a committee on snakes,' and that's what I say about Crew Potalis: just kill it, don't appoint a committee because I can tell you that Crew Potalis will ruin the conservative foothold generations have upheld in Savannah. Now listen, Benjamin Franklin said that a mule will labor ten years willingly and patiently for you, for the privilege of kicking you once, and Crew Potalis is the ass that wants that privilege."

I gasp. The crowd boos. Crew chuckles.

"Life is a play, and Crew Potalis is unrehearsed. He endangers economic security. Hope for the best but if Crew Potalis is Mayor, expect the worst. Archibald Doolittle, III, is the shot in the arm that Savannah needs. We can't allow three generations of political pedigree to go badly awry. Savannah is and will always be conservative."

Crew takes the mic. The crowd cheers.

"Welcome Brothers and Sisters in Unity!" Crew throws his tenor voice.

The crowd cheers.

"World Peace is real!"

The crowd is on fire.

"Folks, at the start of this campaign we were considered a long shot, but the experts are often wrong. They said Clark Gable's ears were too big, and he looked like an ape."

Cheers and laughter.

"I am honored to stand before you under these majestic oaks and share my vision of Sustainable Savannah. We will use Peace and Preservation as our catalyst to overcome greed, economic disparity between individuals, groups, classes, and races and attitudes of superiority arising from hereditary, religious, economic, and political backgrounds.

"We are like-minded positive forces establishing an International Consciousness based on cooperative goodwill, love, and understanding."

Thousands of people shout, "Savannah Shift."

"I quote the late great Rev. Dr. M.L. King, Jr., who said the time is always right to do what is right. Become a dedicated fighter for civil rights. It will enrich your spirit as nothing else can. It will give you the rare sense of nobility that can only spring from love and helping your fellow man. Make a career of humanity. Commit yourself to the noble struggle for human rights. You will make a greater person of yourself, a greater nation, and a finer world.

"Rev. Dr. M. L. King, Jr., your day has come!"

The crowd goes wild.

"We will under promise and over deliver. It would be my honor to serve you, Savannah. Thank you for your vote," Crew says.

The All AME Gospel Songbirds dressed in bright African garb are three hundred voices strong.

Pearle steps up to the mic and hits us in the solar plexus with divine indigo light. Her raspy, rhythmic, resonant voice illuminates our love energy.

The band this year, Sol Torso, is Crew's favorite local band. They kick it off with a four on the floor funk beat that gets everybody up dancing for the entire ninety-minute show. Wise Hoe Woo's silent fireworks display, simple and eloquent, caps off the night.

THIRTY

Cecil is my loyal, loving safety net. Sleeping with Cecil is my life partner fantasy. His quick humor keeps me laughing. I love how caring and polite he is to everyone. Cecil is my whimsy returned.

Wisdom Seeker prepares for our first retreat in the newly renovated Oglethorpe Inn. We're excited that writers, attorneys, musicians, Shamans, and medical doctors have already enrolled.

Benjamin One and Sha Sha will be teaching a one-week course called *Shamanic Ways to Balance Mother Earth.*

We are bathed in a high vibe purification of soul retrieval mixed with meditation, sustainable food production, and plant-based cuisine. Let the love-based revolution begin.

That night Marshall and Rosemarie host our rehearsal dinner. This is really happening.

The next morning we walk down to the dock, greet Ouida, and meditate. After the morning routine, I grab the twelve-foot ladder, hang a dozen of Daddy's Cockspur Lanterns from oak limbs, and accomplish a million other tasks before I shower and slip on my simple bamboo viscose wedding gown.

Lawrence and Ella start Faure Sicilienne. Benjamin One and Cecil takes their places. When we hear "Apres un rêve," Millie, Greta, and Marjorie walk slowly down the aisle tossing daisies and calendulas.

After one measure of "The Swan," Marshall and Crew walk me down the aisle.

Cecil takes my hands. I kiss him. Then I kiss him again. I'm flying. Love, love, love.

"Mary Howard and Cecil Lloyd, I stand before you to honor your decision to be joined in holy matrimony, for all the days of your life, on the spiritual path of awakening," Benjamin One is all smiles.

"Be conscious of the shifting seasons and walk on the earth in a sacred way. View the world as alive and be full of wonder.

"Each day express gratitude by dancing, singing, and giving thanks to your spirit guides, gods, goddesses, animals, plants, and stone spirits."

Benjamin One blesses us as we face west, east, north, and south. He tells us to stand firm in the center of the medicine wheel and heal our pasts.

"The alchemy of intimacy and love making opens our chakras and energize the *Ka* body. Learn the Karma Sutra. Make love regularly for vitality, fire, passion for life, to awaken peace of mind, and become conscious of the spiritual energy that is surrounding you."

Benjamin One smudges us with sage, rosemary, cedar, and lavender. I kiss Cecil mid-ceremony.

"Allow kind thoughts and words to spring forth like flowers blooming in the garden, allowing nature's energy to flow through you."

Before the vows, I kiss Cecil again.

During the vows, Cecil kisses me.

"Mary Howard and Cecil Lloyd, to seal your vows, and as a token of bonding, and the exchange of spirits, as each partner sends a part of their self into the new spouse's soul, there to abide ever after, please kiss one more time.

We lock lips. Wow. Love. Chemistry. My spirit is soaring.

We recess to Ella's original for two cellos. Cocktail hour features Buffalo cauliflower, Shanghai dumplings, eggplant Aji, spring rolls, pad Thai and a sunset that is all the buzz.

We're seated in the clear top dining tent and toast with Veuve Clicquot champagne. Benjamin One and Supreme Chief Isle present us with a transcendental Unity blessing.

Servers pass plates of Tomato-Zucchini Lasagna, Wild Mushroom Crepes, Jicama-Avocado Tartare, Herbed Grilled Portabella Steaks, and Seitan Piccata. Phenomenal.

Pearle catches the bouquet at the end of the night, and Lawrence pops the question right then and there. Love equals love.

The next morning, Cecil and I get a standing ovation when we show up for group meditation. After green smoothie klatch, Fletcher gets our attention.

"Fletcher's asked me for my hand in Common Law Marriage," Bridget says.

"I proved I'd given up coffee and Hershey bars and Bridget said yes."

"Well, Fletcher's pee has been clear for a while now, so with Wisdom Seeker as my witness, I accept Fletcher's proposal."

"Alright, alright, alright!" Fletcher lifts Bridget and flies her around the kitchen. We cheer; the cat and mouse game is finally over.

The next morning we're back spending long days canvassing Savannah. We meet like-minded Crew Potalis supporters who inspire us with their bountiful organic backyard gardens and their healthy lifestyles. Cultural optimism is brewing.

As soon as the polls close we hurry to Crew's house. It's jammed packed. We squeeze into the foyer.

"Settle down. Action," the director says.

"Welcome! I'm Savannah Bright, and this is the *Be Here Now Show*. We're live at Crew Potalis' home on Wilmington Island. There's a full house of energetic supporters shouting 'Savannah Shift.' Chief Crew Potalis, what's on your mind right now?"

"The Savannah Shift is happening now," Crew says.

"The polls just closed and it looks like you have a substantial lead. What's the first item on your agenda?"

"Recognizing, rewarding, and assisting neighborhoods, schools, churches, and individuals, groups, and communities who are promoting peace, preservation, sustainability, one humanity, yoga, meditation, compassionate eating, being of service, giving the needy a hand up, and teaching edible education."

"Excuse me, this just in, we can officially call you Mayor Potalis. Congratulations!"

They cut to a commercial break.

We group hug. I'm in awe that the shift happened so quickly.

The next day we sleep late and meditate at ten. After green smoothie klatch, we load *One That Got Away* and *Driftwood* and head to Wise Hoe Woo Marina.

"Congratulations, Mayor," Wise Hoe Woo says.

"Thanks, I'm ready to make big changes," Crew says.

"Speaking of big changes," Wise Hoe Woo says, "Archibald Doolittle himself stopped by this morning for a wheatgrass shot. He's all about clean colons and fitting into a smaller tuxedo for his next social event."

"Even if you're on the right track, you will get run over just sitting there," I say.

"Have you toured the Oglethorpe Inn this week?" Marshall asks.

"I played the new Steinway Grand in the Victor Howard Concert Hall," Wise Hoe Woo says. "The acoustics are remarkable."

"I agree. I can't wait to perform in that space," Ella says.

"They finished all of the oak paneling and marble-faced fireplaces," Crew says.

"And gold leaf ceiling dome and cast wrought-iron balconies," Rosemarie says.

"The view from the art studio is lovely. How, pray tell, did you get the marble moved?" Wise Hoe Woo asks.

"Beck Atwood's agent took care of every detail," I say.

"A young sculptor," Wise Hoe Woo laughs. "What are the odds? Bridget and Fletcher, congrats."

"Thanks, dude," Fletcher says.

"What exactly is a common law marriage?" Wise Hoe Woo asks.

"Honestly, no two are alike," Bridget says.

"Ours is based on mutual respect, love, and understanding," Fletcher says.

"And since Common Law Marriages haven't been recognized in Georgia since 1997," Cecil says, "I helped them draw up wills."

Wise Hoe Woo makes us wheatgrass shots before we shove off. We motor over to Little Tybee, throw the anchor, and wade to the beach. When the wind changes direction, it's chilly, so we explore the maritime forest rather than swim. I can't remember being this relaxed. We head home just before sunset. The lighting is magical.

The next week, Omar comes to Savannah and irons out the last minute details for the *Wisdom Seeker* and *Omar Victor International Film Institute* grand opening.

"Okay, the moment we've all been waiting for," I say.

"Wrap things up. Guests are arriving," Rosemarie says.

"Remember to address people in a pleasant tone, help kids, and be nice to grown-ups," Pearle says.

We take our seats, poolside, on a make-shift stage.

"Picture is up. Everyone settle, please. Camera ready?" The director asks.

"Ready."

"Sound ready?" The director asks.

"Ready."

"Roll Camera. Action."

"Welcome! I'm Savannah Bright, and this is the *Be Here Now Show*. We're live from the grandeur of the newly renovated Oglethorpe Inn on Wilmington Island, Savannah, Georgias to televise the grand opening of *Wisdom Seeker* and the *Omar Victor International Film Institute*.

"Welcome, Mr. Brew, Green Dream CEO."

"Thank you for your interest in sustainability," Mr. Brew says.

"Certainly. Please tell our viewers about the Green Dream's important mission."

"We aim to stop coal, nuclear power plants, and the one percent wealthy, from prospering through our electric bills."

"What are some of the features that make the Oglethorpe Inn renovation earth friendly?"

"Recycled plastic studs, coolroofs, solar panels, upcycled deconstruction materials, sustainably harvested wood, and locally produced and milled products."

"What is the most innovative technique you used here?"

"Microbial fuel cells that are powered by energy from dirt are being used to pump saltwater from the river into to the Olympic-size pool."

"I like that. Thanks," Savannah says.

"Stand by."

"Follow spot ready?"

"Ready."

"Rolling."

"I'm walking across the expansive lawn with roomed gardens connected by old Savannah brick walkways where Victor Howard sculptures create evocative focal points.

"From here we see rows of organic flowers, vegetables, and herbs, with a backdrop of fruit and nut trees that go all the way down to the river. After Savannah Bright tours the property, it's time for our interviews.

"Pearle Isle joins us now. Welcome."

"It's my pleasure to be here, Savannah," Pearle says.

"What's your take on being a Wisdom Seeker?"

"Plato said that life is but a mere shadow on the wall compared to the complete reality that lies beyond. Since we started Wisdom Seeker, we have approached illusion as a vehicle to discover deeper truths. We utilize the energy of collective thought patterns to create justice, equality, and goodwill. Love-based is mirroring itself. We are powering up to co-create a system that will heal all of humanity."

"Inspirational. Thanks, Pearle. And let's see what the others like best about being a Wisdom Seeker. Marjorie?"

"Exercising free will," Marjorie says.

"Honoring dream analyses," Ella says.

"Listening to our souls for new solutions," Greta says.

"Planting seed bombs and spreading love," Millie says.

Manfred stands on his hind legs for the camera.

"Great messages. Thank you. Next up, Fletcher, Bridget, and Bo. "Fletcher has thousands of subscribers on his Youtube show *Endangered Animal Protector United*. What's trending today?"

"The frog does not drink up the pond in which he lives," Fletcher says. "Every mineral, plant, animal, and human exists within a buzzing ecosystem."

"One love. Thanks, Fletcher.

"Bridget and Bo Alexander, busy with the Thanks-Living Day Grand Opening at Savannah's first One Hundred Percent Organic Raw Vegan Restaurant and Retreat, Good Karma Cafe. What can we expect?"

"Expect to be wowed," Bridget says.

"Our cuisine is seasonal, regional, healthy, hearty, and delicious," Bo says.

"Well, Savannah is ready for fresh, healthy cuisine; I had to pull strings to get a reservation for your opening week. I also wanted to congratulate you for the work you did on *Food Forest,* one of seven films being shown at this week's sold-out *Omar Victor International Film Festival.*"

"Thanks," Bridget says. "The film is powerful."

They show a clip of the film with Bridget tearing out the hundred-year-old croquet lawn the first day we got the Kubota.

"We're joining others to help green up the planet," Bo says.

"First, we tend our gardens, then we help tend our neighbors' garden, and then we unite to feed the hungry," Bridget says.

"Your brand of élan vital is appreciated. Up next, a warm welcome to my good friend, Savannah's Guru of positive thinking, and bestselling author of *My Soul, My Intuition* and *My Thoughts, My Things*, Marshall Portunus. Congratulations, you're back on the bestseller list with, *Kind Kid, Kind Planet.*"

"Gratitude."

"You've illustrated, for more than one million of us, the Power of Positive Thought. To coin one thread you've used throughout the trilogy, 'what now?'"

"We are receptive instruments gaining greater truth through love, compassion, and understanding. We are evolving into a Humanity that honors differences and grants equality via consciousness."

"I'm optimistic."

The director cues me. I'm next.

"Rolling."

"Mary Howard, founder and visionary. I admire your perseverance. What would you like to say to the conglomerates that tried to shut you down?"

"The great pleasure in life is doing what people say you cannot do," I say.

"Wisdom Seeker has been called the archetype for altruism. What makes the magic?"

"Common sense is the knack of seeing things as they are, and doing things as they ought to be done. Each of us is a unique change-agent expanding our intellects, imaginations, intuition, creativity, and the ability to see with our hearts.

"We use nature as our catalyst. When we put our hands in Mother Earth's black gold, meditate, practice yoga, and eat compassionately we heal our own condition so we can go forth in humanity as lamps to radiate love to heal the condition of Mother Earth for the next seven generations."

"That makes perfect sense. How did you write the curriculum for Wisdom Seeker?"

"Wisdom Seeker curriculum is based on the soul's desire to expand our consciousness, patience, and gratitude."

"Tell us about your mascot."

"We adopted the owl as our mascot. We love its distinctive white, heart-shaped face, the fact that it roams freely, has no enemies, communicates when the world is mysteriously changing from day to night, and because we admire his finely tuned senses like binocular vision, binaural hearing, and feathers adapted for silent flight."

"I like that. Thank you, Mary Howard, and thank you, viewing audience."

"Cut. It's a wrap."
We pulled it off.
At high tide, we meet on the dock and jump into the river.
"I am a change-agent."
"I am soul."
"I am love."
"I am source."
"I am free!"
"I am!"
"Unity!"

ACKNOWLEDGMENTS

I give gratitude to my inspiring muses and family of loving co-creators. Steve Green, the love of my life for three lifetimes together. Sally Bostwick (1935-2008), a lifelong resident of Tybee Island, Georgia, naturalist and renowned artist whose Pelican graces the cover and Leslie Bostwick Marlow for her kind permission to print this work of art. Scott Elingberg, my ideal teacher and genius content and line editor. Carole Addlestone, whose love and friendship encouraged me to discover my inner-chef. Debbie Smith, Design Seven Inc., whose artistry and expert engineering made my dream go Newtonian. Adam Chandler Photography, who captured the majestic sunrise-on-the-river. ElfElm Publishing, who cast lovely book magic upon each page. Hear Publishing for catching and releasing *One That Got Away* into the world.